CROSSING THE BAR

Bob Alexander in 1978 on taking silk (*National Portrait Gallery*).

CROSSING THE BAR

The memoir of Bob Alexander QC

Foreword by Jonathan Sumption

Marble Hill London

First published in 2023 by
Marble Hill Publishers
Flat 58 Macready House
75 Crawford Street
London W1H 5LP
www.marblehillpublishers.co.uk

A CIP record for this book is available from the British Library.

ISBN: 978-1-8383036-6-2

Typeset in: Adobe Caslon Pro
Printed and bound in the UK by
Biddles Books Limited

Book and jacket design: Paul Harpin

It has taken us a considerable time as a family to decide to publish posthumously the memoirs of Bob Alexander, QC, who was also, variously, the Chairman of NatWest, President and later Chairman of the MCC and Chairman of the Royal Shakespeare Company.

Past press cuttings about Bob often remarked on what a towering physical presence he was, standing at 6 foot six inches in his socks. But he also loomed large in our family life, and his untimely death in 2005 rocked us all, as untimely deaths can. Hence the pause.

Thankfully, some 17 years on, with the tiny grandchildren he left behind now fully fledged adults, family life has recovered and continued and last year, on rediscovering the files containing the draft memoirs of his life that he had written between 2001 and 2003, it felt the right decision to try and publish them.

We have been lucky to find them a happy home with Marble Hill Publishers. They have had the lightest edit from Francis Bennett but remain entirely Bob's own words.

Focusing on his professional life, the memoirs are a tale of social mobility, a record of the numerous law cases that he was involved in, and a reflection of the financial world in the late 1980s and 1990s, amongst other things. The support he gave to two life long passions – cricket and the theatre – is also covered, in his clear and distinctive voice.

The memoirs were an unfinished work, which explains why they end quite abruptly. Two incomplete chapters, detailing his thoughts on the Iraq war in 2003, and his time in the House of Lords, have been left out.

FOREWORD

Robert Alexander was the undisputed King of the English bar for some 15 years, from the early 1970s until he retired in 1989 to become Chairman of National Westminster Bank. In hindsight, it was a golden age for the bar. It had shed some of the affectations and pomposities of an earlier age – the striped trousers and bowler hats, the unctuous deference to the judge, the continual piling of authority on authority, the indecent joy in plausible but unmeritorious technicalities. The bar's horizons were expanding fast. The eclipse of the economic certainties of the 1950s, the failure of the clubby conventions of English business life and the early symptoms of globalisation had combined to produce an explosion of commercial litigation after many years in which resort to the courts had been regarded as ungentlemanly and rather vulgar. The expansion of the legal aid scheme allowed people to bring grievances before the courts which would once have been borne in silence. The rise of judicial review as a tool for questioning the acts of governments and other public authorities brought fame to its practitioners of a kind which had once been enjoyed only by a handful of stars of the Old Bailey. The demand for talented advocates boosted the earnings of a generation of barristers whose forebears had frequently been unable to survive without private wealth.

This was the world in which Bob Alexander live and thrived. He came from a modest background, which would have hindered a career at the bar a generation before. He worked extremely hard. As a lawyer, he had a range of experience rarely encountered in today's more specialised profession. Crime and tort, business disputes, public law, defamation – he took to them all. His forensic successes earned him a respect for his judgment and presentational skills, which carried him into other fields from the House of Lords to the government of a major bank and the chairmanship of the Royal Shakespeare Company.

Great advocacy is hard to define. There are no rules except honesty. It is an intensely personal skill, whose techniques defy imitation. The impact of a powerful forensic speech is hard to convey outside the atmosphere of the court in which it is delivered. It is, however, possible to identify at least some of the things that made Bob Alexander stand out in a generation of fine advocates. He had an imposing presence, due partly to his appearance (he was 6 foot 6 inches tall) and partly to his transparent integrity and decency. He had a mellifluous voice, a confident charm and a low-key earnestness of delivery which carried conviction. His speeches contained humour but few jokes. They were fluent but without verbal pyrotechnics. His manner seemed so reasonable that to disagree felt uncomfortable, even discreditable. Above all, he had an uncanny ability to take the moral high ground, even with the most unpromising material. It is usually a bad idea for an advocate to believe too strongly in his client's cause. It undermines objectivity and tends to blind him to the vulnerable points of his own case and the stronger points of his opponent's. But Bob had a unique capacity to combine intense belief in his client's cause with a clinical dissection of what might nevertheless induce a judge to reject it. For he was not, in private, the robust and self-assured figure that he seemed to be in court. There was no bravado or swagger. On the contrary, there was a humility, an uncertainty, a fragility about him that made him question everything, including himself. He constantly told himself, and others, that an advocate was only as good as his last case. He sometimes gave the impression of being surprised by his own success, of feeling that he had done things which it would be a challenge to live up to. This was, I think, a large part of the secret of his success.

In these memoirs, one of the most frequently recurring words that their author uses about himself is 'fortunate'. At the bar, as in most fields of human endeavour, talent is not enough. You also need luck. This is a general rule of life, but too many successful people forget it. Bob Alexander did not forget it, and it was characteristic of the man that he should attribute so many of his own achievements to good fortune. But to a large extent, he created his own good fortune. He saw his opportunities and grasped them with both hands. He lived up to his reputation.

I have had more than my share of luck in the course of my career. But my greatest good fortune was to have worked regularly with Bob Alexander in my early years as a junior barrister. We disagreed about most things other than the case in hand. But if I was often in the right place at the right time, it was largely his doing. The many cases in which I was briefed as his junior gave me my first significant professional opportunities. He was an invaluable source of advice. I learned a lot from him, and not only about advocacy.

Jonathan Sumption

CONTENTS

1. HOMES AND BEGINNINGS

There are a lucky few whose lives are shaped from childhood by a driving genius. The poet John Betjeman, destined by his father to be a fourth generation manufacturer, rebelled, because as he famously wrote: "Ever since I could read and write, I knew that I must be a poet." John Gielgud knew no interest but acting and the stage from early childhood to deep old age. Colin Cowdrey, even christened MCC, was predestined to captain England at cricket. But, for most of us, our destiny is revealed more hesitantly, even haphazardly. We are extremely lucky if it turns out that our eventual choice of career happens to chime in with what talents we have. So I count myself lucky that the Law has been at the centre of so much of my life and became the springboard for increasingly varied and exciting opportunities. Fortunate too, that the branch of the Law I chose was advocacy which drew me to the Bar against what seemed natural odds. There was nothing in my background that hinted that I might one day join, let alone succeed in, what in those days was seen as an elite, upper-crust profession. So, let me say a little about where I came from and the fortuitous path by which I got there.

A remarkable cousin, Elspeth Johnson, suggested I should begin as follows.

"In 1942 when you were six, you stole a bottle of milk and carried it carefully home as a present for your mother. The reception was not the gratitude you had anticipated and your mother explained that it was unacceptable to take milk from other people's doorsteps. So with the literal interpretation that marked me for a future in the law, a few days later I carried home a load of bread taken from a different doorstep. This time retribution left no doubt as to the essence of the offence. Nor did it when you engaged in your favourite habit of creeping up behind your aunts knitting wartime sweaters and pulling out their knitting needles. And to cap it, when you came to stay you locked us out of the house, heated a poker and waved the red-hot poker around at us as we stood at the window pleading for you to let us in."

Since I remembered none of this (except faintly the last incident) it seems a good idea not to delve further into my childhood charms and triumphs. So I will keep to the broad picture.

Both my parents came from hard-working, Midlands backgrounds. My paternal grandfathers' family moved in the mid-19th century from Dunscore, in Dumfriesshire in lowland Scotland to Coventry. So well was the farmhouse in Dunscore built of dry stone wall that a fair amount survives today, even although it was abandoned as a dwelling in about 1850. Family circumstances were clearly modest then. The headstone in Dunscore church has the Alexanders sharing the grave with the Brydens, the family from which the wife of one of them, probably my great-grandfather, came. The two families buried together both led stern lives, bent on survival. What caused the migration south to Coventry, or exactly when it took place, I have been unable to discover. At all events my paternal grandfather was for much of his life a coachbuilder. Then, with the coming of the motorcar at the beginning of the 20th century, he adapted his skills to making the coaching work for the modern vehicle.

My father, Samuel James, was born on the 18th of January 1898. His parents were able to send him briefly to Bablake School in Coventry. But, as so many other talented youngsters did, he had to leave school at the then minimum school leaving age of 14. He did a full seven-year apprenticeship as a mechanical engineer with the old Standard Motor Company, which eventually became part of British Leyland. He became a skilled motor engineer and was ambitious, entrepreneurial and keen to create his own garage business. He had drive, determination and doggedness. He was skilled with the lathe and a good amateur carpenter. He was to be a bit disappointed when all practical skills eluded my range of interests or skills.

His mother's family name was Hill, and his uncle, Job Hill, kept a pub in Milton in Staffordshire. This was what presumably drove my father to Milton where he built his first garage close to the village church. His next move was to sell this and build a larger garage at the bottom of Bucknall Bank, Hanley, on the road from Leek to Stoke-on-Trent. His third and final garage business was to be developed at Newcastle-under-Lyme almost opposite the North Staffordshire Royal Infirmary on the main London Road. By the age of thirty he had quite a decent repair business and filling station. His hard work, mechanical skills and ambition was reaping a deserved reward.

My mother, too, came from Staffordshire. Her father, George Windsor Trevitt was born in Wheaton Aston. He was a game dealer and fishmonger with a shop in Stafford. His first wife died leaving him six growing children. My grandmother, Mary Anne, born a Brough was married at 15 to Charles Bailey. They had five children before Charles died. Widower and widow, each with large families, came together and married. After their marriage George handed over the shop to his son, Billy, and became an agent for the Pearl Assurance Company. My mother, Hannah May, but always called May, was born on 30th December 1904. She was the only child of their union, much younger than her siblings, and was not surprisingly made much of as a child.

She also only had the benefit of schooling until the minimum leaving age. But she was bright enough to get secretarial work with Bourne, Bullough, a firm of accountants in Hanley. She was sociable, enjoying jazz and dancing but also loved books and with modern education would almost certainly have gone to university. She also enjoyed tennis, and at the Milton Tennis Club, she met my father. By then he was making a success of his second garage, had a motorcar, dressed smartly, and it was not surprising that my mother was drawn to him. My mother in her turn, was tall by the standards of the time, slim and attractive. They were an impressive couple. They both came from what I suppose would be called the tradesmen class. They were hard-working, made the most of their opportunities, and although neither of them had as adults any formal religious beliefs, could be described as basically serious and indeed of puritanical stock. But then the world into which they were born was a serious world, with little by way of luxury. Everything depended upon the extent to which someone could create their own opportunity. The old Victorian work ethic was deeply engrained as part of their upbringing.

My parents were married in 1931. The business did well enough for them to go to live in a semi-detached house on the Westlands, then as now a well-thought of residential area of high ground overlooking Newcastle. It then overlooked the slag-heaps and smoke of the Five Towns, which have now gone and been landscaped. They first lived in a modest semi-detached house in Kingsway West where I was born on 5th September 1936. But the business prospered even more. The garage was extended to add a smart showroom for new cars. We moved to a bigger, detached house in a smarter road, Abbotts Way. It had a garage, a small front garden, three or four bedrooms, and a back garden large enough at the time for me to draw for long hours on my father's patience as I made my first attempts to learn cricket.

In the Second World War, my father was away in India for several years as part of the Royal Army Ordinance Corps. The garage seemed to tick over with the aid of the foreman, Oliver and I do not remember my mother being tight for money. But wartime rationing was a great leveller in financial terms, since there was only so much that money could buy. My father took up the reins again when he came back from India, and grew the business in the years after the war. Life was settled for the family and pretty good.

Some memories of early childhood, in and after the Second World War are vivid. The regularity of domestic habit. Our meals illustrated this. For Sunday lunch, there was a roast, with sandwiches for Sunday supper, timed for the 8.30 pm reading on the radio of a half-hour extract from a novel. Cold meat on Mondays, which was also invariably wash-day. Shepherd's pie on Tuesdays, the day of ironing. There was the occasional treat to see football at Stoke City, then a fine first-division team with Stanley Matthews on the right wing. An outing to the pantomime at

Christmas. A week in August, often wet, at Rhyl or Llandudno in Wales. My first film, most boringly for my age, taken by my mother to see Wendy Hillier in a tale of female independence entitled "I Know Where I'm Going". Learning to read under the impetus of devouring accounts of war games, or so they seemed to me, as reported from across Africa, Sicily and later Normandy in the excellent local Evening Sentinel. Seeing GIs smartly dressed and calling out at them what we thought was the clever refrain "Got any gum, chum?" Butterflies, especially red admirals in the hot summer days. A cornfield opposite, not yet swallowed up by the surrounding houses, where the tall sheaves with holes at the centre made for endless hours of hide and seek. Air-raid warnings, then the all-clear sounding. There was sporadic bombing of Stoke-on-Trent and I remember the one Sunday, probably in 1941, when we drove out looking at houses which had been destroyed or damaged by bombs, which had probably been destined as part of the savage assault on Coventry. Discovering that my favourite ice-cream kiosk had disappeared, and failing to understand at that age (or for that matter now) what its Italian owner had done to deserve internment. My introduction to Arnold Bennett, the novelist, through his marvellous book, "The Card". Most importantly of all, back in the summer of 1941, shortly before my father went away to India, the birth of my brother Neil.

Then came a turning point and probably a wrong turning in our family life and fortunes. As will be already apparent, my parents had their roots deep in the Midlands. But developing rheumatism, and a tendency to worry, led my father increasingly to complain about the perceived inadequacy of staff and other problems at work. This not unnaturally depressed my mother who was, in any event, prone to introspection and found it temperamentally difficult to counteract my father's moods by creating joy around him. They decided that they would move to the south coast, where they thought the softer climate would aid my father's health. So they sold the garage in 1948 and gave up the trade which my father had worked so hard to build up, and their way of life in Newcastle. This was not insubstantial, given their modest beginnings. My father had become a member of the masonic lodge, and might well have become master which would have been a great source of pride to him. They had taken up golf, gained handicaps, and were both well known at the Newcastle Golf Club. They had a standing in the community which, as it turned out, they were never really able to gain again.

At the end of the war, aged 9, I had gone, at their suggestion but willingly, to boarding school. My parents cared passionately about their children and were determined to give us the best education they could. This was all the more remarkable because of the extent to which their own schooling had been cut off before they had a chance to show what they could achieve. I went to boarding preparatory school at a historical grammar school, Reading School. I was seen as quick, intelligent, but irritatingly keen to impress and highly talkative in class. Passionate to be accepted, I tried too hard, was precocious and not especially well liked. I was asthmatic and had to conduct some of my studies from spells in the sick room which were judged in those days necessary until my asthma attack passed. I was not very sportive. But keen practice of what became my lifelong passion for cricket helped me develop a moderate competence with both bat and ball. By the time I was ready to leave Reading preparatory school, we had moved south to Brighton. I was accepted at short notice for Brighton College.

I was vaguely aware at the time that this was fortunate, but it is only later on that I came to realise just how lucky I was. Brighton was one of the schools for middle class children created at the time of rapid population and prosperity growth in early Victorian England. It was a public school, but one without frills. The school consists now mostly of day pupils, of both sexes. But it was then a school for boys only, about 400 strong, with a fairly even mix of day boys and boarders. The accolades seemed to go mostly to those who were particularly good at sport. Rugby football was compulsory. Short sighted, absurdly tall and thin for my age, I was condemned to a form of living thuggery called the line-out. Eight players from each side lined up. The ball was thrown to me as the tallest in the hope that I would grab it and throw it back to the scrum half. While I was groping in the attempt some fifteen other bodies were licensed to assault me.

But Brighton also had a dedication to education and some very fine teachers. The headmaster, William Stewart who was later headmaster of Haileybury, was an outstanding new, young headmaster. He was a star at games, including cricket. But he also valued poetry and made of the Shakespeare Play Reading Society some of the happiest evenings of my school days. He was a charismatic role model. Those who loved to watch him bowl also rejoiced to hear him sing. My own passions were for the arts, particularly English literature and history. I gave up science, almost certainly wrongly, as soon as I could. My teachers of History and English, Norman Frith and Geoffrey Lees, were both dedicated and often inspirational. They fired in me abiding and sometimes competing interests which have provided a hinterland all my life.

So most of my time at Brighton I was happy and fairly successful academically. Dwarfed only in my chosen fields by Richard Buxton, later to be successively a Law Fellow at Exeter College, Oxford, and a Court Appeal judge, it was thought that I had a good chance of gaining entry to Oxford or Cambridge. There were then many fewer good universities than there are now and the tendency in school was to think that it was Oxbridge or nowhere. Another good history master, Peter Armitstead, who sang in concerts with elan and had been in the choir at King's College, Cambridge, suggested that his own college might suit me better than anywhere else. He felt that the spirit of the college was less conformist, more tolerant, with less emphasis on sport than that of many other colleges.

This was to prove priceless advice. But there are many other reasons why I was lucky in my time at Brighton. There were wide-ranging optional activities: I was secretary of the film society, and captain of chess, a solid rather than imaginative player. What, too, I did not know then was the extent to which the 1950 Brighton's emphasis on sport was only relative compared with that of many other schools. There were encouragements to non-sportsmen to flower although the road seemed sometimes harder and less well appreciated. Brighton, too, helped me pass into King's, an opportunity which as a family we could barely have dared to dream of. Nor did it tame or shackle individualities. Testimony of this is my own boarding house of some fifty boys. Exact contemporaries included Robert Skidelsky, a scholar and biographer of John Maynard Keynes, Timothy Bavin, successively Dean of Johannesburg and Bishop of Portsmouth. The three of us were for a time in the House of Lords together, not bad for one house in one small independent school. My closest friend, John Davison, taught with skill and distinction all his life at Berkhamstead School.

In yet another field David Quayle, one of the founders of B & Q Retail, was a contemporary. There was a time when I experienced the gentle ambience and extraordinary vitality of King's that I looked back unfavourably at my school days. But this was a passing, shallow judgement. School was a fine opportunity, which I took. I owe for it a deep debt of gratitude to both my parents which I'm not sure, that in the callowness and self-absorption of youth, I ever properly expressed.

For it was not only remarkable that they should have this passion that I and my brother Neil, five years younger, should have a fine education. It was also the lengths to which they were prepared to go by way of sacrifice of their own material interests to make certain that this was possible. Their fortunes gradually diminished, not dramatically but markedly, after they left the garage. There was never anything like poverty, but not much affluence either. They were able to be members of the golf club when they lived in Worthing and later near Fleet in Hampshire. But the choice was undoubted between paying for our education and taking holidays. They had no doubt which choice to make, never grumbled about it, and took joy in any success we achieved. One of my own proudest days, which I never forget, now that I preside at graduation ceremonies at Exeter University, is when they came to Cambridge to share in my degree day. They had a similar thrill and sense of pride when two years later I was call to the Bar by Middle Temple.

Not that I minded at all about not taking holidays. My parents bought me a junior membership of Sussex County Cricket

Club. The Sussex team of those days was a fine one, a mix of stalwarts like John and James Langridge, and rising stars such as David Sheppard, Hubert Doggart, and Robin Marlar who came into the team at university holidays. Amongst visiting players were Denis Compton, Len Hutton and Neil Harvey. The ground was intimate, not crowded and I could gape at my heroes at close quarters. A year or two later, when we had moved to Worthing, there was a colts cricket team which nobody else wanted to captain but me and which played on marvellous grounds such as Horsham, Chichester and Middleton as well as having for some home matches the fine Worthing Cricket Club pitch. I was far happier than if we had been able to have a fortnight in the sun at say, the Costa Brava, which was just beginning to become fashionable. These were low-cost fulfilling holidays of happy memory.

There is much more I could write about my parents. But it is probably enough to recall that my father died in 1965 aged 67. The first fifty years of his life had seen solid achievement. The last 15 or so had been markedly sadder. He was a man born to strive, to achieve. He was definite in his views, and sometimes dogmatic and even difficult, as well as mostly deeply serious. He had lost his real aim in life and his ability to continue to enhance prosperity for his family and for himself. Remarkably he never became embittered, nor looked backwards, nor so far as I can remember ever said that leaving the garage and tearing up his roots was a mistake. But my mother took it ever more deeply. She lived on until 1983, an unhappy widow. She had an incisive mind, was immensely clear-sighted, and developed a deep sadness about life. She regretted what she saw as the inadequate opportunities of her own childhood. She felt that my father and she had become less generous towards each other, and more argumentative, in the years since they moved south. She felt that move had been a mistake, and she harboured guilt about her part in this which she could never dispel. What is hard for me is to remember much of either of them in their heyday. Their best years ended before I became a teenager. What I do recall is their deep passion for their children, which became - especially for my father - the most fulfilling aspect

15

of their lives. I have a deep respect for the way they led them, and a particular affection for my father whom I now remember as the stronger source of warmth. But it is wrong to make too much of this distinction: my mother was a good and tireless parent.

Memoirs tend to start with something of a family history, rather like plays with a chorus which allows the audience time to settle into its seat and become comfortable. But perhaps this brief sketch shows some of the influences of my childhood. The Midlands. A down to earth attitude. The belief which is sometimes tedious that, as Thomas Carlyle said: "Work alone is eternal", and pleasure can not be taken except as relaxation from toil. No feeling of financial hardship but a knowledge of what diminished financial means could do. The changes to a southern culture when we moved south which came surprisingly easy, including losing my Midlands accent in the face of teasing at school. A fairly decent intelligence, determination, a sense of seriousness and an underdeveloped sense of fun, plus the will to succeed, and the uncertainty which went with it. With it, too, the lack of experience of really warm, giving, personal relationships which I increasingly realised made me uptight. But by contrast the key sense of the importance of the difference which the dedication and love of a parent can bring to a child. And so far not a single inkling of a wish to be a lawyer.

2. CAMBRIDGE

Cambridge is one of the world's most beautiful universities, all the more remarkable because the fairly compact area of university buildings is set in an otherwise unremarkable town surrounded by a flat landscape. King's has a strongly arguable claim to be the most handsome of many fine colleges, and its Chapel is the finest example of perpendicular architecture in the world, the apotheosis of the gothic churches. It was founded by Henry VI in the darkness of the seemingly interminable Civil Wars of the 15th century, a twin foundation with Eton. Shakespeare's history plays, notably "Henry VI" and "Richard III", remind us of the lawlessness, bloodthirstiness, and triumph of might over right, which were the dominant characteristics of that brute age. Paradoxically it is the work of the unwarlike, scholarly Henry VI, despised by his contemporaries including his more militant wife, which has endured as a beacon of civilisation from a dark age, a vivid illustration of the pen proving mightier than the sword. His statue rightly stands at the centre of the fine lawn in the main court of the college. To stand on the bridge which crosses the river to the "Backs" is to be reminded of the contribution successive generations have made to the modern college. Looking left, there is the Chapel, built across a hundred years spanning the 15th and 16th centuries. Across the centre runs the spacious neoclassical construction designed by James Gibb, the only building of Portland stone in Cambridge, the contribution of the 18th century. Looking right, there runs the great line of buildings which formed the bulk of residential accommodation, embraced the hall, library and the Provost's lodge, which were mostly built in the confident years of expansion of the 19th century, and which were added to during the last hundred years. The overall effect is of a magical setting, space, architectural proportion and harmony, as well as an assertion of the eternal value of learning. Even although I lived in lodgings to begin with, the centre of life, especially dinner, was in the college. Three years enjoyment of the place and the opportunities and atmosphere which pervaded it created a lifelong gratitude, a deep love of the place, and consciousness of its tolerant values.

For there was much more to King's than physical beauty. It was, as Peter Armitstead had said, an unusual college. It had been open only to old Etonians until the beginning of the 20th century, and indeed in my time there were still some closed scholarships for which only Etonians could apply. What marked out the college during the next century of its history was its sheer humanity, lack of dogma, respect for the individuality of its students (then all male), and the total lack of interest in forcing or guiding students into any mould. EM Forster, then a Fellow for life approaching his 80th year, captured these qualities brilliantly in "The Longest Journey". "The college, though small, was civilised and proud of its civilisation. It was not sufficient glory to be a Blue there, nor an additional glory to get drunk. They taught the perky boy that he was not everything and the limp boy that he may be something. And they did everything with care - one might also say with nonchalance - so that the boys noticed nothing, and received education, often for the first time in their lives".

There was nothing hearty in the atmosphere, just a sense of freedom to discover where personal talents or inclinations lay. But exposure to such freedom can be, and certainly in my first year was, bewildering. I joined the Cambridge Union but, although a keen debater at school, felt too shy to speak amongst the apparently polished, worldly-wise, effortless orators who led what were often packed debates. My first term I tried acting, and had a moderate part in an utterly forgettable and rightly ill-attended (largest audience 35) play. But there was no great enthusiasm for my thespian talents. "Don't call us, we'll call you" was never actually uttered, since it was easy for producers to say with some truth, that I was far too tall for many parts compared with the rest of the cast. But I lacked the determination to struggle against rejection notices and faded out of the acting world. But drama has always remained a passion much above any of the other performing arts. It was thrilling in later life to come back to it with my deep involvement in the Royal Shakespeare Company.

I deliberately neglected chess at University, letting it get rusty as I felt the time it took would distract me from more social and convivial activities. Life was gratifyingly free of winter games. Tea was a great event of the day. Crumpets and toast. It was a good way of making friends, and discussions continued until dinner. Come the summer term and there was cricket. This showed again the wisdom of my choosing King's as my college. The competition for our first (and only) eleven was much less fierce than in other colleges. Modest ability, coupled with a fanatical dedication to play in every game as well as a willingness to bowl medium pace on perfect wickets as well as open the batting, plus enjoyment at the bar afterwards, seemed to make me an essential part of the side throughout my three years. But overall I was an unremarkable undergraduate, with few clear goals outside my studies. Yet at least my diffidence, and feeling of gaucheness, was to diminish over the years as I mixed more widely and freely socially, enjoyed life more, and gained a widening circle of friends.

But the serious stuff, for a boy who knew that he needed to succeed academically to make good in the world, was my work. It was a toss-up whether I read History or English, and English just won. The teaching talent at both university and college level was dazzling. CS Lewis, professor of Medieval and Renaissance Literature, on early English studies "Sir Gawaine and the Green Knight," Mallory, "Le Mort D'Arthur" I remember scholarly, clear lectures but perhaps especially an aura of goodness. Professor Joan Bennett taught us the mysteries of the metaphysical poets. Dr FR Leavis delivered tight, complex lectures about the great tradition, as he called it, of writers such as Joyce, D.H Lawrence and T.S. Eliot, the contents sometimes sadly spoiled by apparent bitterness and personal invective against others in the University's English faculty. In the college, George (universally known as "Dadie") Rylands was my director of studies, with his passionate interest and successful record in enhancing the tradition of Cambridge undergraduate acting. He would only see us once a year, sitting with great style in his immaculate rooms full of fine china and treating us to an exciting, declamatory overview. For our regular supervisions he passed us on to FL ("Peter") Lucas, an elegant writer in the 18th century literary figures. He was an entertaining teacher, but his views were firmly fixed and he did not brook or encourage discussion. To a tentative comment from his pupils, hoping for a discussion, he would say, "How interesting, but my view is ....". To this want of enthusiasm for debate he added a total lack of interest in any modern literature. He was firmly of the view that no work under 50 years old should be read. The argument was that there was so much to choose from, time might be wasted in reading modern works, but there was a good prospect that if a work was still known of after 50 years it would be worth reading. He pressed the point even when I pointed out that to stick to this approach would mean that I would not be able to read "Passage to India" for nearly another 20 years. But he was gentle, courteous, and conscientious in the teaching of a not very exciting student, and his own writings on the eighteenth century were elegantly expressed.

EM Forster was one of a race of elderly bachelor dons, a precious breed which is now virtually extinct. These dons, including former provost Sir John Sheppard, the classicist professor Sir Frank Adcock, the economist A.C. Pigou, were frequently seen in college and sometimes entertained undergraduates. I had the immense good fortune to meet Morgan Forster by chance in hall at lunch one day. Shortly afterwards I had a note inviting me to tea. It was the first of some cherished occasions on which we had either lunch or tea in his rooms on A staircase or, when I bought a second hand car, I took him for drives in the Gog Magog hills. He was intensely diffident, gentle, and with a slightly self-deprecating laugh. For him conversations included silences. He hated the telephone because he felt it required one party or the other to continue to talk when they might prefer simply to reflect quietly on what had already been said. There was not in any event much opportunity to telephone. There was barely a telephone in the whole of the college, and only one television set in a small, uninviting, out of the way room.

Looking back I think Morgan was conscious that the well-springs of his literary output, in any event comparatively small, had dried up. But he could gird himself up when necessary. A few years later, improbable as it seemed to some of us then and inconceivable as it must seem now, the publishers of DH Lawrence's great novel, "Lady Chatterley's Lover", were prosecuted for obscenity. Prosecution counsel, a senior Old Bailey practitioner, earned doubtful immortality when he asked the jury: "Is this a book you would wish your children or servants to read?" Morgan attended the Old Bailey, and gave evidence for the defence as to the literary value of the novel. The whole scene, including the nervousness of Gerald Gardiner QC, the outstanding advocate of the day, as he awaited the result of what he saw as a close call, was vividly described in a brilliant essay by Kenneth Tynan.

This brief digression into the law is almost timely. For by the end of my second year at Cambridge, I had to begin to make up my mind as to what I wanted to do in life. I lacked talent or inspiration as a writer of fiction, or as a dramatist. It never crossed my mind to give journalism a try. To be a schoolmaster, which had initially appealed, seemed to do so less and less. FL Lucas's approach to the study of English seemed increasingly arid, and I felt it was time to make a change. One of the advantages of the Cambridge tripos was that it could be broken into two parts, and a decision about a change of subject could be made late. It was at this point that a friend suggested the law, and pointed out that his father had a practice as a solicitor in Crawley, Sussex, which we could both join. This had the incidental advantage that there was a mid-week "conversion" course in the Long Vacation term in the height of summer, which the college generously paid for, with time for much cricket in the afternoon and punting on the river in the evening.

I asked the college whether I could read law. For many years King's did not regard law as a fit subject for a complete university education. No undergraduates in the college were allowed to study law in their first year. Nor had there ever been a fellow in law.

But there was now a research student, Kenneth Polack, who had chosen voluntary exile from South Africa as the apartheid regime deepened its hold on the country, who was assigned as my teacher. He had just completed a pupillage in the Temple with a rising junior, Patrick Neill (later Lord Neill of Bladon, and warden of All Souls College, Oxford) and was excited by the experience and intellectual stimulus it brought. He told me he thought that I would waste my life as a solicitor in Crawley and that it would be much better for me to attempt to go to the Bar. It was a breathtaking suggestion. To join the profession of law in any capacity seemed a challenge enough. To get to what was then seen as very much its higher branch, an elite establishment set in ancient Inns of Court, a career which was surely the province of well-heeled gentlemen, a profession which still wore black jackets, striped trousers and bowler hats, seemed several bridges too far. But here Ken's knowledge, enthusiasm and willingness to take trouble came into play.

What Ken had learned from his pupillage was that opportunities at the Bar were beginning to grow. The numbers in the profession had reduced during the 1950s to less than 2000. Potentially fine advocates, such as Robin Day who later displayed his genius on a wider stage, left the Bar because of the sheer impossibility of making a living. One of the key reasons was that although there was both the criminal and civil legal aids scheme, rates of pay were impossibly low. But this was changing. Gerald Gardiner, when chairman of the Bar, had negotiated a sizeable uplift which was timely to prevent the potential decline of the profession. Ken saw that the time was coming when new entrants of modest means might succeed in making their way, particularly if they were prepared to "moonlight", teaching law or editing law reports in their early years. This was an acute and sensitive judgement, and he had the confidence to press it on me. He also took me to visit the Inns of Court, and to hear fascinating legal argument before Mr Justice Diplock, later to become one of the greatest law lords of my time in practice at the Bar. We had coffee in a Fleet Street coffee house, with a barrister, Rosemary Sands, whom Ken was later to marry. The atmosphere, and the buzz, of the Bar were all around us. It was

22

only the third time I had ever been to London, and that had made it even headier. I was hooked.

Looking back there were massive uncertainties. The need to find a pupillage, and to gain a tenancy. The lack of the wherewithal to sustain me until I gained practice. Total unawareness of whether, too shy to speak in the Union, I would make a convincing advocate. I was, too, still an asthmatic. The daunting, formal quality of the Inns of Court - or so it seemed to the outsider which I very firmly felt I was. But all these seemed utterly irrelevant to my new and passionate ambition.

That Christmas vacation I read biographies of the great advocates: Carson, Marshall-Hall, Isaacs, Birkett, Hastings. I drank in their careers, their successes, and their differing styles. Ken and Rosemary nursed the ambition with me when I came back to Cambridge. I was very fortunate that he was only a couple of years older than I was. We became firm friends. He was rightly demanding: a rigorous lawyer, seeking the purpose of the law, and sorrowfully indignant at facile or untested arguments. So after only one year in the law I graduated with a two: one in part two of the law tripos. Ken Polack soon went on to become the first Fellow in law in the five hundred year history of King's. (Amongst his later pupils were my close friend Nicholas Phillips, who became Master of the Rolls, the senior judge in civil law, and Anthony Clarke, a senior Court of Appeal judge, as well as many excellent solicitors and some academic lawyers). He was a university lecturer in company law and for more than a decade he was Bursar of King's. He had immense energy, administrative skills, and a passionate care for the less privileged undergraduates. He was deeply intense, committed, and found it very difficult when gradually illness which ultimately led to an untimely early death, prevented him from contributing at the pace and to the extent which he would have wished.

Three years at King's passed quickly. I spent two good long-vacation holidays: one in Greece and Turkey, visiting the classical sites and one in Italy centring on Florence and Venice. Plenty of leisure, or so it seemed in retrospect. A lot of time wasted, or rather drifted through, although the casualness and lack of programming may have been deceptively formative. Duffle coats in winter. Gas fires. The cold and damp of the fens. Book shops. Cake shops. Coffee houses. Miller's wine bar. Parties in the Union cellars and the college drinking society. Talented and eccentric contemporaries. Spring and summer on the backs. Even one May Ball. All a marvellously enriching experience. And somehow at the end of it I knew what I wanted to do.

So a winding, haphazard route led me to my vocation. The lack of real talent, or spark for any of the routes which could have flown from English literature. A well meaning suggestion of a friend that I should become a solicitor in Crawley which led me to change to the law. Above all the influence of Kenneth Polack. Others touched my education at important times. But to Ken I owe the deep, lifelong debt, for being a young, talented lawyer in the right college at the right time, with his recent experience of life in the Temple, and the enthusiasm of his advice and for the time and trouble he took to encourage me to embark upon an improbable and tumultuous adventure.

I and my generation had been fortunate as undergraduates. There were some marvellous teachers. The spirit of the college and university was of the best. My youth had not been dislocated, let alone decimated, by the waste of a war. The government had played fair by us: payment of our tuition fees and perfectly adequate maintenance grants, especially when supplemented by a bit of temporary work as a Christmas postman or as a wine waiter. There had been occasional gusts of doubt, such as the Suez crisis and the Soviet rape of Hungary in our first autumn. But mostly we lived in the years which Harold Macmillan, then prime minister, described as years in which "You have never had it so good". And, whatever opportunity I failed to grasp at Cambridge, I left more self-confident, with a passionate calling to a future career, with a reasonably decent degree, and proud parents encouraging me to take the next great leap into the unknown.

What was the impetus which excited me towards the Bar? As the years went on I increasingly recognised and indeed had to defend the importance to society of the rule of Law as underpinning democracy and basic human rights. To sustain our system of justice, it is vital to have a profession of independent advocates: not employed or controlled by the state, prepared to act for and against governments, to represent unpopular causes, and to speak ably and where necessary fearlessly for their clients. It would be good to be able to say that this high-minded understanding of the value of the Bar fired my choice of vocation. I was aware it was a worthwhile calling, but what drove me, fired me, was the thought of the striving, the challenge, the opportunity to argue and persuade. I was fascinated, too, by the mystery. The Inns of Court, with their collegiate atmosphere, wigs and gowns and the majesty of the Law. It was a profession of wonder for me, such as I had not dared to aspire to. Close to the hub of the glittering life of London. This mix of feelings and instincts which made me feel there was no other job for me was not especially noble. But they had led me to the right choice.

3. CALLED TO
THE BAR

The next year after leaving Cambridge was something of an anti-climax. Dull practicalities stood between me and what I saw as the glittering prize of the Bar. The professional examinations, or vocational course, to qualify was fortunately much less rigorous than it is now. But it took a year to grapple by postal course with Roman law, civil and criminal procedure, and the laws of evidence. But if the exams were not arduous, at least the cost of the course was fairly minimal. For part of the time I lived in the household of an affluent English family who wintered in Switzerland for the sake of the health of the bright, agreeable boy who I was hired to tutor for his common entrance exam. Each of us understood that the task was to be necessary rather than enjoyable. This tutorial post with generous spare time saw me started on the way, but the latter part of my study had to be more intense and was conducted in large tranches of solitude learning by rote in a rented basement flat in Hampstead. I shared with my closest friend from Cambridge, a shy, intensely decent, dedicated medical student called Brian Greenwood. He was to devote his future career to rheumatology, working largely in Africa before he came back to lead research at the London School of Hygiene and Tropical Medicine. He became an FRS, and so important was his work that he gained a large grant from Bill Gates in response to what started as routine, round-robin request for funds. His was to be a career of pioneering, deep achievement.

The other obstacle to a speedy call to the Bar was the need to eat dinners at Middle Temple. For centuries the four Inns of Court had exercised jurisdiction over students to admit them to membership and in due course to call them to the Bar. They are all situated fairly close to each other: Gray's Inn to the north of Holborn, Lincoln's Inn traditionally the home of chancery practitioners, in its spacious grounds to the west of Chancery Lane: and south of the Strand Middle Temple and Inner Temple joined (or sometimes it seemed divided) by Middle Temple Lane. The latter two Inns had existed, together with the old Temple round church, since the 12th century, but their relatively modern title stemmed from a charter granted by King James I in 1608. The Inns perform a very similar function to each other: they provide a library, dining facilities, student recreation facilities, and most importantly professional accommodation. In those days they gave no training in advocacy, but nor did anyone else. A young barrister was expected magically to imbibe this key, indeed central, skill in pupillage and through experience and practice. We were exposed on the Spartan hillside to see whether we survived, and the experience, as well as the mistakes we all made, came from learning on the job or in other words at the expense of our clients. Luckily the inexperience of young barristers often drew the sympathy of judges for the clients and they were generally quick to shield them from the rawness of the novices. Now advocacy training, as well as being part of a vocational course, is also one of the principal activities of the Inns of Court. Young barristers are fortunate enough to be taught in small groups in practical exercises by a mix of comparatively young practitioners fresh from their own early experience, very able senior barristers and judges. This personal training by the most highly qualified people is an asset which few professions have and reflects the dedication of so many barristers to maintain the strength of their profession.

With the Inns of Court offering basically similar facilities, my decision which one to join was a simple one. Which, if any, would give me the highest scholarship? Middle Temple did so and I started to eat the dinners which were then considered, and to a lesser extent still are, an essential part of qualification for the profession. My first dining evening at the end of 1958 was an awe-inspiring experience. The Inns of Court have much of the beauty and tradition of university colleges, although they also have the vitality of contact with the pressing immediate problems of individual and corporate clients. Middle Temple Hall is one of the finest buildings in England. Completed in 1572 it is large, well proportioned, with the shields of past Readers on the walls, and with a magnificent double hammer-beam roof. The Inns had been the centre of social life: for law students, actors and adventurers who all lived and bustled cheek by jowl in late 16th and 17th century London. They were residential communities, with the Christmas vacation given over to the highest spirited of revels conducted by so-called Lords of Misrule. The first public performance of "Twelfth Night" is fairly authoritatively said to have been given in Middle Temple Hall in February 1602. Drake, whose table from the Golden Hind is one of our finest pieces of furniture, Raleigh, and Hawkins undoubtedly dined there. So almost certainly did William Shakespeare, whose considerable knowledge of the law, as shown in "Twelfth Night" and the grave-digger scene in Hamlet, to take two examples, must have come from his contact with lawyers. He had a suitable irreverence about the profession, as Rosalind demonstrates in "As You Like It."

> Rosalind: Time travels in divers paces with divers persons.
> Orlando: Who says it still withal?
> Rosalind: With lawyers in the vacation, for they sleep between term and term.

The serious, or rather the most serious, part of all this was that the young barrister was supposed to learn law during and after dinner through readings given by the Readers, who were then the most important officials in the Inns. When thought to know enough law, or to be a good enough fellow who could hold his cups and who would not let the profession down, he was admitted as a barrister. But this serious purpose had ceased with the temporary death of legal education and during the time of the Civil War of the 17th century. Yet somehow the tradition of dining survived as an essential part of gaining the necessary ability and character to practise at the Bar and had lingered on and was hotly maintained as we entered the second half of the 20th century. I arrived for my first dinner slightly daunted by the splendour of the surroundings, but even more daunted by the apparent age and decrepitude - as I

now remember wryly, wondering what modern students think of us
- of the Benchers, the governing body of the Inn. They were highly
courteous, but this did not lessen my embarrassment when about
six of them separately told me gently that while I could continue
to eat my dinner that evening I could not again appear in the green
suit (the only one I owned) which I misguidedly regarded as the
"dernier cri" of fashion.

What was even more disturbing was to learn that I would
not be fit to be called to the Bar until I had eaten twelve dinners
for each of the coming three years, meaning that my call to the Bar
was bound to be fairly long delayed. The dinners were not expensive, nor of bad quality and occasionally I met an interesting fel-
low-student. There was no serious educational content of any kind
given during the evening, except for the occasional debate or mock
trial. The justification advanced for this odd practice, and by senior
benchers, who had probably in their own youth regarded obligatory
dining as an inconvenience, was that we were somehow osmotically
and magically introduced to the culture, traditions and ethos of the
Inn and of the profession. To me it seemed pretty doubtful, but
when I petitioned for accelerated call on the ground that it would
be good to start earning some income, my plea fell on the deaf ears
of the arterio-scelerotic regime.

Over the past 40 years, although at each stage it has seemed
like drawing teeth, this absurd regime has been relaxed. Students
now only have to attend twelve so called "qualifying sessions" in
the Inn over the course of one year when they are studying the Bar
vocational course. Some of these attendees can be notched up at
fine and highly enjoyable weekend advocacy courses at Cumberland Lodge, in Windsor Great Park. Some dining evenings have,
broadly defined, an educational and certainly an enjoyable content.
Guest night and music nights can vary from Humphrey Lyttleton
to Afro-Caribbean. But even until very recently there were some
nights where there was in practice no opportunity to meet barristers, no talk or other special event, at which students simply had
to attend to clock up the requisite numbers. For years I felt that
the offering of these dinners was simply marketing to consumers

who had no choice but to buy, but gradually with the coming of a younger generation the arguments about the maintenance of the ethos sounded ever more hollow. I was glad that when, in 2001, I had the privilege of being Master Treasurer or effective head of the Inn, we were able to introduce some further changes. Now there are half a dozen lectures a year, followed by an informal reception, given by speakers as fine and varied as the great advocate Sir Sydney Kentridge QC, Chris Patten, and Sir David Ramsbottom, shortly after he retired as chief inspector of prisons. The Law, and the world which it affects and is affected by it, is changing rapidly to introduce students to wider and broader horizons. The principle has finally been acknowledged that if, and there is some argument in favour, compulsory qualifying sessions in the Inn are valuable, at least that every one of them should offer a real and valuable opportunity of learning in its widest sense.

This early skirmish with the Inn was thoroughly frustrating. By contrast they generously and promptly granted me a scholarship, some £300 per year for three years which was to be a priceless bridge to the profession. I was to lunch in Hall with friends for years, and my affection for and gratitude to Middle Temple for this timely financial help nurtured a deep affection for the Inn. More than for Brighton College. More even than for King's.

In those days pupillage was not only unpaid but we had to pay a hundred guineas a year to a pupil master. Today applications for pupillage have been largely formalised and it is a complex, bewildering process in which promising applications sometimes unaccountably fail to gain an opportunity in a decent set of chambers. Forty years ago not many new entrants had yet realised what Ken Polack had taught me, that it could be a time of opportunity at the Bar. I gained pupillage with absurd ease, on the old-boy-net. My senior tutor at King's, John Raven, simply wrote to a good friend of his, Roualyn Cumming Bruce, who was what is known as Treasury Junior Council, who then as now did the leading civil work at the Bar for the government. He summoned me for an interview in his 17th century chambers at 5, King's Bench Walk. He was, as I was to come to know, a highly intelligent man with an inquiring, radical mind and a quizzical expression straight out of an 18th century Age of Reason portrait. He asked me why I had only managed a two: one in the first part of the English tripos, but I suspect that this was slight showmanship. What, being a Kingsman as was JM Keynes in a past generation, did I think of "The Economic Consequences of the Peace?" Was I convinced by the arguments of FR Leavis in the English faculty? There was little, if nothing, about Law. But to my relief after ten minutes he simply said that he would be delighted to take me as his pupil. I left the Temple with that hurdle crossed in upbeat mood. Only junior barristers, as all but QCs regardless of their age were called, were entitled to take pupils. And I was to be the pupil of possibly the most respected and highly regarded of common law barristers.

Pupillage is probably the closest and most individual apprenticeship offered by any profession. Nowadays it is more common to become a pupil to a set of chambers and to work in turn with several of its members rather than to be attached solely to one barrister. By convention a pupil had clear rights: to read any, and all if he wished, of the papers of his pupil master, and to have written work specifically commented on, to attend all meetings and conferences as they are called unless the client objected, and to go with his master to court. Walking to court, or travelling by train, gave the opportunity to pepper the pupil master with questions and also to hear about the possibilities and pitfalls of individual cases. So the abilities and commitment of the particular pupil master mattered immensely to the impressionable young barrister. I was highly fortunate. Roualyn's range of work was great. In those days he did all the government work: road accidents involving service vehicles, contract serving, libel, and - although the great growth of administrative work through judicial review was yet to begin - procedural challenges to government under the old prerogative writs of prohibition, mandamus and certiorari. So I saw a broad range of court work performed by an advocate who taught me some extremely basic lessons. He wrote a meticulous note of his proposed argument. This concentrated his mind, even although in the end the flow of debate with the bench might mean that he deployed the material in a different way. He was clear, lucid and succinct. His points followed seamlessly from each other and were rarely repeated. He was an elegant, no-frills, quietly strong and highly effective advocate. He was also, and probably owed this to his initial experiences in the north-eastern circuit, a realist who saw the development of the Law as evolution on a case by case basis rather than the declaration of some great principles from on high. Once when I had worked laboriously on an opinion and produced a tract on the legal precedents, he looked whimsically at me. "You're a great man for the Law, Bob, aren't you? For me an ounce of fact is worth a ton of Law." It was a point well taken. He would I expect have agreed with Cardinal Newman: "I seek not the grand design. Step a time enough for me." I was fortunate enough to practise later a good deal before Lord Denning. To him justice was the end, and the law was the means to arrive at it. The overall merits, the facts, of an individual dispute were key to the imaginative way in which he developed the Law, whether relating to the rights of women or the creation of checks on the power of government. The Law may, as has been said, broaden down from precedent to precedent but it needs to be firmly focused on fairness to the individual who, in a law case, invariably is highly anxious.

Roualyn's whimsicality, his humour, was often like a shaft of light. When I arrived for the first day of my pupillage I was again as I thought dressed superbly for the part. By now I owned a grey suit. But I also sported a splendid, deep red waistcoat. "I cannot hear you" Roualyn said when I greeted him. When he saw that I was nonplussed, he explained that black or grey was the uniform for court and that a judge would not give me audience otherwise. Out went the waistcoat. In came the uniform of black jacket and striped trousers, marking me out on underground trains as an up-market waiter. But I had a perfect alibi to shun the top hat. Being two metres tall, the hat would have taken me above seven feet which seemed a bit excessive.

Roualyn's advocacy only once surprised me. We were engaged in defending a challenge to customs and excise mounted with great élan by Peter Boydell, a planning practitioner. Boydell was in full flow at 2:45 pm on Friday afternoon when Roualyn rose to interrupt him. He apologised with his usual courtesy for doing so and then explained to the judge that he had many responsibilities to perform on behalf of the government, that public offices closed early on Friday, and asked the judge if he would consider rising early so that Roualyn could fulfil some essential tasks. Peter did not object - not surprising on Friday afternoon - and the judge said that exceptionally he would grant this unusual application. On the way back to chambers I told Roualyn that I was puzzled because I had never heard him speak before with the least trace of self-importance or pomposity. He laughed. "I saw the judge at lunchtime, and he told me that he had a train to catch to the country for the weekend and that I was to find some way of getting him out of court by 3 o'clock." A charade, but no harm done, except perhaps to any court officials who grudged the waste of even an hour of court time.

My pupillage went quickly. My finances had looked up because I had found an evening job sub-editing the daily law reports which appeared in The Times every day. Come six o'clock in the evening I went to the old building in Printing House Square in Blackfriars, and read the first prints - called the slugs - which were by then coming up for correction. I annotated them, sometimes rewriting a bit to make them clearer, despatched them to be set as part of the page on the stone by the compositors. That left an hour free for not a bad supper in the staff canteen before it was time to read the full page and make final corrections. I was generally away by 8:30 or 9:00 pm. I learned a fair amount of Law that way, which was fortunate because a combination of one year at university and a fairly rudimentary Bar vocational course had left some large gaps. The hours cut into my social life but that is true of the early years in any profession. It was a good time but the crucial hurdle lay ahead: gaining a tenancy in a set of chambers.

There was never any question of staying in my first pupillage chambers, as they were primarily north-eastern circuit chambers. But the helpful clerk Francis Lakin found me a second six months pupillage. Rodney Bax was a south-eastern circuiteer, an articulate, quick-witted advocate, with a typical knockabout civil and criminal practice. We went to the magistrates' courts, to quarter sessions, and I learnt from him some of the techniques of responding speedily to evidence which came as a surprise and to the style of individual tribunal. Rodney had two of the qualities most important to an advocate: he seemed and was trustworthy, and he was quick on his feet. Occasionally he had a more notable case. One I remember was a challenge by a senior police inspector from Malaysia who had been dismissed from the force for corruption. He appealed to the Privy Council, then the final court of appeal for a large number of Commonwealth countries. His argument was that there had been a failure to comply with natural justice because he had not been granted a proper hearing before his dismissal. It was a strong case, and when the court reserved judgment for a few weeks, we felt optimistic. I was sent to take judgment. This was not a great forensic challenge, since it involved simply going in to the Privy Council chamber in Downing Street when called on, bowing and retreating from the chamber. The police inspector attended and before it was time for us to be called in, we chatted. "I think," said I, "we'll be alright." He responded with a knowing smile: "we are alright." "How do you know?" I naively asked. "I paid the usher £5 yesterday to have a look at the judgment." It is part of the rich tapestry of the Law that two minutes later I was hearing that the lack of fairness to him had meant that it was unsafe to uphold a finding of corruption against such a senior police officer with such an unblemished record of service.

Pupillage is an invaluable, practical apprenticeship. But only experience of court work can show whether the young advocate will be "good on his feet" and feel comfortable in the role. In my own case I could not start until my twelve months pupillage was almost over and I could at last get called to the Bar.

The chance to try out whether I could make it as an advocate came almost too speedily after my call. Call night is a splendid occasion, rather like degree-days in Universities. In the splendour of Middle Temple Hall, with parents including my own proudly present, and standing along with all the new barristers for the first time in our wigs and gowns, it is not an evening ever to be forgotten, nor would the next twenty four hours. I celebrated moderately with my parents until they went home, and then rather more wildly well into the night. The following day I arrived at my pupillage chambers at the unimpressive hour of midday and still feeling distinctly shaky. My clerk offered a token rebuke to suggest that if I arrived this late my career at the Bar would be short-lived. He told me that he had a brief for me. I asked him whether I could read the papers. He told me that the case was due for hearing at the Tottenham Magistrates court at 2 pm. The brief would be handed to me in court. It was an old fashioned committal procedure in which the prosecution evidence in support of a charge would be tested before the magistrates to decide whether there was a case that justified putting the accused upon trial before a jury. Nowadays this stage of the proceedings is generally sensibly dealt with by producing the evidence and only holding a hearing if the defence wished to argue that there is no case to go forward. But the clerk told me my task would be simple: to listen to the evidence, ask no questions, reserve the clients defence entirely, and make certain to ask for both bail and legal aid.

With the help of an A–Z, an indispensable companion for young barristers, I set off. Train to Manor Farm, bus to Wood Green. When I arrived, breathless, fifteen minutes or so before the court was due to sit, I looked for the solicitor's managing clerk who would bring me the brief. Shortly before two he waddled in, unhurried, with an aura clearly indicating that his lunch had not been teetotal. "I hear it's your first," he said with a benign look. I loftily ignored his comment and asked whether I could read the brief. He handed me the slimmest back sheet, as it is known in the trade, tied with pink ribbon. I snatched off the tape to read what the case was about. My instructions were short.

"Counsel will find enclosed a cheque for five guineas and will please represent the defendant." There was little possibility of mishap in the walk-on part I had to play and I was soon on the return journey rejoicing in what was to prove probably the most prompt payment of my fee during my entire career.

Before I could even recount my experience in chambers I was told of a brief the following day. This time there was something to read, and the case was a bit more complex. My client had been caught breaking the plate glass window of an electronics shop and started to help himself to the contents. He had appeared before the magistrates and pleaded guilty but then explained that he had drunk an immense amount, remembered nothing of the evening between leaving the pub and waking up in the police station in the early hours of the morning. The conscientious magistrate's clerk advised the bench that this disclosed a potential defence that he was too drunk to form the necessary criminal intent, so the plea was changed to not guilty, he was assigned a barrister, and a few days later I arrived at the Croydon magistrates' court, to cross-examine the police officer. Not to dispute his evidence of catching my client red-handed breaking into the shop, for there could be no challenge to that end, but to draw out from him gently the usual indications of drunkenness: unsteady gait, smelling of alcohol, total incoherence, the need to be shepherded every inch of the way until he came to rest in the cells. Then to call my client to say how he had spent the evening, how much he had drunk, and that he had no memory of anything after leaving the pub. He came across moderately well. It was then for me to make the first of many speeches for a defendant reminding the magistrates of the presumption of innocence, the burden of proof, and the golden thread which underlies our criminal law that unless the prosecution could prove beyond reasonable doubt the guilt of the accused he was entitled to the benefit of the doubt. The magistrates were impressed enough to agree. I felt for the first time that buzz of excitement which barristers get when they have a "good win" which contrasts with the angst which I was to know when I lost cases in which I thought there was a reasonable chance of success. But what was clinched for me in my own mind was that I felt comfortable in court proceedings, structured as they were, with a clear brief to present, and the basic common sense task of trying to do so persuasively. It is a great stroke of luck in life if the career you think may be right for you turns out in practice to be so. My fortune was that, as my four years or so on circuit reinforce, I had found my metier.

There seemed no particular enthusiasm to keep me as a tenant in this second set of chambers. They had no vacancies and had recently taken on a junior tenant. But they helped me to my goal. They told me of a vacancy in a set of chambers in Pump Court. Enquiries showed that it was quite a strong common-law set, with polyglot allegiances ranging from the Midlands, Oxford, Wales and Chester - notably the rising Geoffrey Howe and western circuit connections. It was the only offer available, and not a bad one at that. I joined the western circuit, encouraged by Eric MacLellan. Eric was a doughty practitioner, incisive, succinct and sometimes pungent in his comments both as barrister and later as a circuit judge. He did not expect too much either from life or practice, although he daily gave thanks for surviving six years in the Second World War sitting cramped in the back of a bomber as a very short-sighted radio operator. He introduced me to the circuit with clear words of advice: "Remember always to get to court on time, remember the name of your solicitor, and to never use Latin in your speeches".

With this, and a good link between chambers and local solicitors, I was on my way, quickly picking up a good deal of work at the near end of the circuit, in Winchester, Portsmouth and Southampton.

Circuit work was not unlike the unpredictable life of the old-fashioned travelling theatre companies. You never knew where you would be next week, or even next day, let alone what type of case you would be doing, whether it would be before magistrate or a high court judge, whether your instructions would bear any relation to the real facts of the case, and what surprises - pleasant or otherwise - might be thrown up by the witnesses. The work embraced criminal prosecutions, defence work, divorce, personal injury and the occasional contract, landlord and tenant or boundary dispute. The hurly-burly of this life and the need to improvise, were and are the best possible training an advocate could possibly have.

It is no accident that many circuiteers have reached the top of the profession. Peter Taylor became arguably the shrewdest

Lord Chief Justice in modern times. George Carman, who began by doing this bread and butter work on the northern circuit, was to become the finest jury advocate of the second half of the twentieth century. It was a marked advantage too, that with the rise in payment for legal aid work, the fees were worth having. A day's contested criminal case at quarter session could be assessed - the assessment was by clerks of the court who generally were sympathetic to the advocates - at no less than £40. Best of all was the first day of any Assize or Quarter Sessions. The pleas of guilty and speeches in mitigation would take place that day. I found after a year that it was not uncommon to have six or more of them to be heard on the same day. The preparation had to be brisk, and the courts with their list expected the presentation to be crisp and clear. Pre-hearing conversations with the clients, generally held in the cells below court, were necessarily brief but they seemed touchingly content to accept my advice and simply trust that I would do my best. Nor was the atmosphere in circuit courts unsympathetic. The judges then may have been more uniformly conservative by instinct than they are now but they knew their geographical area, like a spirited advocacy, and were generally quick to see that misfortunes rather than inherent vice often led to the commission of what were rarely very serious offences.

The circuit atmosphere, too, was traditionally warm and friendly. Rivals we might be in court, but we enjoyed the centuries-old tradition of dining together in Bar mess to the full. We would come from arguing with each other, sometimes strenuously, in court, then dine together but never talk about the case. Once, years later, I described this circuit tradition to Lee Kuan Yew, the Prime Minister of Singapore, when I was acting for him in a libel case in his own country. We were dining together and he said, "I have noticed you drink red wine, Bob. I hope that in Bar mess you gave your opponent red wine but drank white wine yourself. Red wine is bad for the voice and this would have given you the advantage in the morning." I am not sure that this brilliant, utterly competitive statesman would have ever taken to the comradely spirit of circuit life.

There were rich characters amongst circuiteers, and stories of great days of the past abounded. One concerned a trial in the great hall court at Winchester with the so-called King Arthur's table behind the chair where the judge sat in state. A very senior judge, Lord Merriman, with a reputation for being crusty, was trying a case which involved a charge that the defendant had attempted to commit murder with a gun. The defence barrister - and this story which I always thought apocryphal, not long ago appeared as gospel in his obituary - took up the pistol. "Look, members of the jury, look at this old, rusty gun. It is not a serious firearm". He waved it above his head, and more and more excited continued, "Watch while I try to fire it." He did. There was a loud crack and a bullet struck King Arthur's table. There was a temporary alarm, only calmed when the court usher emerged from cover and was heard to say "I thought they'd shot the bugger at last, but they seem to have missed."

Once I represented a pretty harmless, regular, small-time thief. The evidence against him was that of an accomplice. The law required such evidence to be looked at with care and the jury had to be warned that it is dangerous to convict on the evidence of the partner in crime without some form of separate corroborative evidence. The jury rejected our defence and the client, named Smith, was sentenced to a short term of imprisonment. I went to see him, as was usual, in the cells to commiserate and said that I did not think anything had taken place to give us grounds for appeal. He surprised me by responding that he thought the judge's summing-up on corroboration was inadequate. Such evidence had, he thought, to be pointed out with precision and this had not taken place.

I offered to get a transcript and check whether there was anything in his point. But he would not hear of it. He said that he would have more time on his hands than me, and would look it up in the prison library. A few weeks later I heard from the court of appeal that he had applied for leave of appeal, been granted leave, and had - perhaps rather generously - asked for me as his barrister. He was dead right and we triumphed before three judges headed by Lord Parker, then Lord Chief Justice. Smith waved to me happily as he left the dock and some years later asked for me when he was again in trouble.

He was typical of a breed of men of whom there were far too many: ill-educated, no family, without the chance of regular employment, who rather like Autolycus in "The Winter's Tale," went about picking up "ill-considered trifles". He spent, for want of greater imagination on the part of the law, regular short periods in prison for much of his life.

Practice on circuit was splendidly hand-to-mouth. The young barrister depended frequently on a handed-down or "returned" brief from a colleague in chambers whose previous case had overrun. Such briefs came late, and had to be got up in a hurry. I regularly commuted from home to Hampshire and the train journeys, prolonged by delays on the line for which electrification was then the excuse, gave me a chance to prepare the case the night before or on the very morning. This once landed me in a temporary difficulty. I was booked for a conference in Winchester by a local clockmaker. When I opened the papers on the train it appears that some years ago he had written a modest book, privately published, on barometers. His complaint was about a freshly published large work, with beautiful photographs, which the blurb on the cover described as "the only authoritative book on barometers". He saw this as a slur on the slim work of which he was understandably proud. The only snag was that I discovered the author of the book to be Nicholas Goodison, who had already started a fine career which led him to be Chairman of the Stock Exchange and TSB, but who had a passion for the civilised arts. Nicholas had been a contemporary of mine at King's and there was a wise convention at the Bar that you never acted against anyone you knew. I had to come clean with the clerk that I had only just read the papers, and tell him I could not act. He was very decent and understanding.

But it was at least possible to improvise a way of helping the clockmaker feel less hard done by. He accepted my suggestion that I should write to Nicholas Goodison privately explaining the offence which had been given. Nicholas responded at once, said that he was horrified that any book on barometers could ever give rise to an action for libel, and promised to ask the publishers who were responsible for the cover of the book to delete the offending passage from future editions. Not a penny was spent in legal costs. It was an amusing early example of what common sense can achieve by way of alternative dispute resolution.

I tried for a time to combine work on circuit, well paid and varied as it was, with efforts to build up a practice in London. This meant knocking around the magistrates' county courts. This work did not command good fees. Not surprisingly my clerk tried to cram as much as possible into every single day. Sometimes this brought its perils. There was one day when I was briefed in a matrimonial dispute in Feltham magistrates court in the morning and was also to argue a case between a landlord and his tenant in Brentford, not far away, after lunch. I found myself low down the list at Feltham and it was quickly clear that I would not get away in time. In those days I had an informal arrangement with my flat-mate, Nicholas Phillips, that we would cover for each other if we got into difficulties. I telephoned him and he raced out to Feltham where over a pub lunch I explained to him that in our case the landlord and tenant action was invincible. I produced the leading textbook and pointed to a statement, which was backed in the footnotes by reference to the court of appeal decision, which was plumb in our favour. We both agreed that it was misguided from the other side even to be contesting the case.

We went our separate ways and met again in another pub, the Devereux, close to the Temple, early that evening. When Nicholas told me that he had lost the case I waited for an explanation. He explained that he had argued our point vigorously, and drawn attention to the textbook in terms somewhat slighting of the solicitor-advocate who was representing the tenant. The Bar in those days, much more than now, was prone to give itself airs when confronted by solicitors who were regarded as amateur and seen as the junior branch of the profession. But, Nicholas explained, the solicitor then got up and brought out his issue of the same textbook, which proved to be a later edition and showed that the decision of the Court of Appeal on which we relied had been reversed by the House of Lords. So he was forced to retreat in disarray.

A happier, and different experience which Nicholas and I had together was as joint secretaries to a Justice Working Party on "the Law and the Press". Justice was then fairly recently established as an all party law reform group, spearheaded by senior barristers and with an indefatigable secretary, a non-lawyer who was a former champion runner of the mile, Tom Sargeant. This particular working party was chaired by Lord Shawcross, former Attorney General and later senior legal advisor to the Shell Oil Company, in the top of whose tall tower near Waterloo he had a most stylish office - very different from the workaday chambers of the Bar. Nicholas and I took it in turns, depending on who was in court, to produce a not very seamless account of proceedings and to draft a report. Its principal recommendation was to suggest that the Law was too harsh to the Press where an article proved to be untrue had in fact been researched with care and related to an issue of public interest. We suggested that there should be an additional defence in terms for libel over and above that of justification - or truth - provided the newspaper could show that they had published fair information, which they reasonably believed to be true on a matter of public interest. This was similar to the so-called "absence of malice" defence, which was to develop from 1970 onwards in the United States, and mean, in effect, that public figures in that country can very rarely sue for libel. Our suggestion was not then taken up, nor indeed for a long time afterwards. But the influence of the European Convention on Human Rights, and those of its provisions, which recognised the importance of free press, together with our own Human Rights Act, has tilted the law markedly in that direction. In the days of our report Nicholas Phillips could hardly dare to imagine that three decades later, as Master of the Rolls, he would help to mould this new legal thinking.

This work was a welcome change from the day-to-day work of circuit and the lesser London Courts. So, too was the opportunity once a fortnight to go to Greenwich and lecture Royal Navy Officers in criminal law as a part of a mid-career training course. The naval hospitality was superb, their interest in the relatively short lectures polite and unduly deferential, and to cap it all I was transported both ways by chauffeur-driven car.

But it became ever harder to combine London and circuit work. No sooner would I start getting my foot in the door with a London solicitor when the demands of my work in Hampshire would prevent me from taking the next brief from his firm. Nor did my then set of chambers have a particularly impressive London connection. Financially I was doing well. In my first full year at the Bar I booked £2000 in fees, although delays in payment, which were all too frequent, meant that the sum received was only slightly more than half that amount. But by my fourth year fees booked were up to £6500. To give up my circuit work and concentrate on trying to get a decent London practice seemed risky. But the plunge had to be taken if I was to have a chance at getting the High Court civil practice, which had increasingly become my ambition.

So I looked to change chambers. This is commonly done nowadays but less so then and had to be approached tactfully and delicately. The generous help of barristers' clerks had already helped me to a second pupillage and to my first set of chambers. My friendship among contemporaries at the Bar were to help me now. One of these friends, David Vaughan, introduced me to his chambers. They were a small set, although not particularly small by the standards of the day, with a fine tradition. In the past Lord Jowitt, who became Lord Chancellor, had practised from there as had Lords Devlin and Pearson, current law lords. Chambers were then headed by Sam Cook QC, who was a quiet, high quality commercial practitioner with what seemed an improbable passion for the turf. He became a High Court judge but sadly died young. Chambers were then not especially busy. The most effective junior, Robert Gatehouse, to become successively a silk and judge and from whom I was to learn a lot, probably had the busiest practice. But, although there were some good contacts, there was not a flood of work. Chambers were overshadowed by the great commercial sets in Essex Court which then attracted most of the work in that field.

But Brick Court was a lifeline on offer into the commercial field. I hesitated but then consulted Mr Justice Roskill, later to preside over the third London Airport enquiry. I had come to know him because in those days High Court judges often presided in the vacations as chairmen of area quarter sessions. Eustace Roskill was chairman of Hampshire sessions. He had a fine mind, wide experience, was larger than life, keen to provoke those in the profession he saw as promising, and sometimes disarmingly indiscreet.

Our first informal conversation had demonstrated this vividly. I had gone into the courtroom at Winchester before the court sat as I had several cases where the defendant was going to plead guilty and I had to speak to mitigation. I was arranging my papers when he came in to collect his own papers from the bench. He looked down and asked me which cases I was in. When I told him he gave me in turn an indication of the sort of sentence which might seem appropriate for the particular offence. This was of priceless help and enabled me to aim my remarks to achieve the fair, and indeed merciful, outcomes which he had spoken of. When I left court my solicitor said to me that I seemed to have an uncanny knack of reading the mind of the judge. Perhaps not surprisingly I became a Roskill fan from that moment and he was to give me invaluable support and advice at several stages of my career.

When I consulted him about the chambers I was thinking of moving to he expressed his doubts. He was not sure whether there was enough underpinning to help me gain a good practice. But he said that the chambers had an extremely good clerk. This proved to be not only right but an understatement. Barristers' clerks were a mixed bunch, but some were very good. Ronald Burley was the star of them all. His background was typical of that of many barristers' clerks. He had been unable to stay on at school beyond the then minimum leaving age of sixteen. He had come into the Temple as a boy just before the Second World War. He was intelligent, well spoken, and immaculately dressed, and had gained a commission in the RAF during the war. He came back to be clerk to Patrick Devlin for a few years, before he went to the bench, becoming Lord Devlin and writing a classic book "Trial by Jury".

No one can become a good barrister simply because of a good clerk. Clerks can open doors, but the barrister has to go through them. But what a good clerk can do is maximise the opportunities, and the way in which a practice develops, so as to get the absolute best out of whatever talents the barrister has. Burley (some fellow clerks called him Ronald, but this would have been "lèse-majesté" from any barristers in his stable) had the ability to make the most of the smallest opportunity. He would promote his barristers to the solicitor, and if one was unavailable he would make a good case for one of the others. He was a master at judging how much work a barrister could undertake and pacing the development of a practice. He was able to judge how to secure a good fee without incurring the resentment of the solicitor.

He made a point of understanding what the cases were about so as to be able to talk intelligently to the solicitors. But he expected his barristers to give full value. He was unenthusiastic about holidays, for himself and for members of chambers. He felt the disappointment of the client if the case was lost and made his displeasure plain to us. He had strong, right-wing conservative values, which made it sensible to avoid too many political discussions with him. He was, above all, a very good friend to us and committed to our careers.

Over the years Burley played an increasingly influential role in the developing success of chambers. During the next decade we were to build One Brick Court, or Brick Court Chambers as it is now known, into indisputably one of the finest sets of chambers in the Temple. A few years after I had joined, Nicholas Phillips followed, diversifying from what had then been largely an Admiralty, or shipping practice. Between us we seemed to hold on to the solicitors who Burley managed to convince to give us a try. As our success grew we attracted work for chambers on the strength of our own reputation. We were joined by younger, rising practitioners. Notable were Christopher Clarke and Jonathan Sumption. Each of them, as sometimes happened and had happened to me, had not been offered a tenancy in their pupillage chambers. Christopher was to overcome illness in his early career, to develop a wide-ranging practice with some very heavy commercial work and to have the thankless task of leading for the government in the immensely lengthy saga of the Bloody Sunday enquiry in Northern Ireland.

Jonathan was and is a fine historian, and became one of the top practitioners in commercial law.

David Vaughan, too, played a major role. He found it difficult to build up a practice in the common-law field, so he courageously and far sightedly decided to specialise in European law when almost no one at the Bar had come to appreciate its importance. He not only succeeded himself, but encouraged others to do so and chambers now has an immensely powerful European law team.

Perhaps the most remarkable member of chambers was Sydney Kentridge QC, South African, a Johannesburg barrister. He was a Member of Nelson Mandela's legal team in the treason trials which led to Mandela's long confinement. He was a remarkable all-round lawyer and advocate. Skilled in commercial cases, he was also an outstanding jury advocate. Soft-spoken, pertinacious and incisive when cross-examining witnesses, with a mordant wit and deadly phrase in his speeches, he was the finest advocate in South Africa. He represented the Biko family at the inquest which followed the death of their son, Steve, in police custody. His brilliance in laying bare the flimsy police excuses was one turning point in the struggle against apartheid. He came to England in 1975, joined our chambers and speedily established himself as the top-flight of trial and appellant advocates. He rapidly gained silk, was knighted and practised effectively until he was over eighty.

He would have made a superb judge, but was the victim of his times. In another age he would surely have been Chief Justice of South Africa. But he came to England too late to become a judge at the normal age range for appointment. If the Lord Chancellor had been more imaginative he could sensibly have been made an appeal judge for seven years or so. But it was not to be.

By 1966 I had been through two pupillage sets of chambers and had spent four years in my predominantly circuit work in Pump Court. But in Brick Court I now found the professional home which was to be mine until I moved from the Bar into banking some 25 years later. My association with Burley was to be one of the closest and most valued friendships of my life. It had been an uncertain start. I had come to realise what I had wanted to do

46

only late in my undergraduate career. The stately process of eating dinners had delayed my call to the Bar. My circuit experience had been a priceless training ground, a preparation for all that was to come, but I had only slowly realised that the type of work that I wanted to do could only be carried out from London and from different chambers. By now I was thirty. But I had found the best possible home and the greatest clerk anyone could have, when in the Whit vacation of 1966 I moved my desk and law books across Middle Temple Lane and into Brick Court.

4. BRICK COURT

By the time I made the move I had one other asset; growing self-confidence. Success at the Bar called for a good, incisive mind and skilled and sensitive advocacy. I had not managed to get a first class degree, and had not seen myself as a serious player in the top intellectual league. I had lacked the bottle, through a combination of diffidence and a feeling of intimidation from the talents around me, to speak in the Cambridge Union. I was sometimes diffident, and still had slight asthma. But strangely I had always felt that I ought to be able to perform well in the structured environment of a courtroom.

There had been a clear opportunity to change my mind. When marking time whilst eating dinners before my call to the Bar, I had spent three months working in the office of a firm of solicitors. Rowe and Maw was then a small firm, well thought of, with 5 partners. It has now grown to a highly respected medium sized firm and in highly respected areas such as commercial and employment law. It was then dominated by F. Graham Maw, typecast for a starring role as a Dickensian solicitor. Extremely short, highly dapper, sporting a fob watch-chain, and punctilious, he very generously gave me the run of his office for several months and paid me, in an un-Dickensian-like way, £10 week into the bargain. This gave me an opportunity to appreciate that in litigation, solicitors had to deal directly with the problems, the demands and anxieties of their clients and to see the pressures that brought. This understanding was to come in useful across the years when I had to do many cases in partnership with solicitors. And I also learned that there were many aspects of the law, from conveyancing and wills, to negotiating commercial contracts, which were conducted quietly in the office or in meetings and did not demand high profile appearances in court. But it never occurred to me that this was the line of work for me or that I should hesitate to attempt my career at the Bar.

What these months also taught me was that it is a good idea for anyone contemplating practise of the law to spend a period in a solicitor's office and another in a barrister's chambers. This gives them the opportunity to know which kind of work best suits their interests and temperament. It is one of the values of the "mini-pupillages" which the Bar increasingly came to offer over the years.

It is often asked why there should be two branches to the profession. The best answer to that has always seemed to me to be that there are two widely different types of work, each calling for widely different temperaments. There are a small number of barristers who do not practise much in court and have an advisory practice. But most want to seem to pit their wits and skills against adversaries arguing cases before a judge or jury. They need at least to some extent a sense of theatre, and an appetite to engage in high-profile work. For work carried out in court is always visible. There is a saying that you are only as good as your last case, and whilst like most generalisations this is exaggerated, nonetheless a reputation takes a long time in the making and can be lost fairly quickly. Word that a leading barrister is falling off from previous high standards gets around very speedily. The barrister needs to be prepared to take risks in other ways. The Bar is an individual profession. Members of chambers share expenses but barristers do not practise in partnership and so are only paid for the work they do. We are, as I was sometimes to say when I later spent my years in banking, individual small businesses and are on piece work. By contrast much of the work of solicitors is in skilled drafting with a premium of mastery of detail, and solicitors practice in partnership. They need, too, the patience in the handling of client relations for which the Bar is largely insulated precisely because it is the solicitor who is closer to the client, and carries out this role. This is one of the reasons why the Bar is freed up for its specialist work in the conduct of litigation.

My experience at Rowe and Maw reinforced my instinctive dislike of the attitude of those barristers, now a race which is vir-

tually extinct, who looked down or affected to look down on solicitors as the lesser, more junior branch of the profession. I also
can see why some solicitors would want rights of audience to act
as advocates in the higher courts, although it is probably a risky
business for them to do so unless they do it regularly and keep their
skill well-homed. But what I find much harder to understand is
the cry that goes up from time to time that there should be fusion
between the two branches of the profession. The US experience
does not suggest that this leads to more skilled, effective or less
costly advocacy. The availability of an independent Bar, prepared
to represent popular and unpopular cases alike, acting sometimes
for the government or public authorities and sometimes vigorously
asserting the rights of the individual against those same authorities,
ensuring as a profession that all-comers receive decent reputation,
is for me one of the bastions of our system of justice. This is sometimes ill-understood outside the profession, by theorists who would
try to press the Bar to practise in partnership or even organisations
called multi-discipline partnerships

When I was an undergraduate I read compulsively the novels
of CP Snow, centring round the politics of university life. One of
his characters was Lewis Eliot, a barrister, who from time to time
he portrayed as spending long weeks working on a brief. I had imagined that the Bar might bring this intensity of single-minded
study. Occasionally it did, as when in my early years in practice I
was instructed to draft a memorandum for the International Court
of Justice at The Hague for the United Kingdom government which
was resisting a claim over its stewardship of the British Cameroons.
When the Republic of Cameroon was formed, this territory elected
to become part of Nigeria. The French government complained that
this was because the British had simply administered the territory as
part of the old Northern Nigeria and had never focused on its separate identity. My job was to draft a factual history covering a century
of colonisation which refuted this argument. It meant delving into
the archives of the Royal Geographical Society and the relatively in-
frequent articles about the area, which had appeared over the years in
The Times. In the end the case brought me neither a trip to Nigeria

nor a hearing in The Hague. The case petered out after the written memorandums had been put in by the contestant governments.

But for the most part, the life of a common-law junior could not have been more different from the prolonged study of individual cases in depth, which I had fondly imagined from reading CP Snow would be my lot as a young barrister. "Have wig, will travel" was the motto of one of my early clerks. Any case, however small, was experience, produced some financial reward, and perhaps most valuably of all gave an introduction to a firm of solicitors who might send more work in the future if they liked the way that the case was conducted. One vivid example of what this meant was early on when I was sent as far as Workington in Cumberland to appear for a company called Maconochies, who manufactured pickle. They were prosecuted when it was discovered that in one of the jars of pickle were fragments of wood and rock. My task was to make the plea in mitigation, explaining that, although this had quite unaccountably happened, the systems which the manufacturers had in place, were of very high quality. The return journey was six hundred miles. It meant a night train to Workington. The case started at ten thirty and was over swiftly. I had early on received good advice that in general a plea in mitigation should not last for more than about ten minutes. The magistrate seemed bemused that a barrister had been sent all the way from London for such a modest task. By late morning, I was on the return train to London. The fee, which was to include all my expenses, was £25. The entire outing took the best part of twenty-four hours and at the end I was £5 in pocket. But the firm of solicitors came back, not least with more pleas in mitigation for the same company which from time to time left bits of foreign bodies in their pickle, despite the wonderful descriptions they gave me of how their manufacturing system had every safeguard and ought to have been foolproof.

Sometimes these short cases were more memorable than others. One of them, soon after I had moved to Brick Court, was an appearance for the film star Zsa Zsa Gabor.

She proved to be both engaging and articulate to deal with. She had flown from the United States to this country with luggage which included a small hand baggage which she kept with her on the plane. Inside was a small dog which she had sedated and was bringing over for her sister, Eva, in a way which would enable her to avoid quarantine regulations. But as she was passing through Heathrow, and with the sedation wearing off, the hand baggage was seen by a sharp-eyed customs officer to be moving of its own accord. He asked her to come over and open the hand bag. She tried to bluff it out and indignantly refused. The customs officer insisted. Eventually she counter-attacked. She told him he was being over-intrusive and added for good measure the words "what is more you should take your f***ing hat off when you are talking to a f***ing lady".

In the end, the hand baggage was opened, and all was revealed. She was charged with the illegal importation of an animal. To this was added by a prosecutor somewhat devoid of a sense of humour the charge of using abusive language likely to cause a breach of the peace.

We all trooped off to Ealing magistrates' court, where Zsa Zsa behaved impeccably and with a great interest in the proceedings. She instructed me to say, as part of her plea in mitigation, that she deeply respected English laws and loved this country and regretted her excess enthusiasm to bring the dog home for her sister. She asked me to emphasise that normally her language was the soul of courtesy. The magistrates fined her a total of £50 of which £10 represented the maximum penalty chargeable for the language which was in someway said to be promoting a breach of the peace. When we left, she gave a feisty press interview, in which she was good enough to say that she had been very impressed with her lawyer and his "charming speaking voice". I have remembered this down the years as the first public compliment I have received for my advocacy.

One of my most vivid memories of these years when I was building up my junior practice was the sheer variety of the work. From crime, to divorce, to contracts, to personal injury. But after my move to Brick Court there was increasingly more civil work and less crime. Crime is sometimes thought to be the more glamorous form of work for the Bar, but much criminal work is hum-drum and the crimes unpleasant .... The sheer unpredictability, and sometimes humour of the civil cases, brought me enough challenge and stimulation.

Civil claims of relatively small significance were heard in the county courts. But they could be of great importance to the pro-tagonists. One such concerned a bill for the wedding of the daugh-ter of a well-known libel solicitor, Peter Carter-Ruck. Peter was a controversial figure. There were some who said that he fanned the flames of libel actions too enthusiastically, and at considerable cost. But he had many clients, often famous, who placed their full trust in his skills and fearless pursuit of their claims against the media. He had unrivalled experience of the law of libel in which he was an acknowledged expert. His daughter, Julie, had been married from their home near Bishops Stortford. The occasion had apparently passed off successfully on a fine summer day. But when the bill arrived Peter challenged it. He had been charged for three hun-dred and fifty bottles of champagne for approximately five hundred guests. He believed that in the contractual negotiations with the caterers, he had set a limit of half a bottle per head on the cham-pagne that could be served and also believed that nowhere like the amount charged for had been drunk. He was strongly suspicious that full bottles had been spirited away through the back of the tent amongst the empties.

So he tendered by way of defence the amount the bill would have come to if based on two hundred and fifty bottles of cham-pagne. He was also prompted to counter-claim damages for the embarrassment caused to him by the failure of the caterers to pro-vide a red-coated toastmaster. He had stipulated for a member of the Toastmaster's Guild, clad in their habitual outfit of pink, to act as master of ceremonies. But no toastmaster had come. Just before the wedding, someone arrived who had been recruited by the caterers, and whose job in the daytime turned out to be that of the excellent groundsman of Peterhouse College and gone to the back of the marquee to change. He was heard to grumble that he was not provided with a proper outfit. As the afternoon wore on he showed himself to be a very amateur master of ceremonies, but the most embarrassing moment for Peter, as he indicated in his evidence in court, was apparently that when announcing the speeches, he introduced them with the words "Ladies and gentlemen", even though titled people were present. He counterclaimed for damages.

With the battle-lines drawn up the case was fiercely fought at Bishops Stortford county court before a deputy judge who rejoiced in the name of Copplestone-Boughey. The caterers denied that Peter had set a limit on the champagne and claimed that all the champagne charged for had been drunk. We had obtained expert evidence from the firm of Searcey's, who had great experience at putting on receptions and whose evidence was that he had never known more than half a bottle per head drunk at an afternoon reception. For everyone who drank more generously, there were apparently elderly guests or children who reduced the average by drinking very little or not at all. This evidence was there to boost our claim that, whether or not a limit had been set, no more than two hundred and fifty bottles had been consumed.

The caterers acknowledged that they had been asked to provide a red-coated toastmaster but explained that the toastmaster whom they had booked, had rung the night before having fallen ill. After telephoning frantically round the following morning the best they had been able to do in Cambridge was to persuade the groundsman from Peterhouse to stand in for him. They said that they had done their best and disclaimed any absolute liability to provide a toastmaster.

There are few cases more demanding than those for highly experienced solicitors, particularly if the young barrister arguing the case is hoping to attract libel work from that solicitor. It was a demanding two days but eventually the time came when the arguments ceased and the judge was to pronounce. He reviewed the evidence and held that my client had not put a limit on the champagne, adding that he felt that he was too much of a gentleman to do so. But he was satisfied that on the evidence, not more than two hundred and fifty bottles had been drunk. So our defence that we had tendered enough to cover what would have been the accurate bill succeeded.

The judge also expressed great concern for my client's embarrassment about the absence of a red-coated toastmaster, and he did so with a very straight face. But he felt that the only obligation of the caterers had been to do their best to obtain a toastmaster and that they had obviously tried to do so. So there were to be no damages for Peter's disappointment. I shall never know whether the judgment of Solomon displayed a wicked but disguised sense of humour, or was a subtle way of saying a plague upon both your houses to the contestants, or was simply a straight down the middle attempt to do justice as he saw it. But Peter recovered his costs, was robustly content in spite of one or two jocular comments in the newspapers, and fortunately began to send me some libel work.

Much of the work of a junior consisted of settling pleadings, which are the written documents by which parties set out the nature of their case and identify the broad issues involved, or arguing before junior but very important judicial officers called "masters" what further details of the case should properly be provided. Or engaging in other skirmishes prior to the main hearing. It also consisted of advising on the nature of the evidence which was necessary to prove the case. A busy junior had a heavy burden of paperwork. So pure court work was a welcome change as well as very valuable experience. I was fortunate to get the opportunities to appear before the General Medical Counsel in cases where doctors were being charged with professional misconduct. Sometimes I was the prosecutor, sometimes I was representing the doctor. Sometimes in the more important cases I had as a leader Robert Gatehouse QC, from the same chambers as myself, who had a fine career at the Bar before becoming an excellent commercial judge.

One of these cases brought me particular satisfaction, representing a Doctor Browne, a very good medical practitioner from the Midlands. It was in 1971, at the height of what then and since was seen as the emergence of the permissive society. Dr Browne was the long-standing doctor for a family with a young teenage daughter. She went to Browne without the knowledge of her parents and asked him to put her on the pill. He felt he should do so rather than she run the risk of an unwanted pregnancy. But he also worried about whether she might use her sexual freedom in a way which would do her psychological damage and impede her healthy development to maturity. After much agonising he felt he should tell her parents for whose values and judgement he had great respect. The parents were grateful, and felt it gave them the opportunity to know what was happening in their daughter's life and to advise her. In some way which I cannot now recall, what the doctor had done became more widely known and there was a complaint to the General Medical Council. He was charged with the serious offence of breaking patient confidence. Since this is one of the strongest duties of any doctor I realised we had an uphill task.

Dr Browne gave his evidence decently, sincerely and clearly in a way which showed he had appreciated the dilemma and not taken his decision lightly. I argued that although he had broken the confidence of the patient it should not be regarded as misconduct unless he had done so improperly. We suggested that in the exceptional circumstances of the case he had made a reasonable clinical judgement as to what was best for his patient. To my intense relief, for he was a good doctor, exposed both to the spotlight of publicity and to a serious charge, the GMC, chaired by the formidably able Lord Cohen of Birkenhead, accepted the argument and acquitted him. Whilst barristers seek to do their duty properly and thoroughly by every client, there are some cases which inevitably engage the heart more than others and this was one of them.

But not every case went so well. Sometimes an adverse surprise would be fatal. Mr Braune was an inventor, who had invented a motorised hand-held plough, which he had licensed a major manufacturer of agricultural machinery to develop. The manufacturers had the duty under the contract to use all reasonable endeavours to exploit the invention and to make and sell the plough. The crunch came when they declined to do so, saying that they did not think that the plough was strong enough to do heavy work. Mr Braune started an arbitration, which was the procedure stipulated by the contract for resolving disputes, claiming large damages for the failure of the agricultural company to earn what he felt were the large sums available from the proper development of his brilliant invention. We had an excellent solicitor-arbitrator, Ronald Middleton who was then the senior partner in a leading London law firm, who suggested that we ought to have a demonstration as to how the plough worked. One May day we drove to a field outside Cambridge. My clerk, Burley, was with me and as someone keenly interested in mechanical engineering was sceptical about Mr Braune's plough. It was a bright sunny morning and the demonstration started well.

For three quarters of an hour the plough went up and down the field, turning the earth well and making the appropriate furrows. Eventually the demonstration reached its natural end. Burley and I sought to conceal our relief. But Mr Braune had grown in confidence. He asked for the demonstration to continue, suggesting that the plough was capable of even heavier work and sharper turning of corners. He insisted on restarting it. After one furrow, during which he was pointing out with enthusiasm how well it was doing, there was suddenly a sharp crack, the plough came to a halt, and some vital part was found to be broken. We retreated to London with dampened spirits. This vivid demonstration overhung the later hearing of the evidence as to the mechanical qualities of the plough. Neither the arbitrator nor any of the lawyers could rid themselves of the sight of the plough collapsing in a flat expanse in the Fens. The manufacturer offered us £12,500 in settlement. This initially cheered me and I urged acceptance. But Mr Braune told me there was no point in him accepting that sum because his debts were much higher and he would simply be put into bankruptcy. For him the arbitration needed to produce large damages or he was lost. Not surprisingly the case ended in disappointment for him with the total rejection of his claim. But I have been nervous of what may emerge from demonstrations ever since.

But for all that, a view of the scene or subject matter of the litigation is often of great value. Here are two brief illustrations. One day I was sent to a North London county court for a client who owned two modest adjoining houses. He lived in one but had leased out the other. The law gave statutory protection to the tenant unless the landlord could show one of a number of factors which entitled him to reclaim possession. One of these grounds was that the tenant had made himself a nuisance to the adjoining occupiers. The landlord complained that the tenant had behaved as a nuisance to him in a number of ways including using the outside toilet with the door open. The judge asked to see the premises.

My client moved smartly to the window, opened it, and invited the judge to lean out and look to his left-hand side. He told him that if he did so he would see the outside lavatory. The judge just managed to suppress his amusement but clearly this contrived claim of nuisance tainted all the other suggested misdeeds of the tenant and our case was suitably dismissed.

By contrast a fortuitous view of the scene of an accident in Hampshire proved crucial in securing the acquittal of a young man charged with causing death by dangerous driving. These cases are always a heavy responsibility. Nothing can bring back the life of the victim. The other driver inevitably feels a sense of remorse whether or not he is guilty in law. My client had complete amnesia about the way in which the accident had happened so we had to explore the case by testing the prosecution's evidence and looking for possible ways in which the accident had happened. There were not many facts to go on. From the positions in which the vehicles were found, and attempts at reconstruction made, it appeared possible that my client had gone over to the far side of the road and collided with another vehicle which had then gone out of control killing its occupant. There was a police plan which showed a long stretch of road approaching a bend with a double white line in the direction in which my client was driving. On the plan the line started on a slight uphill incline well before the bend. This would have given my client ample caution to be careful to keep on his own side of the road. The night before the case, my hard-working local solicitor, Sam Slater, took me to dinner in Winchester. It was a summer evening and we dined early. When we were having coffee still in daylight, we more or less simultaneously said to each other that we would go and look at the scene of the accident.

When we got there it looked much as it had been described in the witness statements and shown in the plan. But Sam discovered one important difference. The white line did not start in the position in which it was shown on the police plan, but only when traffic was close in to the bend. If the plan were correct my client should have been well on his own side of the road, long before the bend was reached. But with the white lines as they actually were there was a possibility that he was reverting to his own side of the road to get within the lines when the vehicle coming from the opposite direction was well into the bend and close towards the centre line. It was only my theory, and all the evidence was speculative. The police witnesses had to acknowledge the following day that the plan was erroneous and that the white lines as they actually existed were not satisfactory. This encouraged the jury to conclude that there was no certainty about what had happened and that it would be wrong to convict my client. They were clearly unimpressed by the police evidence and this in turn downgraded any reliance they would otherwise have been able to place on police theories about the accident. The outcome was a relief to my anxious young client, and probably the least unsatisfactory outcome to a very sad case.

These examples convinced me that in so many situations a visit to the location of an incident is a great help to the understanding of a case. I would have a site view whenever it seemed even marginally worthwhile. This approach has taken me to North Sea oil rigs, a bacon factory, the grounds of a pop festival on the Isle of Wight, and down coalmines when later on I was appearing in the Belvoir planning inquiry. There is always some understanding of the background or specific experience which comes in useful in understanding and presenting the case.

On one occasion I had to view the subject matter of an action several times. The BBC had asked a publisher if he would allow a party he was giving in a hotel to be filmed as part of a documentary ranging across different social scenes and customs. He agreed, so far as I can remember, for a fee but certainly with the expectation of a modest amount of publicity for his firm. He was dismayed when he found that the film which emerged was one on alcoholism. It began with a scene from his party showing the guests drinking and with the words "the road to skid row begins with middle-class social drinking". From time to time later in the film, more brief scenes from the party and more shots of his guests enjoying themselves with a glass in their hand appeared. The publisher was both embarrassed and angry. He sued the BBC claiming that they had broken the contract by which he allowed them to take the film, deceived him and caused grave damage to his business and friendships. But he was not alone in bringing legal action. A number of the guests who had been shown in the film, relaxing and enjoying their champagne, brought libel proceedings claiming that they had been presented as incipient drunkards. I had to see this sombre morality tale several times with different clients before the BBC decided to pay each of them some damages and make a full apology.

These cases give some indication of the range of my general common-law practice, from death by dangerous driving, to landlord and tenant, to libel, and a growing amount of contract work. These cases rarely took more than a day or two which meant that every week brought considerable variety. Each case was important to the client, involved instant judgements in the way it should be conducted, and was uncertain in its outcomes. All this was very stimulating and a marvellous stage of my practice. But equally I had ambitions to concentrate rather more in certain individual areas, and one of these in which I was increasingly fortunate was libel.

5. KERRY PACKER

Cricket had been a passion from an early age. My long-suffering father bowled to me in the backyard. When we moved south I spent all my summer holidays either watching Sussex at the county ground, Hove, or playing for a Worthing colts' side on some of the beautiful grounds with which the county abounds, such as Horsham, Ditchling, Steyning and Middleton. I had suffered one of the most acute disappointments of my youth in failing to get more than an occasional game for the very fine Brighton College first. But at King's College, Cambridge, not noted for its sport, there had been greater opportunities for me with both bat and ball. When I came to the Bar my team became the Refreshers. This was a club of barristers which had been established before the Second World War. We played on other peoples' village greens, once again on beautiful grounds such as Peppard, and Gray's Green in Oxfordshire and the hidden village of Ebernoe in West Sussex. One day a year we were allowed because of some influential past connection to pit our skills against the barristers clerks at the Oval. We drew a crowd of several hundred, probably as much as the average day at the county match. It was a thrill to play in such a historic setting and on such marvellous turf. The wicket was always pitched for us at the edge of the square which meant that one boundary was very close. With this help several of us had the excitement over the years of hitting a ball clean out of the Oval into the road beyond.

So my schoolboy dreams, the powerful ambitions I can remember of playing one day for England or, for that matter, Cambridge University never had a sniff of reality about them. But at least I was lucky enough to play moderately in good company, to bowl and bat a little, and to revel in the evening life in the pub, which was a highlight of my class of cricket.

I was an avid follower of the first class game. Early memories of winter mornings, as we huddled close to the gas fire, of commentaries crackling over the radio from Australia, are still vivid. So, too, are wonderful days spent watching the Sussex team of the late 1940s and early 1950s. No overseas stars. No players on transfer. All home grown. The Langridge brothers, the Oakes brothers, George Cox, Jim Parks, and in the summer holidays the infusion of the talents from the universities bringing the considerable abilities of David Sheppard, Hubert Doggatt and Robin Marlar. Sussex was the only one of the original teams in the county championship who had never won the pennant until the great victory of 2003. But in the 1950s they came second three times, a fine achievement in the years of the remarkable dominance by the unparalleled Surrey team under Stuart Surridge which won the championship eight times in a row. Sussex played some sparkling cricket and rarely seemed too interested in a draw.

When I came to the Bar in London two friends, Andrew Leggatt and Scott Baker, sponsored me for membership of the MCC. In those days it only took about eighteen months to come to the top of the waiting list. So by the mid 1960s I was a regular spectator at international matches, watching from the Warner stand. So popular has the MCC become that even though it has increased membership numbers the waiting list for full membership is now close to 20 years.

What I could not have known was that my knowledge of the cricketing scene would ever become useful in a case. But then few had anticipated the seismic shockwaves which were to split cricket and fracture friendships when on the 9th of May 1977, the Daily Mail reported that 35 of the world's top cricketers had signed contracts to become what were described as "freelance mercenaries" with a company owned and financially supported by Kerry Packer. Kerry Packer was then, like his father before him, a powerful Australian newspaper owner, and a media tycoon, but his name was initially unknown in this country. During the next few months he was to be targeted, and personally vilified as the outsider who was forcing his way into what the cricketing establishment persuasively described as "our game". Kerry was a large man, of strong, powerful features, with huge hands, and of an overall physique which is well suited to prospering in the Australian outback. What was not obvious from the photographs, generally unflattering, which followed the announcement, was that he has a clear, decisive mind, great business ability, toughness and determination, and a loyalty to his friends and those who stood with him. By the time of the article those who stood with him were some of the world's leading cricketers and in the tempest which followed Kerry was never once to let them down.

Other games have suffered their traumas. Wimbledon, when it could no longer resist the pressure to go professional in 1968. Much later, too, Rugby football went through the battle between the administrators and players who felt that they deserved a greater share of the rewards coming into the game. Each of these sports was to emerge the other side of the conflict with enhanced skills, better rewards for players, more games for the public to enjoy, without losing their essential charm and character. So it was to prove in cricket, although the journey was to be a fraught one. The basic shape of the game had changed very little in the first three quarters of the last century. Test series were played according to a regular pattern. There were no one day international matches at test level. County matches dominated the English summer, with some domestic one day competitions. Similar domestic competitions existed in the other test playing countries which were then limited to Australia, West Indies, New Zealand, India and Pakistan. South Africa were excluded during the sporting sanctions against apartheid. Zimbabwe and Bangladesh were years away from being ready to compete at test level. Even then it was the test matches, and the modest television income, which brought most of the money into the game. In each country the central cricketing authorities who ran test matches subsidised the domestic game in which the players learnt their skills.

There were then professional cricketers only in England. Nor were they well paid. They had a contract for only six months of the year. John Snow, who had by then just ceased to be a test cricketer but was good enough to be signed up by Packer, earned only £3500 in a season for Sussex. The England test party which toured India and Australia in the winter 1976-1977 were paid just £3000 for the whole tour. For other professional cricketers there was little available in the English winter except coaching for expenses, and a small payment in South Africa or Australia. None of the players from other test-playing countries, however exciting and capable of filling the grounds, received anything more than their expenses and modest payments when they actually played in test matches. With the benefit of hindsight this failure to develop the game financially made revolution inevitable at some stage. Indeed Mr Justice Slade who was in the autumn of 1977 to try the legal challenge to a ban imposed on cricketers by the governing body, said in his judgment: "The very size of the profits which could be made out of cricket matches by Packer and his players, involving star players, however, must have for some years carried with it the risk that a private promoter would appear on the scene and seek to make money by promoting cricket matches involving world class cricketers."

The real catalyst for change was the growing importance of television coverage and its growing financial significance to the game. Kerry Packer recognised this clearly and he wanted part of the action. In 1976 he had bid unsuccessfully for television rights for coverage of test matches in Australia which had traditionally gone principally to the Australian Broadcasting commission. He had then bid with eventual success for coverage of the 1977 test matches to be played in the English summer. He achieved this by making an offer far higher than had ever been made for television rights before which simply could not be refused. Yet his coverage was enterprising enough to make a good profit out of the transaction. He felt after these experiences that those administering cricket, who were mostly former cricketers, were not good commercial negotiators, and were selling the game and the players short.

Ill rewarded players and increasingly valuable television rights were a potentially explosive cocktail. Not surprisingly some commercial agent for the players was bound to sense an opportunity. It happened when the agent for Dennis Lillee, one of the greatest fast bowlers the game has known, went to Kerry Packer and suggested that he should promote a "World Series" of cricket matches to be played largely in Australia in their summer involving a galaxy of the world's best players. Kerry saw the opportunity of a lucrative profit and believed that it would be attractive to cricketers. So it immediately proved. So eager were the players that over a three month period from January 1977 eighteen of the very top Australian cricketers were signed to play the world series cricket. So too were cricketers from England, lead by Tony Greig, the then captain, as well as from the West Indies, India and Pakistan. So also as a television commentator was the former Australian captain, the highly knowledgeable pundit, Richie Benaud. By the end of the summer 1977 there were fifty cricketers signed up, including some who would probably no longer be chosen for test matches and others such as Mike Procter, who as a South African was ineligible for test cricket. All the players were granted three year contracts, which brought them a security they had never known, and salaries of up to AUS$35,000 for each series in which they took part. But, and here was the rub, these series could potentially seriously disrupt traditional test cricket.

Not surprisingly the administrators reacted with great concern. For them this seemed like a takeover bid for the game to which they had given so much and cared about so strongly. Their dedication to and concern for the game led Mr Justice Slade to say of them: "I am not surprised that cricket had traditionally been regarded by many as embodying some of the highest professional standards in sport." They were dedicated but proprietorial about the game and old-fashioned in their views of what players deserved to earn and as to their comfort on tour. Their task in meeting the challenge was not made easier because they had to communicate over long distances and respect the formal, cumbersome, structured process for taking decisions which had been built up over many years. By contrast Kerry Packer could move quickly, took all the decisions in his own organisation and had won the trust and the respect of the players who supported him to the full.

The summer was full of high drama. Australia visited England for a test series. The governing bodies rightly allowed the selectors to choose any of the players who had contracted with Kerry Packer for the following winter. They were, after all, totally available for that summer. Tony Greig, regarded as a traitor, was deposed from the captaincy for his part in the affair, to be replaced by the cerebral Mike Brearley. He was an astute tactician who led England to a convincing victory. But for the administrators the enjoyment of the cricket was overshadowed by the need to decide how to respond to the Packer challenge.

Most of them felt that they had to be extremely firm. From early in their discussion they felt that a strong stand should be taken, and that players who did not take the opportunity to drop out from Packer cricket should be banned from test and even county matches. The threat went to the heart of the game as they knew it, and they believed the response must be unambiguous and uncompromising. There were many meetings, legal advice was taken, and from an early stage all the indications were that cricketers who played for Kerry Packer in the Australian winter would be banned from all test matches and, indeed, all county games. The cricket administrators and Kerry Packer met only once, formally, at Lords.

But this single attempt at a compromise, in which Kerry Packer showed himself quite flexible to the surprise of many on the other side, failed because of an irreconcilable difference of approach between him and the Australian representatives. The Australian cricket board were not prepared to accept his request that he should be granted television rights when their current contract with the Australian Broadcasting Commission came to an end.

This led some to say that all the other administrators were sucked in to fighting Australia's battle. But looking back on it, the gulf between the parties and the outrage of the administrators was so great that it would have been a miracle if they had come to any agreement. It was a conflict which was temporarily at any rate bound to roll on remorselessly.

By late July the decision to impose a wide-ranging ban was taken. The West Indian representatives were throughout unsure, and they showed a great sympathy for the players. Their view at one summer meeting is worth quoting in full, because it showed considerable foresight for the arguments which were later to be successfully argued before Mr Justice Slade in the lawsuit: "We feel that it is morally unfair to players who are free to enter into contracts when they did to retroactively virtually declare those contacts illegal as far as cricket is concerned and to find that by entering into contracts freely they have found themselves barred from test match cricket. Feeling as we do that the resolution is morally wrong, we feel that we are giving Mr Packer a weapon with which to fight this conference ...... Mr Packer is offering players a lot more money and most countries are henceforth going to try and ensure that the players will earn more money. This is a plus factor for Mr Packer as he has shown to have improved these circumstances. Who is considered to be fair, Mr Packer or the ICC?"

When the lawsuit came, most of the administrators were to show very little sympathy for the position of their country's players. A notable exception was to be Peter Short, representing the West Indies and one of their most long-serving administrators, who was very firmly to accept my suggestion in cross-examination that the ban was very severe on the players.

Throughout the summer those who saw their world as invaded, including some traditional cricket writers, were merciless to Kerry Packer. One photo of him was described as of "the man in the stocking mask". But for him, as for many who are the victims of populist criticism, recourse to justice was to prove a lifeline.

In the late summer I was instructed for Kerry Packer. In spring 1977 I had gone to Australia to prepare a case. In those days the Privy Council in London, who were the judges of the House of Lords, sitting under another guise, was the final court of appeal for major cases from the states of Australia. My task had been to join a team of Australian barristers and get together the written argument which we had to lodge before the oral hearings of the appeal in London. The visit had excitingly but not coincidentally been arranged so that I could also see two days of the centenary test match between Australia and England. I saw some marvellous cricket in the vast Melbourne cricket ground, with Derek Randall playing his finest innings of 186 for England, and Rodney Marsh making the splendidly sporting gesture of calling Randall back when he was mistakenly given out to a ball which had touched the ground on its way through to the wicket keeper. Marsh was a tough, uncompromising cricketer, but his gesture revealed an aspect of his character which most had not guessed at. He was later to become the most successful director of the first Australian Cricket academy. When much later England decided to establish an academy of their own, they paid Marsh the compliment of turning to him as their own first director. His record in bringing on young players over the years and shaping their characters has been truly remarkable and it does a good deal to explain the success of the Australian team across the last two decades. What I did not know that March day as I sat in the pavilion at Melbourne enjoying cricket, Fosters and the noisy atmosphere, was that negotiations between Packer and some of the cricketers were actually taking place during that match.

My luck did not end with the timing of the visit and my first introduction to a country I immediately came to admire and love. The same Australian lawyers, the leading firm of Allen, Allen and Hemsley, who were briefing me in the case about the price of oil which had brought me to Australia were also the lawyers for Kerry Packer. When the prospect of a ban was raised they suggested that Packer and the cricketers should retain me. One July afternoon Kerry came to my chambers. We sat across the table from each other and sized each other up and explored the facts of the case and attitudes for about an hour. By the end of the talk he felt comfortable that I should argue his case. For my part I was on the cab rank which meant that I was obliged to take his instructions. But I gladly did so, I liked him from the start, and admired his honesty and courage. We first sought an interim injunction to restrain the cricket authorities from implementing any ban prior to the completion of a trial. These applications were regularly made so as to prevent one party to a lawsuit suffering the very damage which he seeks to prevent and was intended to preserve the position until the case had been heard. After a day of robust argument the authorities gave an undertaking that they would hold their hand until a full trial had been concluded. The Evening Standard reported this under the graphic headline "Packer wins an innings".

The speed at which preparations for trial were made were in marked contrast to the slow pace of much litigation. The court ordered an early hearing. By late September teams of cricketers, officials and journalists packed the court of Mr Justice Slade. The judge had the reputation for being cerebral, courteous, incisive, and fully in command of his court. So it proved. He was to preside with meticulous fairness over a case which involved a good deal of emotion on both sides of the argument and which was played out in the full glare of publicity. He commanded total respect of all parties, was unfailingly polite, and quick to take on board both the law and the large amount of evidence placed before him. His judgment was a model of lucidity, and sensitivity to those involved. The only person he felt open to any possible criticism in this drama was Tony Greig, who was then captain of England. But even so the judge was also alert to point out that Greig had no continuing contract in that role and so had to be mindful of his own future. The judgment when it came was to be firm and decisive.

There were three plaintiffs. Greig, as one of the leaders of the players. John Snow, who we chose because he was thought to be no longer in consideration for test cricket and for whom a ban from playing in county cricket, which was in no sense comparative to world series cricket, was particularly intense. The third plaintiff was Mike Procter, who was ineligible for test cricket and for whom a ban from county cricket was similarly illogical except as part of the pressure by the authorities to persuade him to break his contract. Many other players were to pass through the witness box: the Australian Ross Edwards, Pakistani Asif Iqbal, Derek Underwood and Alan Knott from England amongst them.

The defendants were representatives of the International Cricket conference, the overarching governing body for test cricket, and the test and county cricket board, the predecessor of the English cricket board, which by then was responsible for the administration of English domestic cricket. They in turn had some notable witnesses. Raymond Steele, a senior member of the Australian cricket board and one of the prime architects of the ban led the way. Walter Hadlee, one of New Zealand's former finest batsman and father of Richard, and Peter Short from the West Indies were two others who gave views from the perspective of their country. For English domestic cricket the team notably included Douglas Insole, a fine former player, Jack Bailey the secretary of the MCC and Geoffrey Boycott. Bailey was the best witness for the defendants, well prepared, forthright in arguing his points, and well able as I discovered to avoid my attempts to undermine his evidence in cross-examination. He was a credit to the defence case. Geoffrey Boycott was later to describe my style of cross-examination as like that of a "wiley off-spinner". When playing cricket I had bowled off-spin though never remotely well enough ever to have stood a chance of taking Boycott's wicket. The evidence was a touch simplistic. He seemed to think that players should make a straight choice between one kind of cricket and the other, even when there was no clash between the two. He insisted that players "could not have the penny and the bun". But as was to be expected he defended his point of view with stout resistance.

The basis in law for challenging the ban was twofold. First we contended that the restrictions were intended to induce the players to break their contracts with Kerry Packer for fear of no longer being able to play in test or county cricket. At one stage in July 1977 some of the officials had thought that some players were doubtful about sticking with Packer and would abandon their contracts rather than face a ban. This was not so, this was a very determined restraint of trade, going much further than was necessary to protect the legitimate interests of the cricketing establishment. For centuries the common law has guarded the right of an individual to follow his occupation and prevented employers from imposing wide restrictions when the employee leaves his service. The freedom to seek employment and gain a living, or as it has been called the right to work, has been guarded as a fundamental liberty. We castigated the ban in our opening speech, suggesting that it was illogical because it deprived cricket of leading players, that it was dictatorial as an attempt to stifle contribution, and that it was challenging an elementary freedom by seeking drastically to restrict the way in which cricketers could earn their livings.

The case lasted several weeks going on well into October. Another court commitment to argue the rights under an oil contract between BP and the US tycoon Nelson Bunker-Hunt, who was later to try to corner the silver market, meant that I had to leave the case before final speeches. Our final speech was made with conspicuous ability by Andrew Morritt QC, an elegant advocate who was later to become vice-chancellor and so effectively head of the Chancery Division of the courts. The judge had no difficulty in deciding "beyond doubt" as he put it, that there was direct interference by the administrators with the contract between Packer and the players. He concluded that the main aim of the ban had been to pressurise the players into withdrawing from their commitments to Packer. The judge said: "It faced and was calculated to face the players concerned with an acute dilemma : 'get out of your contracts or be banned.'"

The judge was equally strong in holding that the ban was an unreasonable restraint of trade. He accepted that the official cricketing bodies had interests to protect in the organisation and administration of the game. Their case had been best put by Jack Bailey who said that the actions of Packer were "in direct opposition to the heart of the finances of the game ...." And that players who had been nurtured by the game "stood in very strong danger of destroying the game at a test and grass-roots level". But the judge particularly analysed what effect the Packer series might have on the various test-playing countries. He felt that the only real and immediate threat was to Australian cricket ...... that even if this was so there was no justification for a ban as wide as the one imposed or to operate on contracts which had already been entered into. He expressed his conclusion vividly by saying: "It deprived, by a form of retrospective legislation, a professional cricketer of the opportunity of making his living in a very important field of his professional life which was a serious and unjust step to take ...." and that the players who had signed the contracts could not be said to have deserved this sanction.

He also added that such a ban would deprive the public of a great deal of pleasure, and potentially effect income from future test matches. He recognised, as Peter Short in the West Indies had said, that the countries would be making a "considerable sacrifice" in denying themselves the opportunity of playing those cricketers who had signed for Kerry Packer when they were available. He pointed out, as one experienced court reporter, Gordon Cormer had said to me informally during the long hearing, "surely there was a simple answer that selectors could if they wished, decline to choose a player who had decided to play for a private promoter". This should not be laid down in tablets of stone by the governing bodies.

The court case was a bruising one and a considerable reverse for the cricketing establishment. They had understandably appeared sombre and defensive throughout. This even extended to the dress code in court. The Packers players appeared in informal clothes, lunched together with enjoyment, and exuded indignation of the ban and confidence that they would succeed. The administrators all wore suits, behaved with impeccable courtesy and determination but were understandably heavy-spirited at the contest. Once the result had been announced the contest moved to Australia. The established grounds denied Kerry Packer access. He had to improvise by hiring football stadia and innovating by air-lifting in "drop-in" pitches. To start with the crowds were not very interested. By the end of the first season attitudes changed and suddenly about fifty thousand people came to his last one-day match. The Packer matches brought innovations. Floodlights were introduced so that matches could be played in the afternoon and evening enabling people to get there after work. This in turn meant that the traditional red ball was not easily visible and so matches started to be played with a white ball against a black sight-screen. The players wore coloured clothing, which many who had only known cricket played in whites found very difficult to accept. The "dinner-break" was taken at the end of the afternoon and drinks buggies were driven onto the grounds during the intervals. Television coverage became much more vivid with explanation of the game to those who had not previously been interested. Undoubtedly all this brought cricket to wider audiences as offering a more exciting and entertaining atmosphere. The number of women watching cricket grew sharply.

I first saw a Packer match in the second season. His matches consisted of Australia playing a team styled the Rest of the World. The match I saw was at Sydney in January 1979 and seemed to lack passion. It did not begin to compare with the great centenary test match which I had seen at Melbourne eighteen months previously. Packer had no desire to ruin cricket. In time the old adversaries started to talk and the position evolved where the traditional cricket boards administered the game and put television rights out for competitive negotiation. Over time this has reaped dramatic financial results. All this is a striking justification on the law on the restraint of trade. The judge who decides that restrictions would prevent someone pursuing their employment or a commercial activity cannot know the precise effect which this judgment will have. What he can know is that to prevent unnecessary restraints on trading activities is to give dynamic opportunities for economic growth. In this case Mr Justice Slade's judgment meant that individual cricketers could fairly pursue their careers, that their successors had much wider opportunity of earning their livings as professional cricketers and of achieving high incomes, that there would be much more cricket played and available to viewers through television, and that the funds for helping to develop young cricketers to enable the sport to grow were available. The common law had made a notable contribution to secure fair play to Packer, to redress the vilification which had been heaped upon his head, and it also helped shape the future of the sport.

There were two other effects of the impetus given to the game by one day cricket. The need to score fast influenced the development of batsmen. So they began to score faster in test matches and it became a brighter game. VVS Laxman, the star Indian player said: "The influence of one day cricket cannot be denied because most batsmen now are stroke players, rather than those with a defensive mindset. It is good for Test cricket because that's the only way you can attract the public".

The shake-up caused by the Packer case meant that the previously paternalistic attitude of administrators to players had to change. Barry Richards summarised this well when he said in his 2002 Cowdrey lecture for MCC: "Like last year's lecturer, Richie Benaud, I was part of the Packer affair. That would never have happened if there had not been a gulf between administrators and players, a gulf caused partly by lack of understanding and rapport between administrators from one generation and players from another. One tradition we can do without is the squire and peasant relationship between administrators and players."

The crisis over Zimbabwe in the World Cup of 2002-2003 showed that the views of players, who after all bring in the crowds, are vital. So all in all the sound principles of law adopted by Mr Justice Slade helped to influence the modern game.

6. GCHQ

The law has been traditionally reluctant to accept challenges to decisions of government based on national security. In part this reflects that one of the central historic duties of a government has been to preserve the safety of the nation. In part, too, the reality is that in times of national emergency the courts have been even more reluctant to second-guess the government on this sensitive issue. In the Second World War there was an infamous decision of the House of Lords upholding an arbitrary right of detention of aliens by the Home Secretary on his mere statement that they were a potential danger. Nor is this country alone. One of the worst decisions of the Supreme Court of the United States similarly permitted detention of Japanese on the West Coast of America during the same war. In both cases national emergency prompted the laws to fall silent.

In the late 1980s I was engaged in two cases which concerned national security. These did not take place under the shadow of war or other national emergency. But they indicated the importance which the courts attached to security and the government's concerns about security.

Government Communications Headquarters gathers electronic intelligence for the government. On 25th January 1984, the government announced in the House of Commons that staff at GCHQ would no longer be permitted to hold union membership. The Council of Civil Service Unions, in an attempt to overturn the decision, brought proceedings for judicial review.

Two of the principal aims of the Conservative government which took power in 1979 were reform of the civil service, and the reining in of the trades union movement. What became known as the GCHQ case would see those policies pursued in a third area of particular concern to the Prime Minister, Margaret Thatcher: national security.

In 1974, Ted Heath's Conservative government had lost power as a result of a dispute with the National Union of Mineworkers. After a series of strikes, which had forced the government to introduce a three day working week to reduce coal consumption at power stations, Heath called the second election of the year, to determine, as he put it "who governs Britain", the government or the trade unions. Throughout the later 1970s, the TUC leadership would regularly meet "for beer and sandwiches" at number 10 Downing Street, and discuss government policy. In 1978 the government had had to borrow money from the International Monetary Fund. These were conditional upon cutbacks in government spending, and included restrictions on wage increases for public sector workers. This sparked off the winter of discontent in 1978-9. A series of strikes were held by mineworkers, rail workers, dustmen, and the TGWU, amongst others. By the time the Conservatives got back into power, there was wider support for their new, more robust approach to the unions.

They set about a series of reforms to ensure that, this time, they could govern without, as they saw it, being beholden to the leadership of the TUC. Amongst other things, the new government made it illegal for union leaders to call out their members on strike without first gaining their support in a ballot. They banned strikes in sympathy with other strikers, made unions liable for lawbreaking by their members, and forced union officials to be democratically elected. The government's battle with the unions would culminate in the miners' strike of 1984-85, which has been described as one of the biggest defeats in the history of the Labour movement.

At the same time, Mrs Thatcher's government embarked upon a programme of reform of the civil service. The service was stereotypically regarded as the preserve of Oxbridge classicists, immune to the management vogues of the private sector, forever pushing governments into the middle of the policy road. Above all, the new administration regarded the civil service as profoundly inefficient. The Prime Minister appointed the chairman of Marks and Spencer, Sir Derek Rayner (now Lord Rayner), as her Efficiency Advisor, with a brief to implement reforms to the service. Although Lord Rayner left in 1983, his work was continued. By 1987, the size of the civil service had been reduced from 732,000 to 600,000. Civil service pay had fallen below the national average.

The reforms were far-reaching and created considerable resentment during their early years. There was a series of strikes about pay and conditions within the civil service as a whole. In 1983 the government decided it would not tolerate the involvement of parts of the service relating to national security in the strikes. The Government Communications Headquarters (GCHQ) has the important role of ensuring the security of military and official communications and providing the government with signals intelligence. Between 1979-81 workers at GCHQ were involved in a series of stoppages as were other branches of the civil service. The following year the government decided not to take action to prevent further strikes because at that time the existence of GCHQ was not publicly acknowledged. By the end of 1983 that had changed. The government was considering the introduction of reforms to the selection procedure for GCHQ workers. This met with a good deal of resistance from the Council of Civil Service Unions. Before that issue had been resolved the government introduced its ban on trade union membership.

The ban was a dramatic tilt in relationships between the government and the union. From as long back as 1947 staff employed at GCHQ had been permitted to belong to a national trade union and most of them had done so. There was a well-established practice of consultation between the government and trade union sides about important alterations in the terms and conditions of service staff. But in December, 1983, the Prime Minister in her role as Minister for the civil service gave, without any prior consultation, a firm instruction that staff at GCHQ would no longer be permitted to belong to a trade union. Whilst the move was sudden, there had been a good deal of provocation. One CCSU leaflet at the time had emphasised the vulnerability of defence and secret organisations to strike action aimed at the security system of the nation. Sir Brian Tovey, a former director of GCHQ, reported that when the general secretary of the union had been warned of the serious consequences that might follow from the disruption of GCHQ work, the answer was a simple: "Thank you. You are telling me where I am hurting Mrs Thatcher most". The government was understandably alarmed.

For its part the CCSU was incensed. The decision was to them abrupt and without any of the traditional prior consultation which is the normal practice in sensitive industrial disputes. They challenged the decision in the courts. The government was represented in the first two hearings by Simon Brown, then standing junior council to the government, who was to become a fine, shrewd and humane judge and later member of the Court of Appeal. At this stage I read of the case in the newspapers but was not personally involved.

The argument for the union was simple. The decision was unfair, so the CCSU said, because the government had failed to fulfil their duty of consulting staff about the changes. In the High Court, Mr Justice Glidewell agreed with them. He held that the unions had a legitimate expectation to be consulted and so his decision went against the government.

In our country the most senior judges are appointed by the Prime Minister on the advice of the Lord Chancellor. The system depends very much on the integrity of those who select the judges on ability alone and regardless of any political sympathies or other considerations. A small but striking example of the way our system has worked well under a series of different Prime Ministers and Lord Chancellors is that only a month after deciding this important case against the government, the Prime Minister in particular, Mr Justice Glidewell was granted his promotion to the Court of Appeal. Mrs Thatcher as a barrister had a scrupulous respect for the division between the executive and the judiciary. She could sometimes get angry privately about what she regarded as the unfortunate decisions of some liberal-minded judges. But she never criticised judicial decisions publicly. It is a pity that a few later politicians, particularly some Home Secretaries, did not follow her example. What is crucial so long as our constitution remains un-written is that the executive should seek to uphold respect for our independent judiciary.

It was inevitable that the GCHQ case would go to the Court of Appeal. The government raised the argument that the needs of national security outweighed any duty to consult with staff. The Court of Appeal unanimously agreed with them. The CCSU ap-pealed to the House of Lords. I was asked at the start of August 1984, to argue the government's case on this final appeal. It was an exciting challenge, which more than compensated for the need to master the facts and some wide-ranging areas of law about the royal prerogative during the summer holidays. Simon Brown, my good friend from student days with whom I had done so many cases, was to become a judge and would not be available to take part. My junior was to be John Mummery, who had a fine practice especially in intellectual property work and was noted for his sound judgement and thoughtful common-sense.

The case came on for hearing in early October in a setting which would have given plenty of scope for the imagination of Gilbert & Sullivan. Normally an appeal to the House of Lords is heard in one of the very many committee rooms on an upstairs floor in the five miles of labyrinthine corridors inside the Palace of Westminster. Once a year, however, when Parliament is not sitting, there has been a long-standing tradition that a case is argued in the Chamber of the House of Lords itself. Otherwise, or so some scholars advise, the right of the Law Lords to hear appeals in the chamber might be lost through disuse. So to err on the side of caution one case a year was heard in the Chamber against the day when for some reason not easy to conceive, the judges might wish to assert their right to occupy the Chamber more frequently. A brass bar runs the width of the Chamber near one end. During the state opening of Parliament members of the House of Com-mons are brought into the Lords for the Queen's speech. More than 650 of them are crammed behind the bar and not allowed to pass beyond it. In a court case the barristers remain behind the bar whilst the senior judges inhabit the rest of the large Chamber on their own with every now and again a peer coming in to listen. The Law Lords wear lounge suits, but the barristers have to put on full formal dress. That in itself is odd since it meant wearing a so-called full bottomed wig. The flap of this wig is shaped rather like a spaniel's ears and covers your own ears. To hear the soft voices of the judges I found it necessary to lift a flap up with one hand and turn my head slightly to one side. It is an uncomfortable way of arguing a case since there is a considerable distance from the judges and nowhere to put papers or legal books in front of the advocate. The Lords sit relaxed on the benches with little tables in front of them. The whole scene is wonderfully theatrical and historic but in terms of effectiveness of function it is more than a little amateur.

But back to the argument itself. The decision to ban trade union membership had been exercised under what is still known as the prerogative power of the Crown. This is the miscellany of powers which in theory the sovereign still technically possesses in contrast with those detailed statutory laws which have been passed by Parliament. These powers stemmed historically from the absolute right of the sovereign in past times in certain areas of public activity. The prerogative powers were an eclectic mix ranging from the making of treaties with other sovereign states, the grant of honours, the appointment of ministers, and almost incredibly, going to war which means that the government can still commit us to such drastic action without authority from parliament. These days the powers are exercised by the government and not by the sovereign personally. We argued that, as the powers to regulate the conditions of the civil service came under the prerogative, they could not be reviewed at all by the courts. But more centrally we urged that even if review was possible in some circumstances this could not be the case where there was evidence that a decision was taken on the ground of national security. In such an area accountability should be political not judicial. There had been previous industrial action at GCHQ and attempts might be made in the event of consultation to block the taking of a decision by means of further industrial action. Speed of decision-taking without warning was crucial.

Our claim that this was the basis of the decision was supported by an affidavit from the cabinet secretary, Sir Robert Armstrong.

But the banning of trade unions without consultation was a very strong measure to take. The unions had a powerful claim made very well by Louis Blom-Cooper QC, that they had a legitimate expectation to consultation and that the evidence for the decision being taken on the ground of national security was unconvincing. It was a closely argued contest. The judges clearly had some reservations about the lack of consultation but in the end accepted the evidence that the decision was taken for security reasons. This had become the central issue in the appeal, and it was the only reason the government won. In all other ways the decision advanced the powers of the courts in the developing law of judicial review.

The judges held clearly that prerogative powers could sometimes be reviewable and that there was in any event a duty to act fairly. Apart from national security considerations they said that they would have found the decision-making process to have been simply unfair for lack of consultation. But in the end where national security came in it was for the government rather than the courts to decide whether this outweighed the issue of fairness. On the evidence the Prime Minister was held to have balanced these factors in reaching her decision. Lord Fraser of Tullybelton said this: "I am accordingly of the opinion that the minister has shown that her decision was one which not only could reasonably have been based, but was in fact based, on considerations of national security, which outweighed what would otherwise have been the reasonable expectation on the part of the appellants for prior consultation."

So this was the narrow ground on which we won. Lord Scarman said that there was one reason only for dismissing the appeal - the government had made out a case on the ground of national security. Lord Roskill, after a brilliant review of the law of royal prerogative, held that ordinarily the unions would have had a clear right to consultation, but that in this case it would simply have revealed the vulnerability of our security services to strike action. This would have "seriously compromised" our national security. It was a tough case, and it is right that we only succeeded on national security grounds. To be consulted before employment rights are changed is a fundamental aspect of our general law. Exceptional circumstances were needed to lead to its exclusion.

One of the important features of the case was that it restated clearly the basis on which the courts intervened to restrain government action. Judges who resent the courts acting as a check on their powers tend to overlook that the grounds on which the courts do so are narrow. They do not do so for political reasons, for this is simply not the role of judges. But as Lord Diplock said in this case, where politicians and other decision-takers act "illegally" or outside the boundaries of the powers conferred on them by Parliament, or with "procedural impropriety" which means simply an unfair process such as denying someone a hearing or proper consultation, or where they act with "irrationality" which means plain perversity, the courts can and should then intervene to protect the citizen. Interestingly Lord Diplock also touched for the first time in English law on the doctrine of proportionality which existed in continental law but which we had not yet started to explore in this country. Proportionality essentially means that the executive action taken should not be disproportionate to the aim which it was seeking to achieve. The concept was to take root in our law especially after the incorporation of the European Convention of Human Rights. This was the great achievement of the Human Rights Act, 1998. But in those days the challenge on human rights grounds could only be made to Strasbourg. This meant a rather formal argument with the judges asking very few questions by way of intervention. But the compensation was always an evening and good dinner in that fine city. The Strasbourg court had no hesitation in dismissing the application made by the unions and so upholding the decision on the same grounds as our judges.

There was one important side benefit to me personally of this decision. I had become very aware of the need for consultation and the doctrine that people whose rights were affected had a legitimate expectation to such a right. Two years later when I was chairman of the Bar we were seeking an uplift in criminal legal aid fees. The Lord Chancellor broke off the negotiations and decided on a very small rise when it was clear that we had expected proper consultation. I was able to make an instant decision that we should sue for breach of legitimate expectation. This is probably a rash thing for any lawyer to do where he is potentially involved as a litigant. But fortunately it was to prove a right decision and with the help of a court presided over by Lord Lane, the then Chief Justice, we were to gain a right to consultation which in turn led to a markedly higher increase in remuneration.

That was one footnote to the GCHQ case. The other is that the ban on trade union rights at GCHQ was promptly lifted by the new Labour government in 1997. Most members have joined the Public and Commercial Services Union. Stirring events of a decade earlier, and the grievances they created, have been laid to rest.

7. KEN LIVINGSTONE

One Saturday evening in November 1981, in time to celebrate the twentieth anniversary of my call to the Bar, I was returning home from a case in Hong Kong. I had taken a short break in Sri Lanka to see some of the ancient shrines and had been out of touch with the newspapers. My flight was delayed. It was almost ten in the evening before we landed at Gatwick. As I walked out of the arrivals gate, I saw one of the clerks, waiting to meet me. This level of service was highly unusual. My first thought was that there had been some drama affecting one of my children. But they were all safe and well and Nigel was meeting me for a very different reason.

In early days at the Bar I had grown used to dealing with cases at short notice. When young barristers start out and trek between different magistrates' courts it is usual for them to be given the case the night before it is due to be heard in court. But as a career progresses and the cases become more complex they are generally fixed some time ahead and there is normally proper time to prepare to deal with them. Not on this occasion.

"We've got you the brief for the Fares Fair case", Nigel announced. "You are representing the GLC in the House of Lords". He added rather limply that he hoped that gave me enough time to prepare. Out of touch with the news, my first question was what the Fares Fair case was about. My second was to ask how thick was the bundle of papers. In the car I read the press cuttings and glanced at the brief for appeal.

London has grown up from a series of villages, and has done so haphazardly until in time they connected with each other. It was not until 1889 that this assortment of communities first got a government of its own, the London County Council. In 1963 this was replaced by the Greater London Council or GLC, which also became responsible for the wider area than its predecessor. Obviously transport was then, as it is now, a crucial area of responsibility in the capital. There was frustration then as there is now. The average speed of traffic wending its way through London's streets is the same as it was in 1900: 8 mph. The GLC had responsibility for many, although not all, of the roads in London and it regulated London transport. The London Transport Executive was answerable to the GLC. From 1973 the GLC had begun to support, although it had never implemented, policies such as the freezing of fares which were intended to encourage people to use public transport instead of their cars. Whilst in opposition in local government in London from 1977, the Labour party developed a policy of using money from the rates - the local government tax at the time - to subsidise ticket prices on the buses and underground. This policy was to figure prominently in their election manifesto for the GLC in 1981 when they were once again returned to power.

But the ability of successive central local government authorities actually to influence events was not straightforward. Throughout their lives, the LCC and subsequently the GLC had to share powers with the local councils responsible for different areas of London. The GLC covered the same area as thirty-two different borough councils. The broad principle was that the GLC would have responsibility for the things which needed to be coordinated across the capital. But inevitably the different roles of the borough councils and the GLC were not always clear. They regularly clashed over planning decisions, road maintenance and other issues.

These clashes were fuelled by political divides. The LCC was under long periods of Labour dominance for most of its life, and indeed was under Labour control from 1934 until it transmogrified into the GLC. By contrast the outer boroughs, which were added as part of the GLC, tended to be controlled by the Conservative party. The disagreements became so intense that by 1973 Conservative borough leaders were already calling for the abolition of the GLC. The Fares Fair policy was to hasten its demise.

The long-term tensions in London government were fired by changes in national politics. The broad consensus between the major parties as to how to fund local government, which had persisted since the end of the war, broke down in the mid 1970s. Political discussion became more ideological. After Margaret Thatcher was elected Prime Minister in 1979, the Labour party chose Michael Foot as its new leader, and moved so far to the left that a moderate breakaway party, the SDP, was formed, which ran in alliance with the Liberals in the 1983 general election. The Labour party's own manifesto in that election was so radical that it was to be described as "the longest suicide note in history".

Yet in 1981, during Margaret Thatcher's first term as Prime Minister, the Labour party regained control of the GLC. London's government was thus at odds with the government in Downing Street. Into the maelstrom stepped Ken Livingstone. Shortly after Labour took power at the GLC, Ken, backed by left-wing supporters, led a successful coup within the Labour party, to become leader of the GLC. Within a short time Ken was so well known for his socialist beliefs that a man who had mistaken his nickname for his real name once introduced him to a meeting as "Mr Red Ken". It was at a time when some left-wing boroughs such as Islington styled themselves "nuclear-free zones".

Under Livingstone's leadership, the GLC became involved in a wider range of social policies, such as combating racism and promoting workers' rights, consistently advocating strongly left-wing views. Ken Livingstone became a nationally known figure. The GLC became a major opponent of the national government.

It fell to Ken Livingstone's administration to implement the transport policy which the Labour party had set out in its manifesto for the 1981 GLC elections. The plan was called "Fares Fair". It was an attempt to deal with the practical problem of transport in London by encouraging more people on to public transport. The cut in fares would be 25%. Ratepayers would have to provide more than £60 million to pay for this, which in turn would require an increase in rates of 6.1p in the pound. Rates were based on the value of homes. So wealthier people, who were more likely to own cars, would tend to pay more towards the scheme. The outer boroughs were not all covered by the underground system. They also included more Conservative voters. Could the GLC introduce an overtly socialist policy to London, under a Conservative government? Bromley council took legal action to block the scheme. This political debate was to be settled judicially in the courts.

Ken Livingstone was to prove an exemplary client. He was not phased by the fact that I only had a short time to prepare the case. He had no doubt checked me out before instructing me but never felt the need to meet me and discuss the arguments. His executive officers did so and reported to him regularly. There were to be no recriminations or complaints when we lost the case even although it was one which was of very considerable importance to him. When I met him subsequently he was genial and talked about the experience without any apparent bitterness towards the judiciary who had decided so heavily against him.

Because the GLC had lost in the Court of Appeal, we as appellants had to present our argument first. We contended that the policy was fair because it aimed to achieve the general purpose of halting the decline of London transport and building up its services. This was the purpose for which the Transport Act 1969 had been passed. The achievement of this purpose justified the expense to the ratepayers. We also said that the GLC had been entitled to decide on the policy because it had been voted for by the electorate. We relied on the full debates which had been taking place in the GLC to reinforce the fact that it was a legitimate political choice, endorsed by both the voters and an elected assembly. Democracy in action. The courts should not intervene to overrule the view of those who had been empowered to make the decision.

We also argued that the intention of the Transport Act was to meet the general transport needs of Greater London. This was more important than whether London Transport was run at an operating profit. The GLC was acting within its powers, too, in taking account of the wider socio-economic considerations.

In our argument we relied strongly on a then recent case called Secretary of State for Education and Science v Thameside Metropolitan Council. In the 1970s when many grammar schools were being turned into comprehensives, Thameside Council had an election just before this was due to take place in the schools in its area. The Conservatives were successful and the new council followed up their manifesto commitment and halted the change at the last minute.

The Education Secretary had taken the council to court to force through his policy. But the House of Lords had ruled that it was important that the electorate had voted to keep the grammar schools. This gave the council a mandate, which made it harder for the Education Secretary to justify any interference. The council had taken into account the risk that the late change would cause some disruption when deciding to go ahead with its policy of keeping grammar schools.

We suggested that this case helped us in two ways. It showed that the courts would be reluctant to interfere with the actions of elected bodies. The courts are there traditionally in our society to ensure that action is taken in accordance with law but not to second-guess actions which were in the sphere of political activity. The case also showed that just because there were some drawbacks to the policy in the eyes of some people, it was still permissible for the council to decide on the course of action, provided that they did so in a reasoned way. We suggested that this education case had marked similarities to the decision to implement the manifesto commitment to reduce fares in the GLC case.

But these arguments were to no avail. The House of Lords agreed with the Court of Appeal, that the GLC was not acting in accordance with general business principles and so was acting beyond its powers. It was also unreasonable to tax ratepayers to subsidise the underground system. This was especially unfair because the subsidy would trigger a cut in central government funding of £50 million, which would also have to be made up from the rates. Lord Scarman said this: "The Act requires that the fares be charged at a level which will, so far as is practicable, avoid deficit ..... It is plain that the 25% overall reduction was adopted not because any higher fare level was impracticable, but as an object of social and transport policy. It was not a reluctant yielding to economic necessity, but a policy preference. In so doing, the GLC abandoned business principles. That was a breach of the duty owed to ratepayers and wrong in law."

In reaching their conclusion, the House of Lords relied heavily on the interpretation of the one word "economic" which appears in the Transport Act of 1969. They interpreted this word in such a way that they could say the GLC had to govern itself by usual business principles. The consequence of this was a judgment which limited the way in which an elected body could act, even where there was a manifesto commitment which had been supported by voters. The judges considered that the Thameside case was different from this one. In that case the most important issue had been whether the decision of the council was reasonable. But in the Fares Fair case the judges said that they first had to decide whether the decision was one within the legal powers of the GLC. Because it was outside their interpretation of the legal powers, the decision was flawed, since every local authority has to act within the statutory powers conferred upon it by Parliament. Parliament could decide upon and implement any policy it liked. But the GLC, created by Parliament and given powers by Parliament, could not step outside those powers. Accordingly the view of the electorate, and the elected body which had considered the issue, should not be given any weight. No electorate can require, and no assembly can agree, that the GLC could act outside the powers given by the legislation.

It is of the essence of the development of the law that many cases before they are decided are ones in which there are strong legitimate arguments both ways. We have a very high-class judiciary which is called upon to take some difficult decisions involving tough choices. So I have always been reluctant to criticise, especially when I have been one of the advocates and have lost. But of all the cases I argued at the highest appellant level, this is the one in which, to my mind, the reasoning of the court was the most doubtful. It seemed to me a very narrow approach to suggest that the Transport Act, which was requiring a service to be run for the benefit of the public, should confine the GLC to acting like an ordinary commercial company, solely in accordance with sound business principles. If carried to its logical conclusion this might well require the GLC to have charged fares at a level which would optimise overall income.

To my mind the function of public services enables wider socio-economic considerations to be taken into account. The aim of getting the public back onto London Transport and so diminishing congestion on the roads as well as gaining support for the network of public services seemed to me to be not only understandable but positively desirable. It is impossible to know how the policy would have worked but at least it would have been one brave attempt to influence the highly intractable challenge of altering the balance between the use of public transport and private cars. Successive governments and the public often argue that this is a very important aim although few steps have been taken over the intervening years to make any real difference. Ken Livingstone's prompt implementation of the imaginative policy of his party stands out like a beacon as a bold idea to achieve change. The effect of the judgment of the House of Lords is that we shall never know whether it would have worked.

What we do know, some twenty years on, is that there are still major transport problems for London. Bus services have been improved, but the underground system still creaks and has received far too little investment. Traffic congestion has remorselessly increased on the roads in the intervening years. There has been no decisive shift of attitude or bold action to concentrate on the improvement of public transport so as to serve the whole community and also make the roads less congested. Ken's policies might have seemed maverick to some and were certainly brave. I have always felt it would have been healthier if he had been allowed to give them a chance to work.

Meanwhile in 1986 the GLC was abolished and London became the largest city in the world without its own government. So it remained for the rest of the long years of Conservative government. When the Labour party got back into power in 1997, they legislated to reintroduce a central government for London. They did not expect the new mayor to be none other than Ken Livingstone. After failing to secure the official Labour party nomination, Ken stood as an independent. In 2000 he was elected as the first mayor of the new Greater London Authority. The first words of his acceptance speech were: "As I was saying before I was so rudely interrupted some fourteen years ago…"

In the light of the rebuff he had received to his radical transport policy, more than a decade previously, it would perhaps have been understandable if Ken had proceeded cautiously. But this is not his style and he acts on the belief that political power is only valuable if you use it well. By then central government was attracted by the principle of a congestion charge payable by those vehicles which entered the centre of London. Ken decided to introduce this charge to take effect in February 2003. He had to consider a lot of options as to how it would operate. The level of the charge, the boundaries of the scheme, what exemptions there should be, the price to be charged, what improvements should be made to public transport before the scheme started to operate. With the help of Transport for London he had both to consult and decide on these and many other details. He received able legal guidance at every stage, including skilful and sensitive advice from Charles George QC. But this policy, too, was challenged in the courts. In preparing the litigation I stood in for a time for my old client because Charles George was engaged on another case. Every detail of the scheme involved choices, and it followed that criticism could be made of the balance which the mayor had drawn. Charles George had the always demanding task of arguing the rightness of the choices on which he had advised. He succeeded and so this time Ken had an opportunity to put his scheme into practice.

As the day grew nearer, the opposition to the congestion charge grew. Sometimes it even came from the habitually vociferous taxi-drivers in spite of the competitive advantage they were gaining from being exempt. We were told that the technology was not good enough for the scheme to work. The government typically went quiet on the policy which it had previously supported to see whether it worked in practice. Any unpopularity would fall on

Ken. He recognised that if the scheme did not work, and it was very unpopular, he was unlikely to gain re-election. Yet he had the clarity of insight to see that some radical attempt ought to be made to change the pattern of traffic use towards public services. His first attempt had been to increase the attraction of public transport by reducing fares. This had been blocked as it was apparently not in accordance with sound business principles. So he now had to seek a more indirect incentive by increasing the cost of entering the city by car. I regret that the first of his experiments was not given the chance to work. No one can say whether if more of the public had embraced the offer of low fares with enthusiasm, it might have been a catalyst for the tackling of other transport issues. With the same problems existing nearly two decades later, I rather regret that a judicial decision deprived us of the opportunity to find out.

8. SINGAPORE SLINGS

It was always good to travel to argue cases in other Commonwealth jurisdictions. The legal systems in Commonwealth countries were derived from and shaped by English law and jurisprudence. Some countries such as Canada, Australia and New Zealand which have very strong Bars of their own, never or rarely invited English advocates to argue cases. But Hong Kong and Singapore were two which during my time in silk still saw the distinct value of allowing English QCs to argue some of their more important cases as their local Bars developed and grew in strength. The work was interesting, the accommodation and standard of living very agreeable, and it was a wonderful opportunity to learn in a little depth about two very interesting although highly different entrepreneurial societies.

The history of Singapore over the last half-century has been truly remarkable. This former British colony still carries the bag of traditions going back to Sir Stamford Raffles, the explorer who spent no more than six months in the country but established it as a territory with a thriving port and later as a military base. The old Law Courts, the cricket ground and pavilion of the Singapore Cricket Club and the Parliament building have all been retained in the heart of the city. But around them is the vibrancy of the new dynamic Singapore with high-rise buildings, new land being reclaimed from the sea, and a port full of shipping whose lights at night give the impression of themselves being a city. Singapore has a population of 4.1 million, is no more than 728 square kilometres and has virtually no natural resources apart from the harbour. But it has one of the largest economies in the world. The society is prosperous, orderly and is tough on crime, including particularly drug offences and corruption. Facilities, from the Botanical gardens to the mass transit railway and the state of the art new

Changi airport, are impressive. It is almost uniformly a well-ordered society with little dissent and apparent acceptance of the firm disciplines which are seen as having contributed so much to its successful development.

The clear-sighted, dominant, always firm and sometimes ruthless, statesman who has guided and driven this remarkable country for the best part of half a century is Lee Kuan Yew. He is one of the towering figures of Asia. He was a boy in the Second World War and suffered the shattering of the myth of the invincibility of the British when Singapore collapsed like a pack of cards before the Japanese. He was educated at Trinity Hall College, Cambridge where he achieved a first-class degree in law. He went back to Singapore to practise as an advocate and solicitor in 1951. He was immediately active in politics and became Secretary-General of the People's Action Party when it was founded in November 1954. In 1959 the PAP won the majority of seats in Parliament. Lee Kwan Yew formed a government. Since then the PAP has been re-elected to power at every successive general election. Lee Kuan Yew was Prime Minister for many years and when he relinquished this post became Senior Minister, still the dominant figure in Singapore politics.

Opposition politics in Singapore are not strong. There is no Western-style belief that a strong opposition is crucial to a democracy. Nor is there a vigorous, independent press to fill, however imperfectly, the vacuum left by the absence of an opposition to hold the government to account. The two most memorable cases I argued in Singapore both reflected this political and social context.

The first was when I represented Lee Kuan Yew himself in a defamation action. The defendant was another lawyer, J.B. Geyaretnam, who practised as a solicitor and in 1971 became the Secretary-General of the Workers' Party, an opposition party. The action arose out of speeches in a general election called in December 1976.

Lee Kuan Yew fired the opening salvo in the election campaign. He began by saying "The People's Action Party would welcome an opposition in Parliament, but, unfortunately, the leaders of the present opposition parties are inconsequential men with a common denominator - they like to be elected into office but they do not know what they wanted to get into parliament for." He added later scathing comments in the same vein about the opposition leaders.

A few days later, and shortly before polling day, the Workers' Party held a lunchtime rally at Fullerton Square in the heart of Singapore. About fifteen hundred people attended. Geyaretnam picked up an accusation that the prime minister had made that the opposition leaders were not good at the management of their own personal fortunes. He responded, "Well, my dear friends, I feel guilty for that. I am not very good in the management of my own personal fortunes but Mr Lee Kuan Yew has managed his personal fortunes very well. He is the prime minister of Singapore. His wife is the senior partner of Lee & Lee and his brother is the director of several companies, including the Tat Lee Bank in Market Street: the bank which was given a banking permit licence when other banks were having difficulty getting one.. So Mr Lee Kuan Yew is very adept at managing his own personal fortunes but I am not".

These words clearly did not influence the outcome of the general election. The PAP won all the seats with a higher number of votes than in the immediately previous general election of 1972. But Geyaretnam's foolhardy remarks, which may well have been made on the spur of the moment, clearly alleged corruption against Lee Kuan Yew. The prime minister requested an apology. I suspect Geyaretnam would have been willing to apologise but he realised that if he did so the immediate consequence would be a libel action in which he would not have any vestige of a defence. Lee Kuan Yew in any event started proceedings for defamation. The lack of corruption was a badge of integrity on which he had built Singapore society. He was not going to overlook the suggestion that he was personally tainted.

On a visit to Singapore after the action had been launched but before it came to trial, I visited the prime minister to advise him. From what I had seen I had formed the personal view that Mr Geyaretnam may have been rash and foolish but he certainly was not wicked. He had pursued a lonely political career in opposition with some courage. I suggested to the prime minister that it might be adequate for him to accept an apology, moderate damages and payment of his costs if Geyaretnam was prepared to make such amends. It was politely and firmly explained to me that this would not suffice to redress the harm done by the libel. Lee Kuan Yew explained that he had a reputation for being tough and that if he suddenly became conciliatory people would be inclined to think that there must or might be something in the story. The very reputation he had created in Singapore society meant that there was no scope for compromise.

So we came to trial in 1978. My opponent was John Mortimer QC, the fine, fearless criminal barrister and noted writer. His principal creation, Rumpole of the Bailey, by his humanity, passionate commitment to his clients, willingness to stand up against authority, and sheer maverick individuality was probably the best advertisement the profession of barrister has known in my time. John himself was not going to be intimidated by the prime minister. The aura in which the case was held was demonstrated in a small way on the first morning before court started. I arrived early to find a number of people scurrying around anxiously to make certain that the air conditioning worked so that the prime minister would have no ground for criticism.

It was a defamation case to which there was logically no defence. But John skilfully attempted to argue that the real meaning of the words was not as serious as suggesting corruption and that in the less serious sense they were fair comment. This is a straddle that has been attempted in libel actions before and since but is always very difficult and generally fails. John cross-examined Lee Kuan Yew quite brilliantly to suggest that someone who heard the words would simply think that the banking licence had been obtained because of the family reputation for skill and honesty and without pausing to wonder whether there had been any corruption. The first afternoon of cross-examination was pure theatre, and several times John rattled the prime minister. But the next morning it was no contest. Lee Kuan Yew had been back to the prime minister's home, the Istana which had once been the British Government House, and had thought through the cut and thrust of the afternoon. John had, I suspect, dined well and with some relief with his generous hosts from the Workers' Party. Lee Kuan Yew dominated the proceedings for the rest of the cross-examination.

The judge had no difficulty in deciding that the words contained a clear allegation of corruption. He set out his reasons in convincing terms and rejected the defence of fair comment. He rightly said that the charge of corruption was not a comment but an allegation of fact and that if it was baseless there was no defence to the action. He saw this as a serious case. He remarked that "this was a very grave slander which struck at the very heart of the plaintiff's political reputation ...." It was spoken by the principal opposition speaker and a prominent person whose words would carry more weight than that of a lesser individual .... The words would be spread by word of mouth." The judge noted that there had been four other defamation actions arising out of that general election for similar slanders. He awarded the Singapore equivalent of approximately £35,000. Geyaretnam appealed to the Privy Council, the London court consisting of this country's highest judges, the Law Lords, against the amount of the damages. But they got nowhere as it was impossible to say that the damages were excessive and so should be varied by an appellant court.

I had to take it from Lee Kuan Yew that there was no scope for magnanimity in the way I had suggested at an early stage of the case. But by then he had established a formidable position in Singapore and was very well entrenched as prime minister. I suspect that temperamentally he would have found it difficult to resist the opportunity to punish a political opponent's ill-advised remarks. That he was essentially combative was brought out in a small way at the end of the case. He generously invited me to a splendid open-air dinner with the others in our legal team in the magnificent grounds of the Istana. Some of his cabinet were there too although they did not speak very much and seemed more concerned to take their cue from the Prime Minister. It was a warm evening, with open-necked shirts, the case was over and had gone well, and all this encouraged me to drink some excellent red wine fairly generously. At one stage the prime minister leant across the table and said "Bob, may I give you a word of advice?" "Please do, prime minister." "When you are on circuit in England, do you still dine with your opponent?" "We do, and with great enjoyment". Then came the punch line. "When you next dine with an opponent you should drink white wine and give him red wine. Red wine is bad for the voice and you will have the advantage in court the following day". It was a telling small indication of how even in Bar mess one of the most remarkable men of his generation would have sought a competitive advantage.

My next foray to Singapore of any interest was more than a dozen years later. The circumstances were very different and I was pitted against all the least attractive aspects of the system of justice in Singapore.

Teo Soh Lung is a solicitor. She is small of build, earnest and socially committed. She was practising her profession in June 1987 when she was arrested and detained without trial on the ground that she was involved in an alleged Marxist plot. This plot was said to be aimed at subverting the political and social system of Singapore. The power under which she was detained existed under the Internal Security Act which enabled the government to detain someone without trial if they considered that it was necessary in the interests of national security. Whilst, as we have seen in regard to the GCHQ and "Spycatcher" cases, courts are reluctant to intervene and overturn the actions of governments where there is material showing that they are based on national security grounds, this was a particularly tight provision, limiting the jurisdiction of the courts. A challenge could only be mounted if defective procedures had been used in the making of the order or if it could be shown that the order was a complete sham and had nothing to do whatsoever with national security interests. These are tough hurdles to surmount where the burden of putting forward appropriate evidence rests on the person detained.

When arrested, Soh Lung was entitled to make representations to an Advisory Board. She denied all the allegations that she was doing anything which put at risk the security of Singapore. She was a member of the Workers' Party, but contended that she was quite legitimately exercising her civil and political rights. She denied the suggestion that she was using the Law Society of Singapore, of which she was a Council member, as a political pressure group. In a letter, the Law Society said she had done nothing as a Council member which caused it to doubt her loyalty to Singapore.

After making these representations, and after a period of detention, Soh Lung was released in September 1987 along with eight other detainees. The government issued a press statement in which it said it was "satisfied that they are unlikely to resume their subversive activities and no longer pose a security threat". The government also made it clear that they would be detained again if they involved themselves in "subversive activities".

The detainees understandably disliked the suggestion that the government considered they had been involved in subversive activities. The suggestion, too, was obviously damaging to Soh Lung as a solicitor. In April 1988, all those who had been detained made a press statement which simply denied the government's accusations against them. This expression of the right of free speech, which clearly was in no sense of itself a threat to national security, led to the government detaining Soh Lung and her colleagues once again. The revocation order was bare-faced about the reason. It stated: "and whereas on 18th April 1988, the said Teo Soh Lung issued a joint statement denying any involvement in a Marxist conspiracy and whereas the minister for home affairs is satisfied that in view of the statement it is necessary in the public interest that the direction of September 1987 should be revoked ….."

So Soh Lung was taken again into detention. This time she challenged the detention by the time-honoured protection of liberty, an application for habeas corpus, to release her. The ability to apply for freedom from arbitrary detention by habeas corpus was developed by the English common law more than four centuries ago and remains a fundamental bulwark against unlawful imprisonment.

I was asked to argue the challenge for Soh Lung in the Singapore Court of Appeal. We recognised we could not challenge the original detention because of the impossible hurdle of showing that the minister did not at that stage believe, even if totally misguidedly, that the appellant was putting at risk the national security of Singapore. But the position in regard to the second detention was much clearer. In September 1987 the government had recognised that even if in the past Soh Lung had engaged in such activities she was no longer a security risk. Nothing was suggested to have changed between then and April 1988 except that she had the temerity to issue a press statement protesting her innocence. It followed that she had been detained again not on security grounds but for exercising her constitutional right of free speech. This demonstrated that there was no foundation for her second detention.

I have no doubt that this argument would have succeeded before the English courts. The Singapore government appeared to take the same view. For in January 1989, after she had launched her action for habeas corpus, the government amended the law. It declared that any application challenging detention on national security grounds had to be judged against the background of the law of Singapore as it had been in 1971, at a time before the courts of England had slightly widened the grounds of challenge so that there was some opportunity even in cases where national security was involved to demonstrate that the evidence relied on by the minister was insufficient. Even more tellingly the government changed the law to provide that there should be no more appeals to the Privy Council in any cases involving internal security. For good measure, and contrary to all known legal principle, they made this provision apply retrospectively to applications that had been initiated before the new law came into force. In a one-party state there was no possibility of any opposition to these rushed measures which offended constitutional principles so as to avoid the perceived risk that Soh Lung's argument would succeed.

In autumn 1989 I went to Singapore for the hearing of the appeal. By then Soh Lung had been in detention for about eighteen months. I was taken to visit her in the detention centre where she was in solitary confinement.

The detention centre was quiet, tranquil, in no sense unclean, nor was she being deprived of proper food and drink or physically maltreated. But the loneliness was pervasive. She told me that she had become great friends with the spider which visited her cell and which was the only other living creature with whom she had any significant contact. She later wrote some moving poetry about her confinement and feelings. She was not allowed to attend the hearing in court so we went to see her regularly during the case to talk about progress. She had a small body of courageous supporters, notably George Lim, who was subsequently to become president of the Singapore Law Society and Patrick Seong, a talented solicitor. Her family was close and although it must have been hard for some of them to understand why she dared to become engaged in political activities, they were all fiercely loyal.

The hearing was before Wee Chong Jin, the long-serving Chief Justice whose reputation did not suggest that he would easily decide a case against the government. There were two other judges. I opened the case for the best part of two days. In England, or other Commonwealth countries, questions would have been asked during argument to test my submissions. This is elegantly described as the Socratic dialogue and more prosaically in the vernacular as "the verbals". It is normally the key to appellant advocacy. This is the opportunity to resolve the doubts of the court on difficult and decisive issues in the case. All advocates who feel they have a good case, welcome the opportunity to deal with doubts expressed by the judges. In this appeal I was heard in total silence until the second morning. Then after about an hour or so the Chief Justice interrupted me to say he had a question. I was momentarily cheered, as it suggested we were going to get into some real discussion. But hope was quickly dashed when the question turned out to be: "Can you remind me at which page of the appeal bundle the press statement made by Soh Lung is to be found?" My opponent was a Crown Council who argued his case correctly and without any over-exaggeration. He in his turn was asked no substantive questions probing the argument. Our view before the hearing that the case would be a sure-fire winner in England but had no prospect of success before Singapore judges turned out to be correct. The appeal was dismissed in a reserved judgement given in April 1990. Not so long afterwards Soh Lung was again released. She had served just over two and a half years in detention in solitary confinement. She has attempted again to take up the practice which was so dislocated by her traumatic experience. We have seen her and her family from time to time when passing through Singapore. My impression is that she has battled valiantly to put the experience behind her. But she is anxious, nervous and somewhat insecure. I suspect she will never fully recover from an experience that would be shaming to any civilised system of justice.

There is a perception of Singapore justice that has become fairly widespread. In cases between two private parties, a moderately competent judiciary will try cases conscientiously and seek to give a wholly fair decision on the factual and legal merits of the case. But in cases involving the government, however hard some judges may strive to uphold legal principles, there is a pressure working almost unconsciously throughout the system in favour of the government. It is not easy for a judiciary to be fully independent when its appointment is short-term and it has no security of tenure. The protection which exists in most systems to ensure a judge cannot be dismissed other than for absolutely blatant misconduct is a healthy one. It is increasingly seen as an element inherent in the right to a fair trial. The view that Singapore does not meet this standard is a disappointing exception. It is to those qualities in its society, notably freedom from corruption, which make it such a successful marine and financial services centre. I do not want to overstate this point. In many ways Singapore tries to preserve a decent system of justice with respect for appropriate procedural safeguards. But ultimately there is a weakness which it would do well to redress by giving judges proper security of office.

The day the Soh Lung case finished I received a short letter from Lee Kuan Yew. He said he had noticed I had been there to argue the appeal and invited me to call on him at the Istana in the light of our past acquaintance. I did so, and we talked about banking, the international political scene, and legal acquaintances of his going back to the days when he studied in England. We scrupulously did not talk about the case. It was only shortly after the suppression of the riots in Tiananmen Square in Beijing, and there was speculation as to whether this would delay the development of Chinese trade and relationships with the outside world. The prime minister was clear. He pointed out that in every village in China there were television sets. The Chinese could see how the rest of the world lived, and they were amongst the more entrepreneurial and enterprising of peoples. The tide of history would inevitably lead to greater openness. I left once again marvelling at his skills, but at the same time wondering how he and a government he headed could be party to the harsh restraints on harmless people who could not conceivably be even a remote challenge to the stable, successful society of which he had been the inspiration.

9. "SPYCATCHER"

Peter Wright was a member of MI5 who retired in 1976. A decade later his memoirs, "Spycatcher," attracted international interest and the attention of many courts in England and Australia. Mrs Thatcher's government attempted in both countries to prevent publication of the book on the simple ground that Mr Wright was betraying his legal duty of confidentiality owed to the service for which he had worked, and that it was particularly important that this duty should be emphatically upheld in regard to information concerning the intelligence services and national security. This principle was to be upheld by the courts. But in the end it came up against the reality that in the modern world it is impossible to restrain communications on a global basis and that once a book has been widely published abroad and is available to be brought into this country it is contrary to good sense to try and restrain publication of extracts in newspapers.

The history of the lawsuits was almost as surreal as had been some aspects of the conduct of the security services over many years. The work of MI5 had been corroded by the steady revelation of a number of double agents who during the cold war, either for ideological reasons or for money, betrayed this country to the former Soviet Union. In 1951, rightly fearing that they were close to detection, Guy Burgess and Donald Maclean had fled this country to live in Moscow. In 1963 Kim Philby was unmasked and took the same route into voluntary exile. In 1979 Mrs Thatcher was publicly to denounce Anthony Blunt, the Keeper of the Queen's Pictures as a long-standing spy for the Soviets. There were other double agents unmasked during this time, such as George Blake and Michael Bettaney. But there was also a lurking suspicion that treachery had reached right to the top of MI5, to Sir Roger Hollis, who was suspected by some insiders until eventually cleared.

The insidious concern that colleagues might be double agents obviously lessened the effectiveness of MI5 during these years. There were allegations in the press that MI5 had put 10 Downing Street under electronic surveillance while Harold Wilson was prime minister. It was said that some members of the service were suspicious because Wilson had been regularly to Russia after the Second World War before he became prime minister. Some even suggested that the Soviet Union might have caused the sudden death of Hugh Gaitskell in January 1963 so as to allow Harold Wilson to become party leader. In 1977 this was enquired into by Mr Callaghan's government who rejected the suggestion that there had been surveillance of Harold Wilson and Mrs Thatcher publicly confirmed this in the House of Commons in 1987. In the "Spycatcher" case the newspaper editors all accepted that this allegation was without any foundation in fact.

Peter Wright joined MI5 in 1955 and served until his retirement in 1976. He then retired to the deep, deep peace of Tasmania where as the photograph on the cover of his book displayed he sported the fine Australian bush hat which is traditionally said to have the benefit of keeping off both sun and flies. He then wrote his memoirs, which was suggested largely to be out of frustration at the rejection of the view that there was a plot against the Wilson administration between 1974 and 1976 and that either Sir Roger Hollis, or his deputy director-general, Graham Mitchell, was a Soviet agent. He had made this case to a House of Commons select committee which had rejected the charges. The book described, in the graphic language which an Australian judge characterised as being out of "the Boy's Own paper" the work of the service. This included the electronic surveillance of foreign embassies in London with hidden microphones, the bugging of telephones and the investigation of left-wing groups. Most of what he said was in no sense new. About a dozen books had been published over the years about the activities of MI5 by writers such as Chapman Pincher and Nigel West. Indeed Mr Wright himself had given a long television interview in 1984. So there was little new in "Spycatcher". What the government said was different was that this was the first time a serving member of MI5 had breached confidentiality and that this gave the stamp of authenticity to the stories which were already in circulation. The government had not attempted to stop publication of these earlier books and had tended to negotiate with the authors some changes. But it took a fundamentally different stance against Mr Wright to avoid the perception that anyone who dealt with members of the security services would at a later stage have their dealings revealed publicly. It was also designed to deter members of the service assuming that they could write their memoirs without any restraint.

This is not the place for a detailed history of the many and tortuous legal proceedings out of the publication of "Spycatcher". The United Kingdom government started the first lawsuit in Australia against Mr Wright and the publishers who were proposing to bring out his memoirs. The claim was based fairly and squarely on the duty of confidentiality owed by Mr Wright to the security services and his employers. By this time the completed manuscript of the book was in the hands of the publishers but no publication had taken place. In 1985 the publishers gave undertakings that they would not publish the book prior to trial of the action. This is the normal form of undertaking because otherwise the very claim brought to restrain publication could be defeated ahead of trial. In these situations the law seeks to hold the balance so as to minimise the prejudice to either party in the period leading up to the hearing.

In the middle of 1986 The Observer and The Guardian published articles which were simply reports of the nature of the allegations that were made in the book and were to be the subject of proceedings in Australia. There was, I suspect, no intention to circumvent the outcome of the action but simply to report on important litigation which was taking place. The government brought proceedings in this country to prevent further details being given of these allegations on the same principle that to allow publication would partially defeat the rights of the government in the event that they were successful in the Australian litigation. In November 1986, springtime in Sydney when the jacarandas are in their full pomp, the trial in Sydney commenced. It was high courtroom drama. Sir Robert Armstrong, then cabinet secretary, was sent to give evidence for the government in support of their claim. He was vigorously cross-examined by Malcolm Turnbull, a young Australian lawyer. Turnbull had a good mind, great energy and ebullience, and apparently relished the prospect of denigrating the claim for confidentiality and the UK government. He was to suggest in his submissions that both Sir Michael Havers, the Attorney General and Sir Robert had lied in regard to the evidence brought forward to support the claimant. The judge was to reject these contentions although he was critical of some of the evidence which was put forward. Much of the hearing was concerned with the other books which had been written about these allegations. The judge followed Turnbull's wide-ranging submissions with a judgment of great length in which he summarised practically the whole history of the security services. There can rarely have been an account of such a fascinating subject which reads so turgidly. In the end he decided that the effect of the publication of the earlier books meant that what Mr Wright had written lacked the quality of confidentiality. When the case went to the High Court of Australia in Canberra, the final court of appeal for that country, the issue was dealt with much more shortly. The court simply held that there was well-recognised law to prevent the enforcement by a foreign state, even a friendly state, of an obligation of confidentiality on the part of a member or former member of the security service of that state. The court saw it as an attempt to enforce the public governmental interest of the United Kingdom which they considered was contrary to the rule of international law.

The Australian contest attracted a good deal of publicity. Turnbull's attack on Armstrong was outspoken and prolonged and the contrast between their two styles was seen as reflecting the difference between our two cultures. Turnbull was the young, ambitious, able, no-nonsense Australian confronting the very senior, intelligent, civilised mandarin, Sir Robert Armstrong, who as cabinet secretary was uncomplainingly carrying the collegiate responsibility for the entire actions of the government over many years. When questioned about one letter written by the government which was not particularly expansive, he responded that whoever wrote it was "being economical with the truth". He was, as he made plain, quoting Edmund Burke, but this was seized on by Turnbull as displaying typical British duplicity. Civil servants are not normally used to being exposed to a blaze of publicity and to rough questioning. Sir Robert bore up to the task with dignity and stoicism. Nor was this his only experience in the witness box. Almost exactly a year later he had to give evidence in the "Spycatcher" proceedings in New Zealand on the Monday of one week and head home to give evidence in the High Court in the action here on Monday of the following week. He submitted this remarkable feat to the Guinness Book of Records where it duly still appears.

The effect of the case was to make Turnbull become well known in both Australia and the United Kingdom. He had a fine legal pedigree, having recently married Lucy Hughes, the talented lawyer daughter of Tom Hughes QC, one of Australia's leading silks, who practised effectively and vigorously until over the age of 80. Nor did Turnbull hesitate to capitalise on his achievement. In the spring of 1987 he wrote an article in the Sunday Times where he said that cross-examination had obviously been "a humiliating experience" for Sir Robert. He again very strongly criticised Sir Michael Havers and Sir Robert, suggesting that they had engaged in deception. He had earlier colourfully criticised those who were conducting the case in London, allowing himself to be quoted in The Times during the litigation itself as saying "Jeez, I am pissed off with those dumb clucks in London ...." The Code of Conduct of the English Bar does not allow barristers to comment during or in the immediate aftermath of litigation. This is clearly right, since under our common law traditions an advocate is there to present the client's case to the best of his or her ability whatever their private views so that all clients can be properly represented. It seemed to me that Turnbull, who has gone on to become lawyer to Kerry Packer and then to have a highly-successful career in business, did not need to continue the contest outside court in this way.

But the scene now shifts back to the United Kingdom and a rash of applications for injunctions and contempts of court in the summer of 1987. I was only vaguely aware of what was taking place since all my energies at that time were going into arguing the Jeffrey Archer libel action. What essentially happened was that The Independent and the Evening Standard both published information which was said to come from Mr Wright. This time the Attorney-General brought proceedings for contempt of court by publishing the very information which had been restrained from publication in the action brought against The Observer and The Guardian.

The Attorney-General has traditionally had two roles: as senior legal adviser to the government who is also responsible for representing the public interest in an official capacity to promote the proper administration of justice. Successive holders of the office have been zealous to try to preserve the distinction. No one more than Sir Michael Havers. He was the Attorney-General who, after the leak of the letter written by his colleague, the Solicitor-General, threatened to put the police into 10 Downing Street to discover the source of the leak. He was not deterred by the fact that he nursed hopes, later briefly fulfilled, of becoming Lord Chancellor after the following election. But Michael was a man of immense courage, as displayed in the war and his advocacy, and of total integrity. The other curiosity was that the injunction had not been granted against either The Independent or the Evening Standard. There was complex legal argument as to whether in those circumstances the doctrine of contempt of court could apply to someone not specifically bound by the terms of an injunction. The Court of Appeal held there could, although a more recent decision has cast doubt on that principle.

Whilst this important but esoteric legal point was being argued the course of events took a dramatic turn. In May 1987 Viking Penguin, the United States subsidiary of the well-known English publishing house, announced that it intended to publish "Spycatcher" in the United States. There was no prospect of obtaining a court order in that country to restrain publication. The effect of the First Amendment in the United States Constitution which guarantees freedom of speech has meant that it is settled law in that country that prior restraints against publications cannot be obtained. Publication was scheduled for the 13th July. This prompted the experienced and enterprising editor of the Sunday Times, Andrew Neil, to negotiate for the right to serialise the book in his newspaper. But for the legal proceedings the value of the book might have been relatively modest. But the lawsuits had given it the oxygen of publicity and raised expectations that it might contain particularly sensational exposures. The Sunday Times agreed to pay $150,000 for the serialisation rights, contemplating that there would be three or four extracts. Andrew Neil planned the first extract for 12th July, the day ahead of the publication in the United States.

He was a seasoned enough old hand to know that if anyone on the government's side suspected that The Sunday Times intended to serialise there would have been an immediate application for a restraining injunction in this country. So he personally took charge of obtaining a copy of the manuscript. He flew to the United States on 7th July, received his copy, and brought it back into this country, buried in his luggage. He next needed to take special measures to throw the government off the scent and prevent other newspapers trying to rush out what are known as "spoiling" articles based on his extracts in their later editions. So the first edition of The Sunday Times on 12th July had no extract from "Spycatcher". These appeared in the later editions, by which time it was too late for any action to be taken by the government to restrain publication. There would be no time for them to raise a judge from dinner or bed and get what the media had characterised as a "pyjama" injunction.

His plan worked brilliantly. Throughout the evening and the night more than 1.25m copies of The Sunday Times were produced and distributed across the country. No-one, least of all Mr Neil, was surprised at the government's reaction. The Attorney-General commenced proceedings for contempt of court which were upheld by the Court of Appeal. This meant that no further serialisation could take place until after the hearing of the main government action which had been fixed for the coming November.

"Spycatcher" went on sale in the United States. Anyone buying a copy of the book there and travelling to England could in practice bring it into this country. They could pass their copies to their families or friends with impunity. One enterprising person bought a large quantity of the books, tried to sell them in Parliament Square, but failed to dispose of all of them, and was apparently last seen trying to sell them to motorists by the side of the A40. The book was available and could be ordered by mail order, on the telephone from the United States, with the help of credit cards. The dam had burst and the waters were flowing fairly freely for anyone who wished to dip their toe in them.

This development spawned a further round of interim judgments. Sir Nicolas Browne-Wilkinson, who as the vice-chancellor was the senior judge of the Chancery Division, recognised what he saw as the impotence of the courts to continue to safeguard the information in "Spycatcher". He took the view that the government was pursuing a totally unreasonable aim in trying to do so. He saw no point in making an order to restrain further publication when so much had already taken place. He "felt like the little Dutch boy being asked to put a finger in the hole in the dyke when in fact the whole embankment had broken down two hundred yards upstream". If this judgment had been accepted the whole "Spycatcher" litigation would have probably come to a fairly speedy end.

But the government promptly challenged this decision before the Court of Appeal, which took the view that publication in newspapers was more widespread and indiscriminate than in the book form and that the publishers could not simply by a process of erosion destroy the government's right of confidentiality in what it considered to be the important security interest of the nation. This part of the case went through the courts in record time, going from the vice-chancellor to the House of Lords within the last ten days of July. The House of Lords, as sometimes happens, took the view that it was the duty of the courts to stand firm to prevent harm to the security service and to preserve confidentiality in so far as it could until the final hearing of the main litigation. Lord Ackner, a judge notoriously sceptical of the press said: "English justice will have come to a pretty pass, if our inability to control what happens beyond our own shores is to result in total incapacity to control what happens within our very own jurisdiction".

He had put his finger precisely on the issue in the case. The debate arose out of the need to decide whether globalisation, and the reality that news anywhere is news everywhere, should prevent a litigant obtaining what would otherwise be his clear rights under English law. On this conundrum Lord Bridge took precisely the opposite view. He said: "The present attempt to insulate the public in this country from information which is freely available elsewhere, is a significant step down a very dangerous road. The maintenance of the ban, as more and more copies of the book Spycatcher enter this country and circulate here, will seem more and more ridiculous".

So by a wafer-thin majority further publication was even at this stage restrained. The trial of the full English action would have to take place. I had so far had no involvement in any of the "Spycatcher" saga. But in early October 1987 I was contacted by Sir Patrick Mayhew, the Attorney-General, and asked if I would conduct the full action for the government. My wife Marie and I were far away in New Zealand at the time, speaking at the New Zealand Law Conference in the beauties of a Christchurch spring and with the generous hospitality of that country. That day I had resisted one more doubtful feature of that hospitality by refusing a suggestion that I should go bungee-jumping. But I could not resist the challenge of "Spycatcher" even though I knew that it was bound to be an uphill task to restrain further publication. What would be vital would be to establish the principle that a member of the security service is under a duty of confidence not to publish memoirs recounting details of what they and others did during the course of their employment. This seemed to me to be one of the relatively narrow categories of situation where a restraint on the normally invaluable principle of freedom of speech was appropriate. The trial of the full action began promptly in November 1987.

It was heard by Mr Justice Scott. Richard Scott was one of the talented lawyers who had left South Africa at the height of apartheid and practised throughout their career at the English Bar. Richard was a good rugby footballer, tennis player and horseman who was later to conduct the Arms for Iraq Enquiry and to become a law lord. He gave weight to the European Convention on Human Rights even though it had not then been incorporated into our own domestic law, and to the importance of the freedom of the press. He concluded that it was wholly unacceptable that the public in this country should be prevented from reading extracts from "Spycatcher," or copies of the book when it was freely available to anyone who had the determination and wit to seek it out and that it had been disseminated on a world-wide scale. The information was firmly in what the law described as "the public domain" and it would be both pointless and a wrongful restraint on the press to seek to keep the lid partially on its contents. But he recognised the general importance of secrecy saying: "The British Security Service is responsible for the defence of the realm from dangers arising from espionage, sabotage and subversion. It is, and has to be, a secret service in the sense that its affairs and operations require, if it is to operate efficiently, to be protected by a cloak of secrecy. The importance of the service and of its efficiency to the safety of the realm and of its citizens is not in doubt ...."

So he emphatically indicated that Mr Wright had owed a duty of confidence which he had broken by the publication of "Spycatcher."

The case made its way next to the Court of Appeal early in 1988. At the same time as I was arguing the case I had a keen personal interest in a case being held in the very next door court, where there was a challenge to the judgment of the Takeover Panel, of which I was then chairman, because it had ordered Guinness to pay Argyll some £70m in compensation for breaches of the code during the fiercely fought contest to acquire the liquor company, Distillers. I was an advocate in the one court and a defendant, although happily only a representative defendant without being personally at risk for damages or costs, in the court next door. The court in the "Spycatcher" case unanimously upheld Mr Justice Scott in his view that the world-wide distribution of "Spycatcher" meant that a restrain on further publication would be contrary to common sense and inappropriate. They adopted the eloquent expression of Sir Nicolas Browne-Wilkinson in one of the earlier judgements in the case when he said "the truth of the matter is that in the contemporary world of electronics and jumbo jets, news anywhere is news everywhere".

After so many hearings it was perhaps inevitable that the government would want to take the case on to the last lap to the House of Lords. The issue had become well-travelled and rather stale. As the senior law lord, Lord Keith, said "all possible damage … has already been done by the publication of "Spycatcher" abroad and the ready availability of copies in this country."

But there was compensation in the concluding words of his judgment when he stated: "in the first place I regard this case as having established that members and former members of the Security Service do have a life-long obligation of confidence owed to the Crown. Those who breach it, such as Mr Wright, are guilty of treachery just as heinous as that of some of the spies he excoriates in his book."

So the long battle to hold the balance between the importance of maintaining confidentiality in the work of the security services was over. Across three years there had been three major hearings in the courts in Australia and more than double that number in the course of a single year from the summer of 1987 in the English Courts. The case would probably have died if on the interlocutory hearing in the House of Lords in August 1987 the wafer-thin majority for restraining publication temporarily had decided the other way. But once there was a temporary restraint it was obviously important for the government to seek to pursue the principle which it was trying to uphold with great vigour. The strong statements as to the importance of secrecy in the security services and to the duty of confidentiality which had been owed by Mr Wright and broken by him justified this attempt. But the case also struck important blows for freedom of the press. There was a good deal of argument centred round the Human Rights Convention and statements that English law was just as vigilant in upholding free speech.

There was also a memorable passage in the first judgment of the House of Lords where Lord Oliver said: "We do not have a First Amendment, but, as Blackstone observed, the liberty of the press is essential to the nature of a free state. The price that we pay is that this liberty may be and sometimes is harnessed to the carriage of liars or charlatans, but that cannot be avoided if the liberty is to be preserved ..... Ideas, however unpopular or unpalatable, once released and however released into the open air of free discussion and circulation, cannot forever be effectively proscribed as if they were a virulent disease".

Over recent years the courts have been increasingly vigilant to give full effect to the importance of a free press and there is no doubt that the enactment of our own Human Rights Act, the greatest achievement of Lord Irvine as Lord Chancellor, has underpinned and accelerated this robust tendency. There are situations, and the preservation of real confidentiality is one of them, when the restraint on publication is justifiable. But such claims should be rigorously tested particularly when they attempt to restrain publication of serious issues which it is genuinely in the public interest to have exposed or debated. In general as the great United States lawyer Louis Brandeis said: "sunlight is the best disinfectant".

10. THE SUMMERLAND FIRE

It is usual in our country for disasters which cause large-scale loss of life to be followed by a public inquiry conducted by a senior judge. The public, and above all the relatives and friends of the victims, want the facts to be investigated in depth and recommendations made which may help avoid further similar disasters in future. Judges, and as a society we are often in danger of taking this too much for granted, bring skills, authority and above all total integrity to the task. They have no political nor any other axe to grind and their whole training and instinct is to seek to be thorough and fair. Over the years these inquiries have covered a wide range of tragic incidents. The collapse of the tip at Aberfan. The loss of life in the Hillsborough football crowd stampede. The fire in the underground station at King's Cross. The Clapham railway crash. The BSE epidemic. Each of these hearings carry their particular pain and poignancy. So did the Summerland Inquiry which occupied much of my first year as a silk between autumn 1973 and spring 1974.

Douglas, on the Isle of Man, was a typical English seaside resort. Most of its visitors came from the North of England and in particular from the Midlands. It had prospered in the first half of the last century. Holidays had traditionally been weeks or later fortnights. Until the spread of the railways and the coming of the motor car people had generally celebrated them with fairs and entertainments in their own towns. But better transport meant that for the first time ordinary people had the chance of a seaside holiday. Llandudno, Rhyl and Colwyn Bay, all in North Wales were the usual destinations for those who lived in the Potteries. To escape from the grime of factory towns to the seaside was an immense thrill as so movingly told in Walter Greenwood's great

novel, "Love on the Dole.' My mother never forgot her first seaside holiday at Douglas sometime shortly after the end of the First
World War.

But by the 1960s the fortunes of resorts such as Douglas
were declining. People had gone further afield to the south coast
and Devon and Cornish resorts. Some were even going further
still, to the Costa Brava or Ibiza or even to Greece.

So the Summerland concept was developed. It was to be an
imaginative creation to establish an attractive leisure centre which
could counter the obvious attractions of the Mediterranean. It was
to be the much more ambitious, contemporary successor to the old
nineteenth century Winter Gardens. There was to be swimming,
sunbathing, entertainment, dancing, restaurants and all the fun of
the fair. It was all, too, to be available even in the worst days of
the island's unpredictable and often bracing summer. So it was
essential to the building that there should be all sorts of activities
inside but that there should be a great deal of open planning with
a roof which was largely transparent so that the building admitted as much natural light and sunshine as possible. There were
precedents. There were some large advanced glass and concrete
structures for sports stadia and swimming pools already in operation. In the 1967 International Exhibition at Montreal, the US
pavilion had been a huge geodesic dome. The techniques for a
highly-attractive, exciting leisure centre providing as it was termed
"outdoors-indoors" were well available. The building was to be
constructed at the northern end of the long sweep of the Douglas
promenade about a mile away from the harbour. This was to make
it exposed to weather which was very changeable. The wind could
gust at up to 120mph. Rain storms and showers could be both
strong and prolonged. But, as the inquiry also generously said:
"Fine and warm weather can be enjoyed for long periods in a normal summer and the whole climate is clean and bracing".

To achieve the wished-for openness to daylight, the building
extensively used acrylic materials known as oroglas, the product of
Rohm and Haas of the US. The properties of oroglas were very
much the same as those of the better-known perspex. Acrylic was

hard, durable, did not break as easily as glass, and indeed had for generations been used to make the windows of aeroplanes. But it was highly flammable. The south face of the building, and the roof, were entirely glazed with oroglas shaped in several forms of domes.

The building was opened by the time of the 1973 summer season. It had the capacity to hold five thousand people. On the night of 2nd August 1973 it was fortunate that there were only three thousand people in the building. For at about eight o'clock that evening a fire broke out and spread rapidly, devastating the building and destroying most of it. The vast majority escaped amongst scenes of panic and confusion. But fifty people - men, women and children - perished, and a similar number had to be treated in hospital for injuries. In terms of loss of life, it was the worst peacetime fire disaster in the United Kingdom for almost fifty years. An inquiry was promptly established to be headed by Sir Joseph Cantley, a senior high court judge, and two experts in the science of fire and fire prevention and architecture. Where inquiries have really technical aspects it is often of great assistance to the presiding to judge to have assessors who can help him ask the right questions and assess the strength of the evidence.

The fire had very small beginnings. At the eastern end of the terrace on which Summerland stood there were the remains of a broken-down fibreglass kiosk. The kiosk has been used early in the summer as a ticket office for mini-golf on the terrace. But it had been damaged by storm, dismantled and most of it had been taken away. For no good reason one section was simply left lying on its side close to the wall of the building. On the evening of the fire it may have contained paper and other litter which had blown and accumulated in that part of the terrace. Three Liverpool schoolboys on holiday lit a match and started what they expected to be a small fire. It was a prank and not even the most vivid imagination could have predicted the consequences. The kiosk was next to a sheet-metal wall, with a combustible bitumen coating on both sides. Because the sheet-metal was highly conductive fuel vapours were given off on the inside face of the wall and became ignited. This metal wall in turn had a void between it and a fibre-

board lining of the amusement arcade. This meant that the fire
could spread within the board, igniting the lining and its wooden
supports, and so building up over a timescale of about ten minutes
before bursting through into the amusement arcade on the other
side of the fibreboard wall. It was, as the remarkable adviser from
Rohm and Haas Fritz Ragie told us more than once, a variant of a
classic theatre fire. The fire builds up unnoticed behind the scenes
and so appears with great force and speed as it enters the audito-
rium. Not for nothing do most theatres with a proscenium arch
have a fire curtain.

The fire then spread rapidly to the restaurants, the leisure
floors, and upwards and outwards. The oroglas started to burn.
This was captured on camera vividly and frighteningly. So the
initial public impression was that it had played a primary role in
the development and spread of fire within the building. This impression had come almost indelibly from photographs which had
been taken of the fire when it was raging. This showed the roof
to be an apparent fireball. The very name of the acrylic in turn
fuelled this impression as the tabloids not surprisingly christened
it "horror-glass". Challenging this assumption, and showing that
the oroglas was involved in the fire at a later stage, was to be the
primary task of the legal team which I was asked to lead during
the inquiry. It was inevitably going to be a harrowing case, but for
an advocate the challenge was considerable. My clients were cast
as the villains whose highly-inflammable product had gone up in
flames and contributed to many deaths. It was their case from the
outset, and was to become ever-clearer as the inquiry went on, that
this accusation was wrong. Their claim was that most of the deaths
had been caused by asphyxiation before the roof and walls caught
fire and that in the event the burning off of the roof had helped to
lessen the amount of smoke which was putting people at risk.

But all this was to become only slowly clear during the inquiry. What happened on the evening of the 2nd August was a
continuous scene of horror and chaos. The staff of Summerland,
managed by Trust House Forte, was slow to call the fire brigade.
The fire had begun in the kiosk on the mini-golf terrace before

7.45pm. It took more than 15 minutes to develop and move from the kiosk to the metal sheet and then build up within the void in such force that it eventually burst out into the amusement arcade. But it was only then that the fire brigade was notified. Vain attempts had been made by staff to extinguish the fire in the kiosk and their preoccupation with trying to put it out had deflected them from what with hindsight would have been the obvious thing to do. If they had done so properly, so the inquiry found, there was a prospect that the building might have been saved. Ironically the first notification which the fire brigade received was from a ship at sea which had witnessed the development of the fire.

The inquiry began in November 1973. It continued throughout the winter. Winter on the Isle of Man is rugged. The island which displays its natural beauty to considerable effect in summer is sparing of its charms in winter. The sun shines rarely. The terrain is bleak, cold, remorselessly windy and wet. Once in jest a member of our party remarked that the only time the rain stopped falling was when the wind was blowing so strongly horizontally as to drive it sideways. But our team was comfortably housed. We took some cottages on the Ballaugh beach, a part of the island from which when the clouds lift it is possible to see the coast of Northern Ireland and the Mull of Galloway at the south-west tip of Scotland. Our fine solicitor, Christopher James of Linklaters and Paines, as they were then called, looked after the logistics with a quiet and sensitive panache. He imported two talented cooks who ensured that breakfast, tea and dinner were so good that we not only could but needed to miss lunch in Douglas. We were a close-knit, happy team. My junior was Kenneth Rokison, a talented commercial practitioner who was to take silk the following year and become a leading practitioner and arbitrator. He had a splendid sense of humour, and the energy to organise our early morning walks on Ballaugh beach which he cheerfully led whatever the weather.

These physical comforts were very good for our morale. But so was the progress of our case in the inquiry. We had one obvious line of defence. Everyone knew that acrylic was inflammable and there had been architects, contractors, planners, fire-safety experts, and all the panoply of controls and safeguards designed to ensure that safe use was made of every material. In the end it was clear that a combination of poor design, inadequate fire-breaks, lack of proper fire safety precautions, and inexperienced staffing had brought the standard of Summerland far below what the public were entitled to expect. The story was not one of gross incompetence by one single individual. But it was a story of moderate incompetence by almost everyone involved whose skills and experience probably made them out of their depth in the undertaking and management of such a large-scale project. It was the cumulative effect of this incompetence by decent and well-meaning people which ultimately caused the tragedy. But no one could, and the inquiry did not, sensibly blame the manufacturers of a material who simply supply to order a product whose flammable qualities were well-known.

Yet what was even more interesting and satisfying was to dispel through our evidence, and the opportunity to cross-examine other experts, the impression that oroglas had played a large part in causing the fire. The evidence suggested that oroglas first caught fire on the inside from flames which had risen up from the burning amusement arcade. Once the roof caught fire it burnt out in an astonishingly short time, probably as little as ten minutes. It was at this time that the photographs were taken which inevitably concentrated on the burning roof and led to it being thought to be the cause of much of the loss of life. It was also established that the acrylic softened before it ignited so that some panels simply fell out allowing the venting of the fire with a useful removal of lethal smoke. But it was doubtful whether this venting was particularly valuable in the sequence in which the fire developed and its overall timing. The inquiry unequivocally accepted the case we presented.

Para 108 of its report said: "The stage at which oroglas became involved in the fire deserved and received special attention, particularly as there was at one time a widespread public impression that oroglas played the primary role in the development and spread of the fire within the building. This is contrary to the evidence. We are satisfied by clear and positive evidence of eye-witnesses that the oroglas was ignited from fire within the building and was not ignited until there was a very substantial fire in the amusement arcade".

There followed a finding which was very important both as a matter of justice and commercial interest to our clients. The tribunal said at paragraph 149: "It is, we believe, quite possible to clad a building in acrylic safely ..." It was the way it was used, and the extent of its use, which made Summerland a vulnerable building.

The inquiry had taken fifty days. It had been in many ways a fine baptism in silk. There was the sadness of the tragedy and the loss of life. There was the poignancy as the errors made by decent men were revealed, demonstrating how the flawed design, construction and management of the building contributed to the fateful evening. I was conscious, too, that the people who came to Summerland for their holiday came from the part of the world where I had spent my childhood, and from amongst those not prosperous enough to seek out a foreign holiday. We had learned of some fine deeds of courage and daring by people who had attempted rescues. From the personal point of view I had been given the opportunity to compete in an inquiry with some nine or ten more senior silks, and my clients had emerged from the report without criticism. When they were pilloried in the press shortly after the fire they had told me that the evidence would dispel the clamour against them. Their case was sound. But at least I had been able to present it thoroughly and clearly and help them achieve a fair and deserved outcome. And I had survived, and even enjoyed, winter on the Isle of Man.

Another area of life sensitive enough to call for major public inquiries arose from our system of planning applications. In our over-crowded island even small planning applications can attract strong feelings. The instinct of people resident in an area is to oppose change. Since the Town and Country Planning Act (1947) the need for careful control of development has been well recognised. Most planning applications are decided by local councils. But in the case of a major application with wide-ranging consequences the minister responsible for the environment had the ability to "call in" the application and to decide it at central government level. Before doing so there will generally be a major public inquiry so as to give the applicants, who are often a large corporation, and all affected inhabitants, who may often be small groups passionate to protect their surroundings, the opportunity to put their case publicly and cross-examine the other parties. This is worthwhile both to establish what are the really controversial issues, to test the facts, and also enable people to feel that they have had the opportunity both to know what was going on and to have their say.

So the value of such inquiries is both real and therapeutic. Some are on a very large scale, such as applications for new airports or runways at airports which involve wide-ranging change of use of land, increased traffic, and above all potential noise to local residents. Whether at London's Heathrow, Gatwick or Stansted Airport, expansion can change the character of the surrounding area drastically. So, too, can large schemes for the development of road networks. The public inquiries which are held are quasi-judicial and are conducted by an inspector, who is in the most important cases invariably a senior planning silk, who makes recommendations through a written report to the minister. But the minister is not obliged to accept these recommendations. After considering the report with the help of officials the minister gives a decision letter setting out whether the development is to be allowed and, if so, on what conditions. Sometimes these processes can take a long time. The inquiry into the third runway for London's Heathrow Airport took years before there was a decision. The assessment as to whether there should be a nuclear reactor at Sizewell, conducted by the highly-skilled Sir Frank Layfield QC, went on for three years.

Another type of development which not surprisingly was always sensitive was an application to develop a new coalfield. In 1979 I was asked by the then National Coal Board to lead the conduct of their case to develop a new field in the Vale of Belvoir. Coal played a notable part in the industrial history of our country. Production had reached its height by the end of the Second World War where it had been invaluable in fuelling our ships. But demand and production then declined and oil and gas, and to a small extent nuclear power, became substituted for coal. The National Coal Board also had to face competition from imported supplies of cheap coal, notably from Australia. The miners still commanded much sympathy when they demanded better conditions, as Edward Heath's government painfully discovered, but the industry lacked a springboard for the future. But all this was to change for a time with the first oil crisis in 1973, when the actions of a cartel of middle-Eastern producers caused prices to quadruple. The government decided to revive the coal industry with a policy which enthused the NCB called "Plan for Coal". The NCB successfully applied for consent to open a new mine at Selby. This was seen as a very favourable field to work, because the seams of coal contained very little in the way of spoil and could be brought out through gently inclining roads which led to the pit. Then came the application to mine in the Vale of Belvoir.

This was to be a fascinating but complex inquiry. The coal reserves which had been discovered ran under fine countryside in the middle of England about one hundred miles north of London. It was a very important part of the South Midlands and contributed to ensuring the decent space between the sprawling conurbations of London and Birmingham respectively. There were some fine estates in the area, most notably that of the Duke of Rutland at Belvoir castle. The deposits of coal were deep underground and spread out. They extended from Asfordby, already a small industrial town, to Saltby in Lincolnshire, a site in deep countryside which had served as an airfield in the Second World War. The principal deposits of coal were in the middle of the field at Hose, in Leicestershire. The NCB had applied to build pits on all three sites. The inquiry raised a number of major issues. Was there the demand for coal? Could it be economically mined? What was the road system which would need to be put into place? What risks were there of subsidence to the surrounding countryside? How much would it disfigure the landscape to have three pits, all with their tall towers at the pit-head? Where would the spoil go?

We had a team of four and my fellow silk, Lord Colville of Culross who had been a junior Home Office minister in a former government and was extremely knowledgeable about mining, and I divided up the task between us. We were well supported by Jeremy Burford, an experienced planning barrister, and the young Peter Goldsmith. Peter was clearly intellectually bright, extremely conscientious, good to work with, and obviously destined for a fine career at the Bar. He was to become in time a good chairman of the Bar Council. What he gave no hint of in those days was of his political interest which led him in time to support the Labour party and to become Attorney-General. He is widely respected for the integrity and ability with which he gives legal advice to the government. But I, and more to the point many international lawyers, found it impossible to agree with the short summary he published of his crucial advice in March 2003 suggesting that Iraq could lawfully be invaded because of the old resolution passed in 1990 which enabled U.N. forces to expel Iraqi forces from Kuwait. But this was to lie a long time in the future and Peter's ability and personality made him a great pleasure to work with during the Belvoir Inquiry.

Our preparation was thorough, and indeed the immensely diligent NCB team would not have settled for less. We gathered at one of their headquarters at Bestwood, near Nottingham, to prepare our case in September. We visited mines, and spent one day going underground to experience first-hand how mining worked. It happened to be an old mine, with a low ceiling of about three feet to the mining tunnel. It was not perfectly designed for my enormous height but gave me a vivid illustration of what miners had to do to get to work and how claustrophobic it could be when we reached the coal-face itself. In the course of the inquiry a miner was to describe how he, just as much as those who opposed the development, valued the neighbouring countryside. He said that when, after a night's shift, he returned up the lift from the mineshaft to see dawn breaking, he could think of no more beautiful and poetic sight that man could experience. The National Coal Board, with its highly-competent, dedicated and humane management team drawn often from the ranks of former miners and mining supervisors, were a highly-impressive bunch. So were the miners we met, with solid values and accepting arduous and dirty work as part of their lot in life. It was very unfortunate that they allowed them-selves to be led less than a decade later by the articulate but strident voice of Arthur Scargill into head-on conflict with the government.

The inquiry opened during the autumn at Stoke Rochford, a short distance from the A1 in Lincolnshire. I stayed throughout at a pub some miles away called the Black Horse at Grimsthorpe. It was kept by a family called Fisher and was notable for some of the most excellent cooking I can remember. The entire village was the property of the Earl of Ancaster, who owned Grimsthorpe castle in whose grounds I was allowed to walk in the mornings. This was a peaceful place to retreat to and prepare for the following day. It was later to be enlivened by Frank Layfield, leading counsel for the objectors, who came to stay there, as for a brief time did Ian Glide-well, representing other objectors. Our clients had no difficulty in accepting that we would not have dreamed of discussing the case and indeed we had much more amusing and sparkling topics to talk about during the evenings and at breakfast.

The inquiry took some six months. One of our principal tasks was to establish the demand for coal. This in turn meant that we had to provide some assessment of its competitiveness against the price of oil. In autumn 1979 there was a second oil crisis, which caused a further large hike in the prices of oil. We called a witness from the European Commission who gave competent evidence that he thought the price of oil would never again fall below $32 per barrel. In the light of what has happened since this has struck me as a clear indication of the dangers of relying too strongly on expert evidence. The local objectors relied on the authority of the Duke of Rutland and the stylish personality of the Duchess who was a regular attender at the inquiry. The deference factor was still present in the Midlands and even affected the urbane Peter Boydell QC, appearing for the Duke. In the middle of his meticulous final speech he suddenly said: "Now, sir, I come to the evidence of our Duke, if I may say so our excellent Duke".

Life, too, was brought to the inquiry by the sporadic appear-ances of Gilbert Gray QC, appearing for the local town council. Gillie was a sublime, old-fashioned jury advocate. He was not needed at this planning inquiry very much because his clients' interests coincided in many ways with those of other objectors. The day before Gillie had to make his final speech he telephoned me and asked me whether I could try to influence the inspector to alter the order of speeches. He explained that he was double-booked in a jury trial at Leeds on behalf of an alleged IRA bomber and had received a telephone message telling him that if he was not present to make the final speech he would be "knee-capped". This concentrated our minds wonderfully and we managed to arrange that Gillie could make his speech to the inquiry on the day after the jury trial ended. Another light moment was when Peter Goldsmith and I took the afternoon off to go to visit Belvoir castle. This impressive, 19th century pile, set in wide-ranging grounds is far from the finest of English country houses but was well worth the visit. We knew that if permission was granted to mine the coalfield there would be some mining and a small risk of subsidence at one distant part of the estate. The house, gardens and view would be wholly unaffected. So we were amused to find on leaving, a prominent petition displayed and inviting signatures with the introduction: "If you have enjoyed your visit to Belvoir castle and wish it preserved for posterity, please sign this petition against the development of the coalfield." This plea had drawn a good number of signatures but was a graphic illustration why petitions of this kind carry very little weight with decision-takers.

Most of the issues we raised at the inquiry went well. One of the toughest parts was our proposal for the disposal of spoil from the mine. The NCB were keen to minimise expense by placing the spoil near the mine and contouring it with sensitive landscaping. Coming from Stoke-on-Trent I knew just how difficult this was to achieve and how ugly slagheaps were. The objectors raised the convincing argument that the NCB should be obliged to take the spoil by train to old brick quarries in Bedfordshire where they would provide useful infill. The brickworks were willing to take them for a fee, and the cost would not have added to significantly to the price of the coal.

After the inquiry there was the usual wait for the inspector to produce his report and for the minister to consider it and to issue his decision letter. We were relatively confident of the inspector's report, and our speculation was right. He accepted that the need for coal was established, that the three pits should all be developed so as to provide an economic way of mining the coal, the overall environmental consequences were not unacceptable but that the spoil should be taken to Bedford brickworks. Michael Heseltine, then Secretary of State for the Environment, did not wholly agree with this, and in his decision explained why he took the view that in the first place the only mine which should be developed was at Asfordby, which was by common consent the least environmentally attractive of the three potential mines. This decision did not make the NCB position easy, because to mine from Asfordby alone would probably prove uneconomic and they had no guarantee that they would be permitted in the end to mine from the other sites.

It was only years later, when reading Nigel Lawson's book "The View from No.11," that I learned of what had apparently gone on behind the scenes before Michael reached his decision. Nigel explained (pages 144 to 146) that when in 1981 he became Energy Minister he discovered that Michael, with the full support of Mrs Thatcher as Prime Minister, was about to refuse the NCB application entirely. The Prime Minister was said to be "adamant against touching the Vale of Belvoir".

Nigel was concerned because a future conflict with a strike was obviously a real prospect. He pointed out in a letter "that the Midlands miners were the most moderate of all the miners, and that it was vital to keep them on our side if we were to have any hope of preventing the NUM gaining a mandate for a strike. I explained how important Belvoir was to them, and how - especially since the inquiry had come out in favour - a refusal to allow the seam to be mined would be seen as a slap in the face for the Midlands miners from a government they would inevitably regard as hostile to them". He also sought to allay any fears that the only real hostility was to mining in the centre of the coalfield at Hose, and that if permission was limited so that Hose was excluded Conservative held Leicestershire seats would not be put at risk.

Lawson continued that he then met Michael Heseltine and agreed a compromise. He believes that the decision to grant permission was "a necessary sacrifice in the battle against Arthur Scargill" and "the crucial decision of the Nottinghamshire miners to carry on working during the coal strike of 1984-5 fully vindicated it so far as I was concerned."

So, on this account we had a long and meticulous quasi-judicial inquiry but the real discussion was taken behind closed doors for political, and mostly party-political reasons. Needless to say the decision letter gave absolutely no hint of these manoeuvrings.

There are comparatively few planning applications which are so important that the Minister calls them in for his personal decision. After the Human Rights Act 1998 was passed a court challenge to the role of the minister was launched on the ground that section 6 required "civil rights" and obligations to receive a fair and public hearing and to be decided by an independent and impartial tribunal. This, so it was agreed, would exclude the role of the minister. But the judges in the House of Lords decided in ex parte Alconberg that the underlying decision was an administrative one and that a minister who was democratically accountable should be able to take the final decision. The inquiry process was there to enable facts to be established and views of applicants and objectives to be heard and commented on. The recommendation of the inspectors was to assist the minister but not to be binding. In the end the decision was left to the minister.

In practice ministers do not often disagree with the inspector's reports, but I agree they should be free to do so. What is not remotely fair is that machinations of the kind Nigel describes of raising issues extraneous to the planning process can take place without the parties knowing what is going on. Somehow this account, if it is the whole story, leaves a sour taste.

11. NEW ZEALAND DISASTER

The 28th November 1979 was one of the saddest days in the history of New Zealand. On this early summer day, a DC10 aircraft operated by the national airline, Air New Zealand, left Auckland on a sight-seeing trip to the Antarctic. Later that day news reached Auckland that the aircraft was missing somewhere in Antarctica, after the time had passed when all the fuel on board would have been exhausted. The aircraft had crashed at a height of one thousand five hundred feet straight into the lower snow-clad slopes of a twelve thousand foot high volcano, Mount Erebus. All the two hundred and thirty seven passengers and twenty members of crew were killed instantly.

How could this possibly have happened? Air New Zealand immediately started an internal investigation by the Chief Inspector of Air Accidents. This kind of investigation is held in private. By 12th June 1980 the Inspector had completed his report which was published. This report essentially put the principal blame for the tragedy on Captain Collins and the pilot team. He said: "the probable cause of this accident was the decision of the captain to continue the flight at low level toward an area of poor surface and horizon definition when the crew was not certain of their position and the subsequent inability to detect the rising terrain which intercepted the aircraft's flight-path."

But even by the time of publication of the report it was recognised that there had to be a much more exhaustive, authoritative investigation. So a Royal Commission was established at the same time as the publication of the initial report. Royal Commissions, in this country and in New Zealand, are means by which a government can conduct a major, wide-ranging inquiry into disasters or sometimes into the wider policy issues of whether there should be changes of policy on issues which may vary from reform of the House of Lords to relaxation of the law of gambling. When the inquiries are into disasters they are normally conducted by a senior judge.

So it was with the Royal Commission on Mount Erebus. The judge appointed, Peter Mahon, was able, distinguished, capable of forming strong judgements, and as his book of letters to his son "Dear Sam" showed, a man of wide-ranging interests and deep humanity. But his reputation was to be in the end adversely touched by the Mount Erebus tragedy. In its aftermath the crash tarnished for a time the reputation of the pilots, and of Air New Zealand itself, in addition to the tangible loss it brought to so many families and friends of the victims.

The judge was set the demanding task of reporting within less than six months. Obviously everybody wanted the issue to be cleared up quickly. But haste can sometimes be the enemy of justice and the timescale for the inquiry was rightly extended. Even so the judge produced his report within a year of the start of his inquiry.

An inquiry of this kind is very different to ordinary civil litigation which is the regular task of judges and on which their experience and approach to decision-taking has been gained. In civil litigation the parties put forward their evidence and the judge has to decide where the truth lies in the result of conflict of evidence. By contrast an investigative inquiry enables the judge to pursue lines of evidence for himself. Some avenues lead only to a dead-end. In other cases it may lead to the discovery of facts throwing a fresh light on what actually happened and why. The evidence may emerge piece-meal. This sometimes makes the task harder than the traditional judicial role. Some say that was true in the case of the Profumo Inquiry conducted by Lord Denning in 1963. More recently there was similar criticism of the inquiry for Lord Scott into Arms for Iraq. In the case of the Mount Erebus Inquiry the judge brilliantly investigated the facts of the disaster and reached conclusions which carried total credibility. But he was to go on to make harsh findings against Air New Zealand and its employees that they had conspired to cover up the truth after the accident. It was this which was to cause a challenge to the fairness of the judge's conduct of the inquiry. This challenge succeeded in the Court of Appeal of New Zealand and so the judge appealed to the Privy Council. This court still hears appeals from some Commonwealth countries and is comprised mostly of judges who also sit as members of the House of Lords Judicial Committee, our own highest appeal court. It was this Privy Council case which was to take me to New Zealand for the first time, to prepare it with the New Zealand legal team and then to be argued in the Privy Council building in Downing Street in the summer of 1983.

What the judge did so well was to piece together the reality of what had happened and caused the accident. The fatal flight of 28th November was the fourteenth in a series of sight-seeing flights which ANZ had undertaken to Antarctica. The flights went down as far as a United States military Antarctic base known as McMurdo, did some sight-seeing, and then turned round and returned direct to Christchurch in the South Island. McMurdo is on a peninsula which forms the most southerly point of Ross Island. On the island are three mountains of which Mount Erebus at twelve thousand five hundred feet was the highest. Ross Island merges into the Ross ice-shelf which forms the southern boundary of the Ross Sea. A part of that sea, which is over thirty miles wide, is known as McMurdo Sound. This separates Ross Island on the western side from the part of the Antarctic continent which is called Victoria Land. As summer advances the ice breaks up and water is visible between the ice floes. Most of the previous flights, conducted by very skilled and experienced pilots, had flown down to McMurdo Sound at a height which would best serve the purpose of sight-seeing. This was an open well-known practice. No-one suggested that flying down that sound at levels ranging from between fifteen hundred and three thousand feet in good visibility was not perfectly acceptable.

So the flights plans which were programmed into the computer of the aircraft, and given to the pilots, regularly provided for the aircraft to go straight down the sound at a low height. In the case of the fatal flight the captain was given some eighteen days before the flight computerised flight plans that showed a longitudinal heading of 164 degrees 48' East. This was tracking the aircraft down McMurdo Sound. Captain Collins in the intervening days before the flight actually drew out the flight-path on a map on his wall at home from the briefing papers which he had been given. What he and his fellow crew were not told was that shortly before the flight the computer was re-programmed so as to provide a longitudinal direction of 166 degrees 48' East. This was simply and tragically not reported to the air crew. But it was to put the aircraft straight on course for Mount Erebus.

But why, flying as they were on the computerised programme called "Navigation Track", were the crew to fail to notice Mount Erebus ahead of them? To the change of programme, of which the crew negligently had not been informed, was to be added another fatal circumstance: the phenomenon of "white-out". This is an optical phenomenon experienced in polar regions. In certain meteorological conditions, which unfortunately prevailed at the time of the crash, the landscape ahead appears like flat terrain and the pilot believes that he has unlimited visibility ahead. White-out prevents changes in the level of the ground over and towards which the aircraft is flying from being perceived by the pilot even although he is approaching as large a mountain as Mount Erebus.

So, unaware of the change in the computer programming, Captain Collins believed that he was flying down the flat lands of McMurdo Sound. In fact he headed directly towards and into Mount Erebus which was invisible to him because of white-out. These were convincing conclusions and have been unreservedly accepted as the cause of the accident. They were reached with such clarity only because the judge carried out an outstanding investigation. He concluded "the dominant cause of the disaster was the act of the airline in changing the computer track of the aircraft without telling the air crew ...." He wholly exonerated the captain and other members of the flight team from any error.

Inevitably the enormity of the tragedy, and the strong feelings surrounding the Chief Inspector's report, had meant that the inquiry was conducted in a fairly short space of time, in a tense atmosphere, and with the whole of New Zealand watching and awaiting the result. It may be that this led the judge to go on to make a sweeping, hostile finding against Air New Zealand and many of its senior staff. For whatever reason he came to think that Air New Zealand had tried to cover up the real cause of the accident, to destroy or be selective about documents, and to lie in the evidence they gave to the inquiry. He used his fine command of language to devastating effect when he said: "…. the palpably false sections of evidence which I heard could not have been the result of mistake, or faulty recollection. They originated, I am compelled to say, in a predetermined plan of deception. They were very clearly part of an attempt to conceal a series of disastrous administrative blunders and so …. I am forced reluctantly to say that I had to listen to an orchestrated litany of lies".

In his report he identified a large number of senior Air New Zealand employees as being party to the conspiracy. They included the Chief Executive, Mr MR Davis, Captain Eden, the Director of Flight Operations, senior officers employed in the department responsible for flight operations, and four members of the navigation section. It struck at the heart of Air New Zealand's reputation for integrity at a time when it was already damaged by the deserved criticisms of it for incompetence. The comments potentially spelled ruin for the careers of those named as being part of the plan of deception. The report of the Royal Commission was covered by the legal doctrine of privilege, and so none of these people could fight back by taking an action for libel.

What Air New Zealand could do was to commence in New Zealand an action for judicial review. This brought into play the dividing line between the proper discretion of the Royal Commission to make findings of fact and the over-riding legal obligation to ensure that there has been fair play in the process. There was some doubt at the time, although with the wider development of judicial review and public law there would be none now, as to whether the findings of the Commission's report could ever be attacked in a court of law. But, in the typical way in which the law sometimes advances, the courts did not need to meet this challenge head-on. The judge had made an order for costs against Air New Zealand which he had justified on the basis of his view that Air New Zealand had sought to mislead the inquiry. So the order for costs which was clearly a decision, would be the formal peg on which to hang the challenge.

The Court of Appeal in New Zealand unanimously upheld the complaints that the judge failed to do natural justice in making the resonant finding that there was "an orchestrated litany of lies". When the judge appealed to the Privy Council I was asked to go to New Zealand to lead the strong local team which had been conducting the case so far. Some years previously I had acted with one member of that team, David Williams, when advising on a case involving allegations of corporate misconduct against a leading New Zealand businessman. In February 1983, following a short case which I argued in the High Court of Australia, I went to New Zealand for the first time.

To travel away from home to prepare a case had the advantage not only of working closely with the other lawyers involved but ensured the ability to concentrate on that case alone without distractions from any other part of my practice. Never had this been more necessary. It was important to read all two thousand pages of the transcript of the enquiry, the supporting documents, to understand the principles of flying and navigation, and to master the way in which the procedure had gone at the Royal Commission Inquiry. I was fortunate that the legal team included Richard McGrane, who later came to England and became a highly-skilled partner in the firm of Dibb Lupton, and who was a qualified pilot. It was priceless that Richard understood the technicalities of flight, although I suspect he felt that it would be quite a long time before he succeeded in getting me up to speed.

It was impossible to visit New Zealand without realising the impact which the tragedy had on that country. As someone said to me there was barely anyone in New Zealand who did not know someone killed on the flight. This was particularly poignant in an eminently decent, caring close-knit society. Marie joined me for a short holiday at the end when we went up to the Bay of Islands, in its splendid late-summer beauty and to the evocative setting where the Treaty of Waitangi ceded control of the country from the Maoris to the English under the guise of a treaty of protection. We were later to get to know New Zealand even better. In 1987 we were guests of the New Zealand Law Conference, held in Christchurch in the finery of its spring. I was asked to make the closing speech at that conference, and immediately ahead of me without any warning the Prime Minister of New Zealand, David Lange announced that they intended to abolish the right of appeal to the Privy Council within the lifetime of that parliament. All I could think to say rather limply in response was that this was a step which a mature democracy like New Zealand should take when it felt right to do so and that I hoped the growing internationalism of the law would mean that there was still valuable contacts between English and New Zealand lawyers.

But to return to the case which was heard in the Privy Council in London in June 1983. It was probably the most important case to come before the Privy Council since, as Lord Diplock the presiding judge said at the opening of our argument, "the great challenge to the Australian banking legislation back in 1948". The court was an extremely strong one including, as well as Lord Diplock, Lord Keith, Lord Scarman, Lord Bridge and Lord Templeman. Lord Diplock presided, and was to show from the outset the total mastery of the issues of fact and law which made him one of the outstanding judges of the second half of the 20th century. For me he stands with Lords Reid, Denning and Wilberforce as the outstanding figures who shaped English law and the renaissance and growth of administrative and public law. Their judgement provided the inspiration for fine successors such as Lords Bingham, Hoffman, Steyn and Phillips. But it was Kenneth Diplock as much as anyone else who helped bring our public law out of the dark ages which it had voluntarily confined itself to in the first half of the 20th century, and assert once again the proper role of the judges in supervising the legality of executive actions.

It was this that the Mount Erebus Appeal was all about. The task of a court in such a case is not to second-guess decisions of the judge sitting as the Royal Commissioner. That would be a usurpation of the proper role of the judge himself. The job of the court in such cases is to enquire as to whether there was natural justice, or due process, or put more simply, fair play. Fair play has two elements. Any potentially adverse findings which could affect an individual or company must be raised during the course of the inquiry so that the person potentially affected has a chance to deal with them. There must also be some evidence on which the judge can properly base his finding of fact, otherwise the process of an inquiry is clearly flawed. Lord Diplock set this out in his judgment in terms which go to the heart of the way in which the courts police the proper boundaries of executive action.

"The rules of natural justice .... can be reduced to two .... The first rule is that the person making a finding in the exercise of such a jurisdiction must base his decision upon evidence that has some probity of value ....The second rule is that he must listen fairly to any relevant evidence conflicting with the finding and any rational argument against that finding that a person represented at the inquiry whose interests (including in that term career or reputation) may be adversely affected by it, may wish to place before him or would have so wished had he been aware of the risk of the finding being made."

Most of the judgment then consisted of the application of these principles to the complex facts. My opponent, Patrick Neill QC, then the warden of All Souls College, Oxford and later as Lord Neill of Bladen to be Chairman of the Committee on Standards in Public Life, opened the case for four days understandably selecting those parts of the evidence which were favourable to his case. This always called for some restraint on the part of the opponent, and on the third day I was about to remonstrate with him for omitting something which I thought he ought to have read when Lord Diplock simply looked at me and gently said, "Don't worry, you'll get your turn." When, with the feeling of nervousness, adrenalin and frustration at waiting which all advocates know, I began my argument I quickly realised that he had so mastered the details of the case as to be wholly aware of most of the answers to the points which Pat Neill had emphasised. His command of the case, his beautifully gentle control of the way it was argued and his dominance of what was a very high quality tribunal represents the finest example of presiding judgeship which I have ever come across. By the end of the third day of our argument Lloyd Brown QC, the leading New Zealand silk who was working with me, telephoned Air New Zealand to say simply, "the tide has turned, and we are going to win". Our arguments were to be tested, but in essence the court was to hold conclusively that the criticisms which the judge had made in his report had neither been put to the witnesses to give them an opportunity to respond, nor were they backed by any evidence to justify them. It was sadly an example of a case where because the judge was involved in the investigations as opposed to conducting the normal judicial role of weighing evidence put before him, he had gone outside the boundaries of the material available, worked himself into a state of indignation, and ended up with conclusions which assassinated the characters of Air New Zealand and its senior team.

The hearing was an emotional time for many people. For myself at a personal level because my mother had a stroke and died, and we had to ask the court to adjourn for a day for her funeral. For Mrs Mahon, the wife of the judge, who very bravely came to the case and sat through the entire hearing in a dignified way. It was a hot summer and I used to stand on the steps of the building in Downing Street to get a bit of sun at lunchtime. She came and joined me once or twice and we chatted and she showed no sign of animus at all towards me as the person who was seeking to uphold the criticisms of her husband. I am not sure whether it was she or someone else who said that the tragedy of Mount Erebus had gone on and on for New Zealand affecting the families of the dead pilots, the employees of Air New Zealand, her husband's reputation, and her families' feelings. Some years later in Christchurch I met her son Sam, a sculptor, and was able to buy one of his small pieces. Peter Mahon went wrong in the findings he made against

Air New Zealand, but it was a single high-profile blemish on a fine career. Overall he should be remembered as a good advocate and judge, who did an immensely important service for New Zealand by analysing in an absolutely cast-iron way the cause of the Mount Erebus disaster and so clearing the reputation of Captain Collins and his fellow pilots.

The value of the Privy Council as a court of appeal for Commonwealth countries can be long-debated. Almost all of them have now decided that their own cases should be decided by their own highest courts. But there was no doubt that it helped opinion in New Zealand in the Mount Erebus case that the final decision was taken by one of the strongest group of judges in the world, who were wholly distant from New Zealand and whose leader could set out the facts and the reasons with such authority.

As I have said it was a few years after this that the Prime Minister announced the intention of speedy abolition of the right of appeal to the Privy Council. But such is the unpredictability of politics that this has not yet taken place. It surely will soon for the standards of law and instincts for justice are as well developed as anywhere I know.

12. JEFFREY ARCHER: TRIUMPH AND TRAGEDY

The law has for centuries been alert to protect a person's good name or reputation. Shakespeare put it with vivid passion into the mouth of Othello:

> Good name in man and woman, dear my Lord,
> Is the immediate jewel of their souls;
> Who steals my purse steals trash ; 'tis something, nothing:
> 'twas mine, 'tis his, and has been slave to thousands;
> But he that filches from me my good name
> Robs me of that which not enriches him,
> And makes me poor indeed."

For good measure in Richard II he puts into the mouth of the dying John of Gaunt this sentiment:

> "The purest treasure mortal times afford
> Is spotless reputation; .....
> Mine honour is my life ; both grow in one;
> Take honour from me, and my life is done.

The importance of "honour" explains why libel is still one of the very few civil cases which can be brought before a jury. Traditionally defamation actions have been great theatre.

In the early years of the last century, before the counter-attraction of the talking, moving pictures, crowds used to flock to watch orators such as Isaacs, Hastings and Birkett in full flow. There is still the element of theatre about these cases, which can bring spectators into court, and the Jeffrey Archer libel action was to be no exception.

I had done a good deal of defamation work as a junior but not much since taking silk. In 1976 there was a memorable contest for Robin Herbert, a Welsh landowner, against Christopher Brasher and the BBC who had accused him of trying to drive tenants out of their farms by imposing too harsh a schedule of repairs. It had been notable because we uncovered a technique under which the BBC would ask witnesses questions, record their answers, and then doctor the questions so as to make it appear that the answers were evasive. The dislike understandably felt by the jury for this technique helped us attain what in those days was the substantial award of £30,000 damages.

It was a decade later when I was approached one Sunday at the end of September by the solicitor Lord Mishcon who asked me to buy and read an article about Jeffrey Archer in The News of the World. This described in graphic detail how Jeffrey had some long telephone conversations with a prostitute, Monica Coghlan, after which he agreed to pay £2,000 to her so that she could leave the country for a time. The payment was made by one of his aides, Michael Stacpoole at Victoria Station. In the article Archer denied having met Miss Coghlan, and said that he had foolishly allowed himself to be trapped into paying the money. This immediately raised the issue: why should he pay if he had not in fact slept with her?

The telephone conversations were extensive over a period of a fortnight and had been taped by the News of the World. The delivery of the money had been photographed. The newspaper very carefully attempted to skirt around the direct suggestion that Jeffrey had sexual intercourse with the prostitute. But it was hard to see what other inference could be drawn. But before I could meet Jeffrey a newspaper, The Daily Star, published a derivative article which had a much more direct inference of sexual intercourse. It suggested that on the night of 8/9 September 1986, Archer had met Miss Coghlan between midnight and 1 am, in Shepherd Market. He had then followed her and another client of hers by car to the Albion Hotel in nearby Victoria. He waited while the other client had his assignation, but was said to have approached her as she came out of the hotel and then paid her for sex. She had not at the time recognised Jeffrey Archer, but he had been identified for her later by the previous client.

A few days later I met Jeffrey Archer for the first time. I knew that his career so far had been eventful, with its peaks and troughs.

He had been an international runner who secured the Beatles for a charity concert and had then become a GLC councillor. He was born a showman, indeed an exhibitionist, with a passion for politics. In 1969 he had won a by-election for the Conservative seat of Louth and became at the age of 29 the youngest member of the House of Commons. But his first reverse was soon to follow. In 1974, after the failure of the Canadian company Aquablast, in which he had invested, he came very close to bankruptcy and resigned his parliamentary seat. He recouped his fortunes by writing his first, some think best, novel "Not a Penny More, Not a Penny Less" within ten weeks. It was to be the start of an immensely successful career as a writer.

But Archer remained passionate about politics. He did not return to the Commons but was very committed to the Conservative party. He started speaking at meetings across the country. He had immense drawing power in the constituencies. He was once to tell me proudly that he had attracted 400 people on one occasion, talking in a constituency to be followed next week by a senior cabinet minister who had apparently only drawn 33. In 1985 he was appointed a deputy chairman of the Conservative Party.

My first meeting with Jeffrey took place in chambers at the end of September. He had felt he had no choice but to resign as a deputy chairman so as to limit any harm to the party. It was clearly not going to be an easy case. Appearances were against him and people would inevitably look closely and sceptically at any innocent explanation. I was concerned that he should know the difficulties and also that he should realise unambiguously that a case in a court of law was not just a question of who could be the finest story-teller. I told him that the processes of justice, like the mills of God, grind slowly but surely. Any falsehood would in the end be likely to be exposed and for this to happen would clearly be the end of any public career. He asserted robustly that he was innocent of the charges and that he had a clear alibi for the night in question.

In the end it was almost 15 years before my predictions about the dangers of giving misleading evidence were to be fulfilled. For Archer was to triumph in the libel action in 1987, only to pay a heavy and bitter price for doing so when he was convicted of perjury at the Old Bailey and sent to prison all those years later.

My spirits rose when I was told that day in chambers that there was a clear alibi. I assumed he might have been 200 miles away addressing the Conservative party faithful. But he told me that he had dined in the Caprice, a buzzing, fashionable restaurant, off St James's in the heart of London. I immediately pointed out to him the journey from there to Shepherd's Market simply involved crossing Piccadilly and going a few hundred yards. So, if he was in the Caprice, the time at which he was last seen there would be critical.

The newspaper articles had said that the events occurred on the night of the 8/9th September. But when we had filed our claim an extraordinary and wholly innocent mistake was made by the barrister settling the defence. This document stated that the events had occurred on the 9/10th September. This, as we shall see led to the complexity of Archer creating another alibi to the effect that on this night he had been dining in a different restaurant with a freelance television producer, Ted Francis. But early in 1987 the legal team for The Daily Star realised the mistake they had made and changed the date back to the original one of the 8/9th September. But the affidavit which Archer had procured from Francis to cover his tracks on the evening of 9/10th September was to be the cause of the later challenges to his alibi and the perjury trial. But for this slip by the defence team the investigations which led to this trial would probably never have been started. It was to be a twist of fate at least as ingenious in any of Archer's novels.

We had decided to concentrate our action against The Star because it was absolutely clear that it was claiming that Jeffrey had not merely paid off the prostitute but had also slept with her. We decided to ask the court to expedite the hearing of the case because it was putting Archer's career as a politician in baulk. The judge agreed, and so the hearing was fixed for July 1987. The case was not burdened with documents, since the issue was a straightforward one of fact as to what had taken place on the night of 8/9th September. But clearly the tapes which had been made by the News of the World of conversations between Monica Coghlan and Archer were of critical importance. There were several conversations of up to 15 minutes. The gist of them, and in this Coghlan had no doubt been coached by the News of the World, was that she had slept with him and that there were people who knew this and were trying to make life difficult for her and persuade her to disclose her story publicly. In the tapes Archer was guarded, making enquiries as to the details of what was supposed to have happened and when, but at no stage did he accept that he had ever met Coghlan. He categorically said that he had not done so. This was heartening, but what was puzzling was why he had continued conversations with her and eventually offered to pay her money to go abroad while he tried to find out who was trying to blacken his name. Most other people would probably simply have denied the allegation and put the phone down. But Archer continued to receive the calls and eventually fix the appointment at which his assistant delivered the money. The Star also asked for Archer's diary to be disclosed for the 8th September and after some skirmishes between solicitors a few weeks ahead of the trial, it was admitted that Archer had a diary for the night in question.

The tapes had fully borne out the explanation which Archer had given me earlier on as to what had taken place during the conversations. Monica had said that she was afraid of the people trying to get her to tell her story that she had slept with Jeffrey Archer and had asked for money to help her disappear for a time. Archer had in the end consented because he wanted to clear up what was a disturbing issue. He had told me that he had no idea that the press was monitoring every word that he said, but he had assured me that the tapes would be fully consistent with his story. I hoped at an early stage that he was right. When in time I came to hear the tapes he was proved accurate. The jury were to hear the tapes themselves, and clearly to be impressed by this explanation as to why he had paid the money. Why did he play along with her in conversation? Was it his instinct to flirt with danger? Was it that bizarre situations simply appealed to him? Or did he somewhere in his past have something to hide and therefore wanted to try to control the situation?

I saw little of Archer during the months between October 1986 and the trial of the action. The solicitors prepared as was customary the statement of evidence. The issue was a devastatingly simple one particularly in a branch of the law that is sometimes very technical. We simply had to claim that the articles published were defamatory and that it damaged his reputation. It was then under English law for the defendant, in this case the newspaper, to set out their argument that the libel was true. It was also a very interesting and busy time for me. I had recently become chairman of the Takeover Panel, the body then sponsored by the Bank of England which held the ring between rival candidates in contested takeovers to try to see fair play and provide decent orderly treatment of shareholders. I was also to defend in June the first person accused of insider trading under new legislation.

Geoffrey Collier was a successful trader with Morgan Grenfell who was caught in a clear case of insider trading. Such clarity was rare. There had been few prosecutions and fewer convictions for insider trading previously. Indeed for many years, the City had prospered on tips or the leakage of advance information and habits died hard. The Collier case was to put a message out that it was wholly unacceptable and Collier, a senior employee of Morgan Grenfell, was widely expected to go to prison. We presented a strong case in mitigation. We relied very much on the destruction of Collier's valuable career in the City which he had brought upon himself as to contributing to his punishment. There was very strong testimony from his very supportive wife that this was an aberration and indeed from a string of witnesses who described his reputation in their local community and the work he did there. He was obviously terrified, and visibly shaking in the dock at the prospect of going to prison. The judge, a very experienced but humane criminal judge Mr Justice Farquharson, imposed a suspended sentence. The whole episode did not totally appeal to the media. The judge was criticised for leniency and for not making an example of an insider dealer. I was criticised on the basis that a chairman of the Takeover Panel should not seek a lenient sentence for someone who had offended against the law of the City. This ignored the fact that I had already accepted the case before I was asked to become chairman of the Panel and it would have been unthinkable to let Collier down. I do not know what happened to him afterwards, although someone once told me that he had rebuilt his life very successfully either in the United States or Singapore. I simply never understood why he fell for this temptation, not least because he had a high income and the potential reward was small.

Back to Jeffrey Archer. The case opened on Monday 9th July in a packed courtroom before Mr Justice Caulfield. By then he was an extremely senior judge not far off retirement. The senior judge traditionally allocated cases between judges sitting in the courts in London. In keeping with other senior judges before him and since, Mr Justice Caulfield allocated this high-profile libel case to himself. He was a keen follower of the theatre and saw a jury in action as a remarkable piece of theatre in which he had one of the thespian roles. He was a very experienced presiding judge and controlled his court without any apparent effort. He immediately showed his acuteness. Two jurors made excuses for not reading the oath, saying they had left their spectacles at home. Sensing that this might well be an excuse because they were embarrassed that they could not read, he immediately released them. It was then for me to open the case to the jury explaining how Archer had been led to make the payment and invite them to listen to all the conversations so assiduously taped by the News of the World.

Then Jeffrey gave his evidence, competently, clearly and with conviction. He explained that on the night of 8th September he had dined in the Caprice restaurant with the then editor of his books and his wife. When they left about 10.30pm he went "table-hopping" talking to people he knew, then joined his television and film agent who was at the bar, Mr Terence Baker. He said he drove Mr Baker home to South London about 12.45am then returned to his flat on the Embankment and went to bed alone. When the call came through from Monica Coghlan two weeks or so later, his initial reaction was one of surprise and disbelief but he said he believed her when she told him she was in trouble and that it was not unusual for him to receive calls from people in difficulties. His wife, Mary, was with him in court as she was to be for the entire hearing. He told the jury that she was "remarkable" and throughout conveyed the impression that he was a happily married, faithful man. He told the court that he had not realised that the News of the World had taped all the telephone conversations saying "I always thought myself quite sharp, but I hadn't even worked out by then that the News of the World had set me up. They had been tutoring this girl on the phone how to deliver every line. This had gone on throughout six telephone conversations."

Jeffrey was cross-examined at length by Michael Hill QC, a very senior criminal barrister who had been a feisty colleague on the Bar Council. Throughout his life Michael gave tireless service to his profession and in his later years spearheaded training for barristers in advocacy. He was a dogged, tough examiner. Inevitably the relationship between himself and Archer became distinctly sharp. Michael at one stage suggested that there were already rumours circulating of a sex-scandal involving Archer.

Michael accused Jeffrey of trying to "wriggle off the hook" and avoid answering difficult questions by launching into long speeches in the hope that the jury would forget the question. Jeffrey responded by telling Hill he was becoming "aggravating". At one stage Michael pressed Jeffrey on the way in which his official diary had been compiled. The diary which had been disclosed near to trial showed an alibi and Hill asked why, if this was a genuine alibi, reporters had not been told of it at the time. The only part of the diary which Hill was shown was that which covered Monday 8th September up to noon on Tuesday 9th September. There was no suggestion by Jeffrey that this was other than an original, genuine diary. These exchanges about the diary seemed at the time simply standard form, probing the alibi, and it was years later before it became apparent that they disclosed a much more complex and damaging situation for Archer.

Hill then put The Star's case quite clearly to Archer. He suggested he had approached Monica Coghlan in Shepherd Market in Mayfair, a notorious red-light district, had then followed her in his car when she went with another client by car to the hotel in Victoria. When she emerged from the hotel with the client, Archer approached her, they made their bargain, and had sex in room 6A. He suggested that Archer told the woman he was a car salesman, and paid her a basic £50 with a further £20 for an unspecified "extra service".

Mary Archer followed her husband into the witness box. In a breaking voice she said that she had a "very happy marriage". She said that when told of the charge against her husband she was "more dumbfounded than anything else. The thought of my husband consorting with a prostitute is preposterous. Anyone who knows Jeffrey would know that far from him approaching a prostitute, if one accosted him he would run several miles in the opposite direction very fast." Mary made a considerable impression in the witness box. She was attractive, elegant and supportive. She was conscious of the element of theatre involved in the trial. She was bravely in court throughout, and the couple went to the theatre together most evenings to try to take their minds off the case. I vividly remember that when the time later arrived for Michael's closing speech she appeared dressed in black. She told me that the following day she would wear white for my closing speech and she duly did so. She was calm even as we were waiting for the verdict for several hours in my room in chambers. She asked Lord Mishcon to explain to her the court system as a way of passing the anxious time before the jury gave its verdict. By contrast Jeffrey and I watched cricket on the television, as England had a rather bad session against Pakistan.

The supporting evidence for Archer was to be crucial to his case, particularly that of Terence Baker. It was clearly not enough for Archer to show that he had dined in the Caprice that night because of its proximity to Shepherd's Market. What was crucial was the last time he had been seen there. The witness who best covered the critical time was Baker, and his evidence was clear and precise including the statement that after Archer had taken him home he had looked at his kitchen clock and saw that the time was 1.15am.

Monica Coghlan was the first witness for the defence. She had been kept in hiding by a "minder" for some days or weeks before the trial to ensure that the press could not get at her, and to secure firmly that she would turn up to give evidence. This later led to several press articles about the curious role of the minder or guardian in that situation. She told us she came from Lancashire, worked in London mid-week, and, as I recollect, that she had a child to keep. She was composed and clear in her evidence. She told the court that she went into the Victoria hotel with another client, a solicitor called Aziz Kurtha, who later identified Jeffrey Archer for her. The name apparently meant nothing to her until this identification although she said that the face was vaguely familiar. She was intrigued that Kurtha had told her that Archer was a well-known author and MP. This was why she asked him what he did for his living and he told her he sold cars. She identified Archer in court as the person she was describing. A week later Kurtha contacted her again and told her she had "hit the jackpot" with Mr Archer and shortly after that got in touch with her, suggesting that she spoke with journalists and that she would get a fee of some £700 or £800.

She was to say in cross-examination that Kurtha hounded her to go to the press. She went on to describe the telephone conversation where the News of the World had coached her what to say.

So ended the first week of the trial. I remember it as an anxious time, and the case seemed to me absolutely wide-open. Over that weekend I was able to have some very fine help from my doughty and supportive junior, Julian Malins, whose help throughout the case was invaluable, in preparing our cross-examination. On the Monday we were able to dent her evidence to a significant extent, but in no way conclusively. We tried to treat her firmly and courteously, which some people thought was for effect. In fact I have always thought that cross-examination is the privilege of an advocate and that questions should never be more offensive than absolutely necessary. Nor does haranguing a witness appeal to the sense of fair play which is an instinct of judges. What matters is asking the right question and because - unlike in a television interview - a witness is obliged to answer, the substance of the question is much more deadly if put quietly.

There were some obvious criticisms we could make of her evidence. We established that £6,000 was paid to her by the News of the World, so we could suggest that she had an incentive to provide a good story. We made the point that she had shown herself an accomplished liar by jesting on the tapes that people were threatening her and making life uncomfortable by trying to force her to support accusations against Archer. She also helped our case by saying that most of the article which The Star had written describing her life, on which they had never even contacted her, was pure fantasy. She said that the only true part of the story in The Star was that "I went to bed with Jeffrey Archer. The rest is fantasy". This clearly enabled us later to test vigorously The Star's standards of journalism in the presence of their editor Mr Lloyd Turner who sat silently in court throughout the case and gave no evidence. This led me in my closing speech to describe him as "the silent Mr Lloyd Turner". Our criticisms of The Star were also to be sharpened by the fact that each day it carried an account of the case on its front page, and so we could suggest that it was using the libel action and the anguish of the Archer family as a cynical vehicle for making money.

But, dents as these were in the case for the defence, Monica Coghlan stoutly stuck to her basic story. She said that she recognised Archer once she had been shown a photograph by a News of the World reporter and heard his voice on the telephone. She was categorical that there was no case of mistaken identity since she had remembered the face of the man she had lain on top of. She did say that the News of the World had asked her to lie about a number of issues including the existence of a picture of Archer's car outside her hotel. This suggestion did not scare Archer and was clearly a point in favour of his assertion that the whole charge was untrue.

We had by no means won the case when she had finished her evidence. But that was soon to change.

The turning point was the evidence of Mr Kurtha. He was a solicitor who told the court that he had been for many years a member of the Labour party and that he had acted out of the conviction that Archer's personal behaviour was completely at odds with Tory party policy. He did not say one way or the other, nor did I ask him, whether he considered that his own behaviour was fully consistent with Labour party policy. He said that the Conservatives "had stated very plainly that they believed in Victorian values and the strict sanctity of the family. So his activity was total hypocrisy and against party policy, and humbug. I believed it had to be exposed." He said that next day he had written a humorous, if malicious little article anonymously for Private Eye.

His evidence was shot through with inconsistencies, and at several stages some of the jurors appeared to be laughing at him. They did so when he said that he had been no further away from Archer than four feet, but that Archer put his hands over his face so as not to be recognised. He said that Archer had gone into the hotel with Monica in full view of Kurtha. When asked whether it surprised him that Jeffrey had been as bold as brass in this way, he responded that he would not have done so but that Archer was a gambler. He managed to feel that the News of the World had double-crossed him in some way, failing to acknowledge that without him they would have no story. But then the judge turned on Kurtha with the following question: "You knew this story would kill him. You know what I mean - destroy him." The overall effect was to create the image of someone who appeared at the same time both maliciously willing to damage but also rather ludicrous. This was the critical corroborative witness, and this inevitably tarnished the whole case for the newspaper.

We had a long weekend ahead of us because the judge gave us until Tuesday to prepare our closing speeches. This was welcome because my own habit was to write out every word, and then practise the speech, so that I felt I knew the material very well. Unlike my friend George Carman, I did not find it profitable to practise in front of the mirror but I shared his view that it was important to know the speech very well and to have decided how to deliver it. By then I was optimistic. We dined with our friends Michael Priest, the interior designer, and his wife Jilli at a restaurant in Oxfordshire on the Saturday night. Michael asked me what I thought the result would be and I said I believed that we would win and recover £500,000. But a confident dinner-time forecast did not dispel my own nerves when it came to the final speech.

On the Monday there was a distraction. Over the weekend a visitor to the National Gallery had shot the Leonardo da Vinci cartoon. Neil MacGregor, the new director, took me, as a trustee, through the incident during the Monday afternoon and we were able to consider whether he was taking all the right steps to deal with the incident. In time the cartoon would be remarkably restored by Eric Harding, working for years in virtual solitude, with meticulous skill and care and total modesty. His otherwise unknown work was reward by an OBE. Serious as the incident was, it provided a not unwelcome distraction from the tension of the trial.

The following day Michael Hill made his spirited closing submissions. He accused Archer of lying throughout the trial. He said that Archer had, prior to the trial, given different alibis at different times. He suggested that the alibi given by Terence Baker, the key witness, differed from the account of the evening given by Archer himself. Michael was quoted by The Times as saying that Jeffrey's shifts in alibi were born "out of the same desperation that produces fiction rather than fact". As for Mrs Archer, "sympathy is not the basis for judgement as to where the truth lies".

On the Wednesday it was my turn. The judge called out my name loudly, as he had done for Michael at the start of his speech, rather like an impresario introducing an artist. I relied strongly on the behaviour of The Star. I pointed out that the editor, Mr Lloyd Turner, declined to give evidence even though Monica Coghlan herself had described much of his story as fantasy. It was surely evident to Lloyd Turner, who sat there throughout, that Mr Kurtha, a key witness for the defence, had spoken nonsense. Yet he was content to rely on his evidence. I said: "You may think that this silence is as eloquent as any of the witnesses we have heard. They did not give a damn if what they wrote was true or false. Mr Jeffrey Archer must be brushed aside in the great cause of selling newspapers". I said that, as Miss Coghlan did not know Mr Archer from Adam, it was Mr Kurtha, the only other person to have allegedly seen him, who had planted the idea that it was him in her head. As far as the tapes were concerned, she had acted and acted and acted. She was acting again in the witness box. I pointed out that the jury's decision would decide Jeffrey Archer's reputation for the rest of his life. A public figure would have been crucified by a popular newspaper, part of the multi-million pound newspaper group. The paper had hit a man when he was down. Its conduct had been cynical and wicked. Massive damages were appropriate.

The trial, and indeed some of the comments afterwards, turned in part into a critique of the ethical approach of newspapers. I asked: "Was it right that one of its journalists should, for weeks on end, act as a minder and live "hugger-mugger" with a prostitute? Or that the paper should pay her large sums of money and finance her foreign holiday? Or arrange for her to sell topless photographs?" I argued that "journalistic methods like these create a terrible risk of a man being framed". Was it right for The Star to cash in on all this, and then cynically defend a libel action just to provide yet more titillating stories out of the degrading accusations which day after day were made about Mr Archer?

I also set out the details of the case laid against Archer, concentrating on the suggestion that he followed Kurtha and Coghlan to her hotel, a journey during which Miss Coghlan had characterised the solicitor's driving as fast and reckless. "Jeffrey Archer is no relation of Nigel Mansell, nor has he been trained by Starsky and Hutch. Yet he is said to have driven in this same crazy way. Has real love at first sight ever led to such recklessness?" By this time we were able to portray the payment of Miss Coghlan by Archer as the act of a generous man trying to help a woman in trouble. I pointed out too that no evidence had been suggested that Archer was other than a "very happily married man with a strong family life" and there had been no suggestion that he was someone who had affairs or had been with prostitutes before.

Appearing before juries is a curious exercise. They have to remain effectively silent throughout the whole period of the trial although they can ask a written question of the judge. It is only gradually that you begin to see from their expressions what they may be thinking. I had felt by the end of the evidence, and did again during my closing speech, that they were strongly sympathetic to Archer and disliked the charges against him and the ruthless way in which the newspapers had pursued them.

Looking back at it, my closing speech reads like strong stuff, totally different from the sort of language used before judges in civil cases when they sit alone. But a jury is ruled by its instincts, and expects a bit of passion. Perhaps it does not always expect as much brio and passion as came from Mr Justice Caulfield's summing-up. He began by telling the jury what the stakes were for Archer. He said: "In material terms he can be described as rich. At this moment in reputation you may think that he is a pauper. And if your verdict goes against him you may think he is destined to endure the rest of his life as a social leper in a social workhouse for hypocrites". He summarised the evidence fairly throughout, which is fortunate as for him to have done otherwise could have led to a successful appeal. But he commented strongly in favour of the Archers. He said of Mary: "Your vision of her will probably never disappear. Has she elegance? Has she fragrance? Would she have, without the strain of this trial - a radiance?" He invited the jury to consider whether Jeffrey, with all this going for him, had been "in need of cold, unloving, rubber-insulated sex in a seedy hotel". He pointed out that if Archer had followed Kurtha, he could not have known where Monica was being driven and when he arrived there have no idea how long Kurtha was going to remain with Coghlan. He pointed out that Kurtha, who admitted that he was colour-blind, said that Archer's car was either red, green or brown although it was in fact dark grey. He had written in the Private Eye article that it was green. He laid in to The Star for the inaccuracies in their article and for the editor for failing to defend their conduct. He continued his summing-up throughout the day and briefly into the following day so as to give the jury the best part of a full day to consider its verdict.

Michael and I had different reactions to the summing-up. Michael would for the rest of his life feel that the judge's summing-up had tilted the case against his clients. But I felt concern the other way. Juries do not like being told what to do by judges.

There is always a risk that if a judge sums-up too strongly in favour of one party it may cause a reaction the other way by the jury. Before summing-up I was very confident we would win. Afterwards I was still confident but nervous that the jury could react against Archer because the judge had gone over the top. The jury were to take four and a half hours. When summoned we had to push our way through serried ranks of cameras to get back into the courtroom where the buzz was intense. There was a gasp when the jury found in favour of Archer, and an even stronger one when they awarded £500,000. We were granted the costs of action, and Jeffrey and Mary made their way from court with the crowds disappearing, leaving Julian Malins and I sitting there quietly for almost half an hour in a mixture of sheer relief and contemplation of all the drama we had seen there in the last few weeks. I should have been elated that weekend but I was too drained. There had been a lot at stake for the Archers and I had given the case my all.

It was all the more disappointing to learn years later that there were claims that Archer had not told the full truth at the hearing. In the intervening years Marie and I had been regular guests at his eclectic Christmas parties where the prime minister was likely to be found chatting to Frank Bruno and the Archbishop of Canterbury in animated conversation with Joan Collins. Jeffrey stood by the door and greeted all the guests as they came and went enjoying the shepherds pie and Krug champagne and colourful company. He also invited us to one or two family celebrations. Otherwise we saw little of each other although we chatted warmly once we had joined the House of Lords and we would meet in its corridors. I, like the rest of the world was puzzled about the truth of the suggestion of insider-trading over the share dealings in Anglia Television, of which Mary was a director, which cast another shadow over his reputation. But it was still a marked surprise when one Saturday afternoon a friend who worked as a legal adviser for a newspaper telephoned me to warn me that Archer had just stood down as candidate for Mayor of London because of suggestions that he had committed perjury in connection with our libel action. He had kindly telephoned me so that I would be on the alert if journalists got after me for comment. I promptly plugged in the answer phone.

Once it became apparent that the police were investigating the evidence given by Archer at the libel trial I said to him, and he agreed, that he and I should not talk even socially until the issue was finally resolved. We have not spoken since. Our only exchange has been when he sent me a copy of "A Prison Diary" describing his time in prison, his relationship with other prisoners, and the petty degradations of the system, which vividly brought out how some people who are originally unfortunate fall for a life of crime. This struck a chord with me from my days doing criminal work on the western circuit. I wrote to Jeffrey that it was probably the most moving and valuable book he had ever written because it tells the story so vividly that people who normally would be uninterested in prison conditions may want to read it. I was later to disqualify myself, as chairman of the MCC, from sitting at the hearing of a motion to suspend Archer from membership. There would clearly have been a perception of conflict of interest. My colleagues decided that he should be suspended for seven years, whereas my vote would have been simply to suspend him for the length of his prison sentence. Society has a tendency to treat someone who has committed an offence as something of a leper and visit further small punishments on them, and this has always seemed to me to be unattractive.

I was to follow the perjury investigation and trial only from a distance. But what seemed to give it impetus is that Ted Francis, who had sworn the affidavit for the night 9/10th September saying that he had dined with Archer at the Sambuca restaurant, went to the publicist Max Clifford. Francis apparently had a grievance that Archer had promised to pay him a substantial sum for his support and had only paid him part of it. He also said that he regretted his own part in the affair and wanted to own up to it. The police also interviewed Archer's former secretary, Angela Peppiatt. According to Francis, Archer had said that he needed the alibi for the 9/10th September to help Archer out of a marital scrape with Mary because, so Francis said, Archer was having dinner with a girlfriend, Andrine

Colquhoun, on that night. In the event Archer never needed an alibi for that night because it only figured in the libel action through the mistake of The Star defence team and by the time of trial everything was to focus on the night of 8/9th September.

But Miss Peppiatt told a story which explained why Archer had need of an alibi for 9/10th September. According to the evidence of Miss Peppiatt at the perjury trial in April 1987 Archer gave her a blank A4 size 1986 diary and a paper with six hand-written entries on it. She was told to copy six entries into Monday September 8th in the new diary. About the same time she wrote another three entries up to noon on Tuesday 9th September on Archer's instructions to correspond with Archer's actual real engagements that morning. Miss Peppiatt told the court at the criminal trial that she had photocopied the forged pages and the original diary for 1986. Archer's lawyers did not know about this diary at the time of the libel trial, since it was kept back from them but Miss Peppiatt kept copies of the entries and may even have kept the original of the diary.

In fact the diary contained a potentially ruinous entry for Tuesday 9th September: "Terence Baker, Caprice/Sambucca 8pm". The prosecution suggested that Archer had simply brought forward his meeting with Terence Baker by one day so as to provide himself with the alibi for 8/9th September. This meant that once The Star mistakenly suggested that the incident had actually occurred on the 9th September Archer needed to create a false alibi for that evening as well because he had already used up his genuine one. He was mired in the perils of complexity and untruth. The trial must have been a nightmare for Archer, for Mary, and for their two loyal sons. It must also have been a heavy burden for defence counsel. Archer instructed that Miss Peppiatt should be attacked strongly on the ground that she had misused his credit card to pay some of her own debts. This partially backfired because she responded that in some cases the money had been spent on presents for Archer's girlfriends.

The picture that Archer had presented at trial of someone who did not have affairs was shown to be flawed. But what was critical were the diaries. Michael Hill, as witness for the prosecution, said that if the original diary had been available at trial, Archer's alibi would have begun to "unravel like an old sweater". There was great force in this, and the impression was confirmed when Archer did not take the opportunity to give evidence himself. The jury retired for several days before they convicted him. But on the evidence put forward it was hard to see what else they could have done. The judge, Mr Justice Potts, sentenced him to four years imprisonment. This seemed to me to be right at the top end of the scale although an appeal against sentence was unsuccessful. Jonathan Aitken, for his perjury in the action against The Guardian, had been sentenced to 18 months imprisonment. I would have thought that in a more flexible system Archer could have been more sensibly dealt with by the same term of imprisonment and a swingeing fine of several thousand pounds. It appeared a bad case of perjury, but it also seemed to me to be a savage sentence.

Jeffrey Archer continues to protest his innocence. But whilst he was in prison he accepted that the original verdict which we had obtained at the libel action should be overturned. He agreed to pay back the damages and costs, together with accumulated interest, and the total bill was close to £2 million. He is a creative, energetic man with an ability to profit from misfortune. Sometimes I wonder whether his story-telling talents lead him to believe that what can be made to sound convincing is in fact true. He and Mary have come through this together, which is a great credit to them both. She is a talented woman, cleverer and more deep-thinking than Jeffrey, and has sometimes appeared willing to support him at almost all costs. I found her unfailingly courteous and cool, but her personality remains a total enigma to me.

Barristers always strive to do their best for their clients. But I found Archer's case particularly anxious because so much was at stake for him and he was so convincing in his assertions that he had been unjustly treated. There were many strange features of the charge against him, including the part played by Kurtha and the improbable car chase, which still make me wonder exactly what happened on the night of 8th September. But for all that I felt that

Archer had hidden some key areas of the truth from me. In one sense barristers should take this in their stride because they are paid to put forward the defence advanced by the client and not to judge that defence. But for all that I felt a bit let down.

There are now moves afoot, initiated by the current Lord Chancellor, Lord Falconer, to have Archer expelled from the House of Lords. What is put forward is the proposal that those who have been convicted of serious criminal offences should automatically lose their seats, as they do in the Commons. This is clearly right for the future. But it is specifically aimed at Jeffrey Archer and this is why the government proposes that it should operate retrospectively. I am against legislation aimed in this way at single individuals, and a retrospectively imposed extra penalty for a crime seems untenable. After all Archer has served his long sentence. Nor did his barrister, since his proposed action was not known at the time, have the opportunity in mitigation of reminding the court that part of his penalty would be the risk of losing his peerage. The judge might have taken this into account and somewhat reduced the sentence. The proposal is petty and unworthy of a government which claims to defend human rights.

13. THE TAKEOVER PANEL

One of the special charms of the Bar is its sheer unpredictability. We are on piece work and often have no idea what our next case will be. In 1986 I had argued a case for Hong Kong Land against the Government of Hong Kong in their Court of Appeal. We had won and the Government appealed to the Privy Council, still the final Court of Appeal from overseas United Kingdom territories and some Commonwealth countries. After the advocate for the Hong Kong government had argued its case I was told by the judges that there was no need for me to respond. Such an indication was always welcome because it meant that the appeal would be dismissed. The conventional way of the judges saying this was to use the words: "we need not trouble you, Mr Alexander". By the time I got back from the hearing room in Downing Street my clerk, Burley, knew the outcome and told me that he had accepted a brief for the following day to act for the Takeover Panel. There was an application for judicial review which had arisen in a hurry and he optimistically told me I could prepare it overnight and during the hearing itself whilst my opponent Jeremy Lever QC, an unrivalled expert in competition law was mounting his argument.

I knew little then of the Takeover Panel. Nor did I have any inkling that six months later I might find myself as part time Chairman. So I had quickly to learn the role of the Panel. I discovered that it did not exist to pass judgment on the economic merits of take-over bids which was to be left to the judgement of the shareholders. Nor was its task to rule on public interest issues, such as the effect on competition, which was ultimately a judgement for the Secretary of State for Trade and Industry. The task of the Panel was the more focused and modest one of trying to ensure the proper and orderly conduct of a takeover bid, and to hold the ring during the contest. The primary concern of the Panel was fairness to shareholders. It was a very British creation. It had been set up by the Bank of England in 1968 at a time when its influence over City conduct was immensely powerful and valuable. It was prompted by a concern that the growing aggression in some bids had meant that the interests of all shareholders were not being properly taken account of. In the first twenty years the Panel monitored some 5,000 bids, although many of those were agreed and uncontroversial.

Because the Takeover Panel was an informal creation there was scope for flexibility in its rule book and in the way it did its work. The essence was to see that all shareholders of a particular class should be treated equally and provided with full information. Those who acquired effective control of a company, which was judged to be 30%, could be obliged to make other shareholders an offer for their shares. There had to be an orderly timetable for the bid so that the documents put out by the advisers to the contesting parties could be properly considered by the shareholders. Those documents had to be full so that shareholders could have enough information to consider a bid for their company. These underlying aims formed the general principles under which the Panel operated. But to give greater precision these principles were supplemented by detailed rules giving clear guidelines as to how they would generally operate in practice.

The Panel had a small but highly effective team located in some style on the top floor of the Stock Exchange building in Threadneedle Street. Their task was to give advice and initial rulings on the proposed conduct of the contesting parties. For its role was not simply the somewhat arid one of passing judgement on conduct after the event. Its main work was to be done during the course of the bid, by acting as an advisory body available for consultation. It was to be a referee fully engaged during the match. Under the code, financial advisers had an obligation to consult in case of any doubt as to the way in which the Panel would view their work. In the event of one party not agreeing with the ruling of the executive, there would be a full Panel hearing with wide-ranging representation from City and business institutions. Membership was drawn from right across the financial spectrum so as to create an in-built safeguard against cosiness. From the outset it included representatives of organisations which had different interests: financial advisers, investors, banks, the CBI, and independent members. So it was not really self regulating but more about non-statutory regulation.

The chairman of the Panel has generally been a senior lawyer. For many years after its creation, Lord Shawcross was the chairman and did an immense amount to establish its authority. He had a clear view that for the Panel to operate effectively it had to take a purposive approach and not act legalistically. He once wrote: "The code operates by a broadening down from precedent to precedent and is obligatory in the spirit as well as in the letter." In days when city regulation was less open to legal scrutiny, he was famously said to govern by the use of his formidable eyebrows. Nor did he allow lawyers to appear at hearings and once famously refused to make an exception for Lord Goodman, then at the height of his fame as advisor to Harold Wilson's government. He believed in making the participants and the financial advisors personally responsible for the arguments. He also felt that in this way the dispute would be resolved more speedily. When I became chairman of the Panel he strongly advised me to maintain this robust approach and I was able to do so.

The court challenge to the Panel, which I took on at short notice, had one central, important novel point of jurisdiction. For the applicants, Datafin plc, it involved a challenge to a ruling that certain purchasers of shares during the course of the bid were not acting in concert with each other. The relevance of this was that the bidder had to offer a price as high as any other purchaser of shares during the bid who they were acting together or "in concert" with. The rules prevented a bidder avoiding his obligation to offer equal prices to all shareholders by simply getting allies to make purchases at higher prices. But the important legal issue was as to the informal status of the Panel and whether this made it susceptible at all to review under administrative law. It was a ground breaking case, and came before a Court of Appeal led by Sir John Donaldson, then the Master of the Rolls.

The great concern of the Panel was that the ability of parties to start legal proceedings during the middle of a bid might be thoroughly disruptive of the orderly process in the markets. Obviously one party or the other might want to consider whether it would be of tactical value to take proceedings even if they did not think there was a great chance of success. So for this reason the Panel argued that the jurisdiction of the courts in public law did not apply because it was a body established privately by the Bank of England. It fulfilled an important public function but was a self-regulating body. As I argued: "The Panel may be required to take decisions swiftly and finally. When a ruling is asked for in the course of a bid, it may affect the outcome of the bid before or after it has succeeded. If the latter, then the shares will already be traded under the new name ..."

There was an overwhelming need for speedy finality which meant that the court should decline jurisdiction. Jeremy Lever countered this argument by pointing out the importance of a decision of the Panel to the parties and that the work of the Panel was closely meshed in with and supported by that of other recognised city bodies some of which, such as the Bank of England, existed under legislation.

Sir John Donaldson was a commercial judge of unrivalled shrewdness and practicality. He began his judgment in these vivid terms: "The Panel on takeovers and mergers is a truly remarkable body. Perched on the 20th floor of the Stock Exchange building in the City of London, both   literally and metaphorically it oversees and regulates a very important part of the United Kingdom financial market. Yet it performs this function without visible means of legal support."

He went on to point out that the reality was that the members of the Panel had the power to force other people to comply with a code of conduct. He rightly recognised that the Department of Trade and Industry or the Stock Exchange would exercise statutory or other powers to penalise anyone who transgressed the code and refused to comply with the decisions of the Panel. So, he asked, whether this remarkable body should be "above the law". In particular the Stock Exchange had the power to withhold the listing of shares in the event of a breach. He ruled that the Panel was performing an important public duty, which affected the rights of citizens. The Panel could not go on its way "cocooned" from the attention of the courts which were entitled to scrutinise and rule on the legality of the actions of the Panel. But with his usual acuity he accepted the arguments of the Panel that it would be disruptive of its work if the courts were to intervene regularly. He indicated that it would be extremely unlikely that they would interfere during a bid and that they would normally only consider a case at the end of the bid process. He said: "I wish to make it clear beyond a per adventure that in the light of the special nature of the Panel, its functions, the market in which it is operating, the timescales which are inherent in that market and the need to safeguard the position of third parties, who maybe numbered in thousands, all of whom are entitled to continue to trade upon an assumption of the validity of the Panel's rules and decisions, unless and until they are quashed by the court, I should expect the relationship between the Panel and the court to be historic rather than contemporaneous".

This would provide a "workable and valuable partnership between the courts and the Panel and the public interest" and avoid all the perils of legal proceedings being used as a ploy to disrupt the bid. It was a brilliant solution to what he later confided to me had been an extremely difficult problem. It also reflected the flexibility with which the courts are able to fashion the development of public law.

In the Spring of 1987, some months after the decision and after I had ceased to be Chairman of the Bar, I was approached to become part time chairman of the Panel itself. It happened in the very pragmatic way in which jobs were offered in the days when they did not have to be advertised, and before Nolan procedures and the ever increasing plethora of rules about corporate government. A senior representative of the Bank of England came to chambers one day to ask whether I would be interested in the appointment. I responded positively. The Panel enabled parties to receive speedy advice, for long contested hearings to be avoided, for the market knowledge to be put in to play and perhaps above all, for problems to be resolved ahead of action, before the train came off the rails rather than, as so often happens in litigation, trying to pick up the pieces after the accident. Add to this that cases were to be decided purposively in accordance with broad principle and that the rules were to be adapted, to ensure that it was the spirit rather than the letter of the law which prevails. This would not have been acceptable if the parties had not been able to obtain an advance ruling because it would have created too much uncertainty. But, when combined with the obligation on the experienced investment bankers to seek advice before action, it was the most constructive and valuable form of dispute resolution process which I have ever encountered. I was glad when Robin Leigh-Pemberton, then Governor of the Bank of England, duly invited me to become Chairman. I was in the event to hold the post for two and a half years at a time when the work of the Panel was high profile with a large amount of contested takeover bids during the heady days of the Lawson economic boom. My belief in the value of the informal, flexible system was confirmed when at a legal conference later in 1987, I was able to see the extent to which under the Australian system of strict law there was much litigation during contested takeovers and an inability under what they called "black-letter" law to resolve disputes flexibly. The Australians have since started to reverse this process.

There was an immediate crucial challenge for the Panel. Over the months before my appointment there had been a bitter and contested bid for the drinks company Distillers. There were two bidders, the Guinness Group headed by Ernest Saunders and the Argyll Group led by the late James Gulliver. As the climax approached, the two bidders were neck and neck in their race for control. Stockbrokers and investment advisers were in voracious competition to acquire the support of the market for their side. Guinness just pipped Argyll at the post and succeeded in becoming owners of Distillers. After the bid there were widespread market rumours that some of the purchasers of shares in Distillers who had supported Guinness had acted in concert with Guinness and paid a higher price for shares than was offered to the shareholders. To treat individual shareholders differently from the others was a serious offence under the rules. Argyll complained retrospectively to the Panel. At the same time a criminal investigation was launched. There was a suggestion that the Panel had been deceived by the advisers to Guinness who were leading City figures, and that it had not controlled the bid strongly enough. Its authority was seen as being temporarily weakened and it had to respond positively to the request to look at the complaint in detail.

Guinness attempted to delay the Panel action by arguing that we should not decide the issue until the end of any criminal proceedings which might be brought against Guinness, the share purchasers, and its advisers. They suggested that only at the end of this lengthy process would the true facts be known and that it was unsafe and inappropriate for us to act earlier. We rejected this invitation to procrastinate which would have been a sign of weakness and more importantly, unfair to Argyll who were claiming compensation. This was particularly so because there was no significant dispute about the facts which showed the clearest possible breach of the code. We clearly could not unscramble the takeover or declare victory to Argyll but we could do the next best thing and order Guinness to pay them appropriate compensation. In the event we ordered Guinness to pay Argyll £85 million.

Since all this was taking place after the bid, it was open to Guiness to challenge this decision by judicial review, and it did so. The challenge was heard in January 1988 at the same time as I was arguing the "Spycatcher" case for the government in the adjacent Court. At the end of the morning argument I would move swiftly to see how I was faring as a litigant in the neighbouring court. Our case was very well argued by Roger Buckley QC, one of my close friends later to become a fine judge, and he succeeded in satisfying the court that the bold course we had taken of acting promptly without waiting for the criminal prosecution was fair. In July 1988 Lord Donaldson, as he had become, upheld the judgment. This strengthened our authority and also was prompt proof of the wisdom of his earlier decision allowing the important decisions of the Panel to be considered by the courts. The Court of Appeal decision reinforced the authority of the Panel's conclusions. The £85 million was duly paid, giving weight to the earlier view that in reality, commercial parties had no choice but to comply with the judgments of the Panel.

By then I had learnt the effectiveness of the way in which the Panel did its work. It had a director-general, who was a merchant banker on secondment for two years. In my time, John Walker-Haworth and Antony Beevor successively held this key role with just the right balance of strength, market understanding and appreciation of the constructive way in which our work should be approached. They had two long-serving deputies, Peter Frazer and Peter Lee, and a fairly small staff some of whom were on secondment from city law firms and accountants. They worked tirelessly, at all hours of the day and night, and were quite devoted to the work of the Panel. There was a pride, eagerness, skill, lack of bureaucracy and low-cost efficiency which exceeds that of any public body I have known. What is good is that over the intervening years the work continued to flourish and give public satisfaction and be largely exempt from the ever-increasing trend towards more bureaucratic and legalistic regulations.

I will only touch on a few examples of notable bids during my time as chairman. One illustrates the value of flexibility. In October 1987 there was a dramatic fall in the stock markets on what became known as "Black Monday". At that time the Government was seeking to market its remaining shareholding in BP. The market fall meant that there was grave doubt as to whether the issue would succeed. Nigel Lawson, working with the Bank of England, decided to offer to buy back the partly-paid shares at a price of 70p for a period which was, at that time, unspecified. But the shares which the government was offering totalled over 36% of BP. This gave a difficulty with regard to rule 9 of the code, which provides that, except with the consent of the Panel, a person who acquires 30% or more of the voting rights of the company must make a mandatory bid. Otherwise it could gain effective control without having to make a bid to all shareholders. But in the BP case the government decision carried the risk that the Bank of England would have to repurchase, if all shareholders took advantage of the offer, the full amount of the newly released shareholdings. This could therefore involve the Bank of England in being required to make a general offer for all the shares. This would have led to the ironic, even boomerang, effect that a partial privatisation of BP would in the event have led it to becoming fully nationalised. The Panel was consulted and promptly gave consent that, if called on to acquire more than 30% because of the repurchase obligation, the Bank of England should not be obliged to make a full bid, provided that it agreed only to vote 29.9% of any shareholdings. In the event only a small number of shareholders took advantage of the offer. But our ability to deal sensibly with this market problem shows both the value of a flexible code and the speed of service which the Panel could give.

Another illustration also related to BP. It made a bid for another oil company, Britoil. But the government held a special share in Britoil which carried a majority of the voting rights in the event that anyone offered to acquire more than 50% of the ordinary shares. This meant that the Panel had to decide the way in which to operate rule 10. This rule provides, in effect, that an offer must be capable of becoming unconditional unless the offerer acquires shares carrying over 50% of the voting rights. This is to make sure that the proper premium necessary to obtain control must be paid, and clearly this is only achieved if over 50% of the voting shares are acquired. What was to be the effect of the special share? If applied rigidly, rule 10 could prohibit any bid. Yet BP's offer would comply with the essential objectives of the rule. The Panel sought to interpret the rule in accordance with common sense and fairness. We did not think it right that shareholders should be deprived of the opportunity of considering a bid for their company on its merits. So we ruled that BP could proceed with its offer excluding from the acceptance conditions any votes attributable to the special share. This flexible, innovative, but necessary decision also gave a vivid example of the ability of the Panel to work speedily. The

problem was raised on a Friday. Full written submissions were prepared by the parties and the executive team of the Panel over the
weekend. Oral argument was heard on the Tuesday. The decision
was published in an orderly way in time for the opening of the UK
markets at 8.00am on the following day, all this, too, in the week
immediately leading up to Christmas. The decision was published
on the 23 December, with the effect that the festive season may
have been somewhat disrupted but the bidding process was not.
The Panel executive team had worked as usual long hours, out of
hours, and at weekends.

The bulk of the bid issues was dealt with by the executive and
normally parties accepted its rulings. But on important or novel
issues, either the executive might want to refer an issue to what was
called the full Panel or the party which disagreed with the initial
decision would wish to appeal. The full Panel was presided over by
the chairman with two deputy chairmen of great City experience,
in my time Mr John Hull and Sir Philip Shelbourne, together with
very senior nominated representatives from a wide range of business
interests from the banks to the CBI. This not only gave the Panel
credibility but also meant that there was no in-built cosiness in
the regulatory system because of the divergence of the view points
and interests of the members. After hearing the arguments for the
parties which were generally advanced by their investment bankers,
the Panel would give a ruling with its detailed reasons. In cases
of exceptional novelty or difficulty there was also a right of appeal
from the full Panel to an Appeal Committee, which shortly after
my appointment, I persuaded my mentor and friend, Lord Roskill,
to chair. One high profile and groundbreaking case, which went
from the Panel to the Appeal Committee was the bid by Hoylake
plc for BAT Industries plc.

Hoylake was a company used for the principal and so far as
I am aware only purpose of mounting a takeover bid for BAT. It
emerged in a somewhat improbably bid launched in September
1989 towards the end of the heady days of the Lawson boom when
any form of creatively financed acquisition seemed feasible. The
principal investors in Hoylake were a colourful and diverse trio:

Kerry Packer, Sir James Goldsmith and Jacob Rothschild. They were all former clients, but so were BAT and everyone consented to my taking part. The issue arose because BAT owned a United States insurance company, Farmers. Hoylake needed to obtain regulatory consents in nine states before they could complete the bid. BAT and its subsidiary, Farmers, vigorously opposed the grant of such consent in the US proceedings.

It became clear that the regulatory process would not be completed within the timescale laid down by the code for the completion of the bid process. Hoylake applied to the Panel complaining that the actions of BAT in lobbying politicians and other people who might influence the outcome of the offer in the United States, and taking part in the regulatory process did not amount to what is known under the code as "frustrating action". This is one of the most valuable features of the code because it prevents a defending company putting in place a "poison pill" defence which prevents shareholders getting a proper opportunity to consider an offer for its company, but we took the view that for BAT to exercise its legal rights in regulatory proceedings concerned with a company it owned in the earlier United States jurisdictions fell well short of what was intended by the code.

Hoylake also applied for a dispensation under the code. Normally where a bid lapses for any reason the bidding company is precluded under the code from making another offer within the following 12 months. This is to prevent a defending company being under a perpetual state of siege and distracted from the primary task of managing its business. It had become clear that the regulatory proceedings in the nine states were not going to be completed within the timetable prescribed by the code for the bid. The effect of this would be that shareholders would not have been able to consider a bid on its merits. Hoylake invited the Panel to allow it to lapse its bid but permit it to make another bid within the 12 months during which it would normally have been prevented from doing so if the regulatory processes were completed. We agreed. It was a novel situation, but which appeared likely to occur more frequently as companies increasingly become multi-national, and the way in which the time scale of the code interacted with foreign regulatory processes would need to be considered. There would often be a mismatch between timetables which had to be sensibly resolved so that shareholders could have a proper opportunity to consider a bid for their company. The Appeal Committee of the Panel agreed with our decision.

In the event Hoylake never bid again for BAT. Whether the regulatory processes in no less than nine states dragged on, or the viability of the bid ceased as "boom" turned dramatically to "bust", I have no idea. The idea that the regulatory processes go through all the hoops within the 12 months had always seem improbable. The issue was important in creating some precedent as to how the Panel would approach such a cross-border situation. It also provided an amusing hearing. Kerry Packer sat in a corner of the room smoking and looking monumentally bored for most of the time. He only came to life when Sir James Goldsmith asked if we would allow him to cross-examine the witness for BAT. Sir James then demonstrated in short order how he would have been a brilliant success in my own profession. Jacob Rothschild sidled in looking almost as if he did not want to be noticed and was rather apologetic about his part in what seemed to me an over-imaginative bid.

Another case with cross-border implications and its amusing side was a bid by GC & C brands for the Irish Distillers Group. GC & C had made an initial bid about which Irish Distillers complained to the European Commission. GC & C was a company in which the ultimate majority ownership lay with Allied Lyons and Grand Metropolitan. It had been created to make the bid for Irish Distillers and, if successful, jointly to produce and distribute its brands. This was argued to be in breach of the competition provisions of article 85.1 of the Treaty of Rome. The Commission took the view that the complaint was well founded. So GC & C undertook with the Commission to restructure its offer in a way which would deal with these concerns. They asked the Panel to confirm that they could proceed with their restructured offer. Irish Distillers protested that the offer should lapse, and that GC & C should be prohibited from making a further offer for 12 months.

We were careful to make plain that we had a very distinct and different role from the Commission - we seeking to observe fairness to shareholders, whereas they were driving for market competition. We took the view that the offer should lapse because clearly the revisions made it a new and fresh bid different from the one which had already been launched. We took the view that the 12 month rule applied to prevent a fresh bid soon after the expiry of a bid which had run its full course but had been rejected by offeree company shareholders. The intent of the 12 month rule was to avoid a prolonged attack which would have distracted management for an unreasonable time and create general uncertainty adversely affecting the development of the company. So there was flexibility to dispense with the 12-month cease-fire period. We ruled in the circumstances it was right that the shareholders of Irish Distillers should have an opportunity which they had not so far been given to consider a bid. But we shortened the timetable so as to limit the uncertainty which would surround the company.

But the saga did not end there. There was a counter-bid from the French company Pernod-Ricard and GC & C claimed that this competing offer entitled it to exercise a right it had reserved to increase its otherwise final offer for Irish Distillers. The offer arose later in the day and Pernod-Ricard were regarded as a friendly suitor. At a weekend at the beginning of September, Pernod-Ricard indicated to certain shareholders that it would make an offer for Irish Distillers if it could obtain in advance irrevocable commitments to accept its proposal from enough shareholders. Shareholders were contacted on the Saturday and Sunday by word of mouth by representatives of Irish Distillers and Pernod-Ricard. Shareholders were asked to go to a large meeting held at the brewery on the Sunday. Word spread quickly and the meeting was well attended. I doubted at first how much weight we should have attached to anything which happened there until we were told firmly that no alcohol was served. GC & C argued that Pernod-Ricard had gone about approaching shareholders in a way which effectively circumvented the code, meaning that those shareholders who had not accepted the Pernod-Ricard approach would only get its offer after control had passed and without any opportunity of a higher competitive bid. The Panel agreed with this argument. This decision was clearly good for shareholders since GC & C raised its offer, but Pernod-Ricard then came in with a higher formal offer and acquired the company. But not before the Panel had considered an application by GC & C that the directors of Irish Distillers had not properly exercised their discretion in advising shareholders because of the way that they had cooperated with Pernod-Ricard. Overall we took the view that the directors and the shareholders had been given a proper opportunity to consider the rival bids and that it would be inappropriate to reopen the process to give GC & C yet another opportunity. So Irish Distillers went to its preferred suitor.

I was highly fortunate in my time at the Panel. It was a very active period with a number of interesting and significant contested bids raising important points as to how the code should be adapted and applied. In recent years the number of bids as a whole has diminished, and hostile bids have become much more rare. But the Panel remains authoritative, operates efficiently and to the same very high standards, and keeps as far away from statutory regulation as is possible. Otherwise, flexibility on the purpose of approach which makes this the most impressive means of dispute resolution I have ever come across will be lost, and maybe the ability to give the tireless advice at very short notice. But in a flexible system this advice must be available so that people can know where they stand before they act. As Antony Beevor, my fine second director-general wrote, "the executive consultancy service lies at the heart of the non-statutory system of regulation offered by the Panel". The Panel is now 35 years old. When it was created the Bank of England thought that it would last for about 20 years. In a world of ever more complex legalism, and in a city which is more tightly controlled than in the past, it is strong, respected, and a beacon of excellence. It is important that this should continue. Otherwise something special from past standards will be lost. Sir Nicholas Goodison, a notable chairman of the Stock Exchange and generous supporter of the arts, once said: "there is no financial system in the world which does not depend to a large extent on the moral standards and disciplines of self-regulation". The long saga of the European Union takeover directive, which the Panel helped to shape, should not end with over-tight legislation which deprives the Panel of its informality and flexibility.

These values are not easy to carry over in to the modern, ever more acquisitive jungle of financial services. But when these values still exist, they should be treasured as precious. Working for the Panel, although my time there was cut short by the move to NatWest, and helping to restore its reputation after the Guinness incident was one of the most satisfying and worthwhile of times.

14. NATWEST:
CULTURE SHOCK

One cold Monday in January 1989 Lord Boardman, once a cabinet minister in Edward Heath's government and now the chairman of National Westminster Bank, came to see me in chambers. I had read somewhere that he was planning to retire at the end of the year. But it never even remotely occurred to me that the aim of his visit was to suggest that I succeed him. I was so unprepared for this idea that all I could do was to offer him some more coffee, ask some elementary and disconnected questions and suggest that we had a further talk in a week or so.

I had never thought of going into business or the City. My practice had brought me into contact, sometimes prolonged, with large commercial organisations. Some of these cases had been about banking law. But none of this had made me feel remotely like changing course and becoming responsible for the affairs of a major business. Nor had my past contacts with National Westminster Bank impressed me. From my time as a young barrister until my early years as a QC, I had banked at one of their branches in Fleet Street. There had been an extremely decent assistant manager, a Mr Hall, who subsequently went on to manage a branch at Wimbledon. He always took the trouble to chat with me when I paid in cheques. He epitomised the old-fashioned, solid banker who cared about his customers and wanted to understand any way in which he could help. I had virtually no contact with the senior manager of the branch. My one encounter was less than impressive. Before taking silk I was concerned that there would be a drop in my income for a time before clients needing a QC would think of briefing me. Such a drop used to be quite normal. So I built up a good balance of fees to tide me over. In the event I got off to a very smart start in silk and so looked around for a tax-efficient investment for these fees. Investing in forestry was then popular with barristers and attracted generous tax relief.

So I went to see the senior manager at my NatWest branch and asked him for a loan to help with an investment in tree planting in Wales. He was very disappointing. To my bemusement he told me the saga, which I already knew, dating back some years when town dwellers had been enticed to invest in rearing pigs. It turned out that there were nowhere near enough pigs for all the townies wanting the occasional sniff of the farm. So different individual labels were attached to the pigs each weekend, according to which owners were coming to view them. This brazen deception led to new legislation to prevent future fraud of this kind. What on earth this had to do with well-recognised schemes for investing in forestry escaped me. But the manager counselled against my purchase, and politely declined the loan.

Fortunately I was introduced by a friend to the admirable Clydesdale Bank who understood the merits of the investment, offered the loan, and promptly gained my main account. In the years which followed National Westminster Bank never seemed the least bit concerned to follow up why, from maintaining a substantial banking relationship, I had reduced my contact to a tiny current account which enabled me to draw money from the service till near my office. From this experience, and other tales I had heard, it seemed a solid but fairly dull and sleepy institution.

But what had always seemed unquestioned was the bank's integrity. I believe this is important for the success of any business, but it is crucial for a bank. At the end of 1987, this reputation had been dented. The merchant or investing banking arm of the bank, then called County NatWest, had been promoting a rights issue of shares in an employment agency business called Blue Arrow, in connection with its bid to takeover Manpower - another employment agency. The proposed issue of shares at a fixed price had looked as if it might well be a success until the dramatic stock market fall of about 11% in October 1987 which became known as "Black Monday". The result was that the issue of shares looked as if it would not be fully subscribed. County NatWest was intending to hold a certain number of shares to trade as part of their stock-broking activity, on what was called their broking book. This was legitimate and perfectly normal. But in this crisis, they also agreed to hold a significantly greater percentage on their broking book than they would need for broking purposes. They used this device to suggest that more shares had been taken up by investors. Legal advice apparently suggested that this was permissible. But to many experienced lawyers and merchant bankers it would have seemed highly artificial and so pretty dubious.

Reports of what had happened began to filter out and Nat-West decided to hold an internal enquiry. This compounded the initial mistake. It is now accepted practice that investigation of suggested improper practices within a company is conducted by an outside organisation, usually by chartered accountants. The findings of the NatWest internal enquiry were seen as being insufficiently rigorous. The Economist newspaper, which is mostly a weekly journal of commentary, unusually ran a highly critical piece of investigative journalism. The Department of Trade and Industry set up an official enquiry, chaired by Michael Crystal QC. There were even suggestions that the chief executive of the bank itself, Tom Frost, had known of or even been party to the decision to inflate the broking book so as to give the impression that the issue of shares had been fully successful.

These charges struck right at the heart of the bank's reputation for probity. It was, as I quickly realised, for this reason that they had decided that a senior lawyer, who they regarded as having contributed to the speedy restoration of the reputation of the Takeover Panel, and knew his way a little around the City, was the right candidate to guide this issue to its conclusion and ensure the appropriate strengthening of management and systems within the bank. I was encouraged to respond positively to Lord Boardman's approach by those I spoke to at the Bank of England who were responsible for the integrity of the banking system. In particular Eddie George, who was to be an outstanding governor for most of my time, and for whom I have always had a great respect and liking, was very encouraging about my appointment.

The decision was hard, and Marie and I discussed all angles. I would be stepping out from the secure world I knew and largely leaving the law, which had been my only profession. I would be exchanging an individual profession for a large company. I would be moving from working amongst friends to a large corporation where I knew virtually no one. And I would be taking charge from my first day when it was in crisis. Did I want it? Could I cope? Why go into commerce when deep down I was attracted by some form of public service? Such were the many doubts. But then the positive arguments would surface.

Whilst the bank was a commercial organisation, it seemed to me that there was a clear challenge with a worthwhile element of public interest in trying to help it through this difficult time. I was finding City contacts, which the very different work of the Takeover Panel brought, stimulating and enjoyable. At the same time this part-time post was precluding me from accepting some of the more interesting cases involving companies or issues which might come before the Takeover Panel. With relatively rare exceptions, I was not approaching my work at the Bar with the same zest as I had done since my term as chairman of the Bar when I had become engaged in the wider issues affecting our profession. The return to ordinary practice suddenly seemed rather narrow. As the same time I still had no wish to become a judge, involving as it would a more isolated life. So the attraction of entering into a different field, with a worthwhile organisation in difficulty, where my own skills might make a difference, seemed to me a challenge worth taking up. After a fortnight wrestling with the arguments, my instincts came down on the side of taking the job.

So, I agreed to succeed Lord Boardman at the end of 1989. I immediately became a vice-chairman of the Bank although this was something of a titular role, since I had a full workload of cases. I worked in court for the next few months. But even so, I was surprised at how little seemed to be required of the board. Indeed my first board meetings were probably amongst the greatest culture shocks I had ever had. Meetings were then held after lunch and no-one could criticise the quality of generosity of the fare. The headquarters of the bank were in Lothbury, a solid and serious building in the shade of the Bank of England. The dining and boardrooms were extremely sombre. But within them drinks were offered before lunch, and lunch was of the highest standard, the wines were of the best, and decanters of vintage port were on the table. When I arrived for my first pre-board lunch, I knew very few of the other directors. One noted businessman kindly escorted me to the table. After the white wine had been served, he offered me some claret with the main course, encouraging me with the words : "I always like a couple of good glasses of Chateau Latour 1970 before a board meeting". Barristers are not noted teetotallers, but drinking at lunch-time is virtually unheard of. Indeed the lunch-break is a scramble from court across the street to chambers to go over notes and hastily munch a sandwich. Relaxation and drink are generally kept for the evenings when the day is largely done.

Nor was the board meeting which followed lunch any the less improbable. Lord Boardman sat at the top of a long table, around which were seated no less than thirty directors. Most of the business was formal: receiving minutes, noting the extent of large exposures to clients, and approving certain transactions which had to be decided formally by the board. There were a few minutes of anecdotal discussion when one director expressed his disappointment at the quality of one of the London branches. There was no discussion of the Blue Arrow issue, nor of the progress of the economy, even though Nigel Lawson's boom had begun to founder, nor of what the bank's profits might be. It was all in all a gentlemanly, old-fashioned occasion with little discussion of anything.

I was later to realise acutely that there was an unhealthy attitude on both sides between directors and the executive management of the bank. Directors were traditionally grandees, and a world apart from those who had started work as school-leavers and worked their way up the ranks of the bank. Executive management, sensitive to this, and probably of the lack of understanding of some of these grandees, were not eager to keep them fully informed or take their advice. Lord Boardman had started to bridge the gap by bringing a number of the senior management on board as executive directors. But there was far to go.

I was quickly to discover that there were glaring gaps in the information given to directors. Their opportunity to contribute in any serious way to the work of the bank was stunted and stifled. There had been no regular reports at all on the problems thrown up by Blue Arrow and no proper board discussion of how they should be handled. Nor was the board kept aware on a running basis of how the business was doing. There were no monthly management accounts. Directors would arrive in August and be told the figures for the first half of the year, of which they had been given no prior indication. There was keen anticipation of what management had achieved rather as if awaiting the delivery of a birthday present. When I set about changing this habit, I was at first told that it was impossible to have monthly accounts because they could not be provided with enough precision. When I insisted, this difficulty faded away and we started to receive monthly financial statements, as do all properly run companies. But these archaic first board meetings and practices made me realise speedily that there was much more that needed to be done at NatWest than working through the consequences of Blue Arrow. And we started by holding meetings in the morning, before the claret.

I do not know how these quaint habits compared with those of other banks. I had once been for a celebration lunch at Lloyds bank after a case, where I had to leave for another appointment during the main course shortly before three o'clock. And I learned since that Lord Carrington described board meetings at Barclays in those days as being "High Mass without the vestments".

The time for me to take the chair was advanced by the publication of the Blue Arrow report. This was heavily critical of the way in which senior people in County NatWest had dealt with the potential shortfall in the share issue. Indeed some of those criticised were later prosecuted, although all were eventually acquitted by the Court of Appeal in 1992. The report also criticised three senior main board directors of the parent bank itself, and suggested that their conduct fell short of what was to be expected of directors of a major bank. This was seen by some, including myself, as rather harsh, because they had been told that legal advice had been taken to the effect that the practice was permissible. These directors properly felt that they had no alternative but to resign. Lord Boardman, who was not individually criticised in the report, also honourably decided to bring his retirement forward as a gesture of sympathy for those directors.

So in the autumn of 1989, I moved my workplace from Middle Temple, where I had been for practically thirty years, where I had so many good friends and colleagues, to the sedate and then rather depressed atmosphere amongst the bankers at Lothbury. I inherited a senior secretary who was shortly to retire, and then to be replaced by Elaine Walker, a much younger and more modern person. She, together with my young personal assistants were to provide a loyalty and friendship which I very much needed in this large organisation.

I also had to get rid of some of the formalities of a chairman's office. There was a lift reserved virtually exclusively for the chairman to carry him no further than the first floor. This lift had a permanent attendant of fixed habits. When I entered the lift, he would shut the door, turn his right foot outwards as he pressed the lift button and pass whatever comment was appropriate for the weather of that day. There were also two elderly retainers in the chairman's corridor to meet any conceivable need I had or to greet visitors. I discovered that when I retreated to the toilet they put their head into my secretary's office and uttered the rubric: "chairman's down the corridor". All this was symptomatic of the formality and the surfeit of messengers at that time. I was able to retire or re-deploy the three of them and have one really bright younger man in Andy Thompson who did not comment on my every move and indeed had a wider range of duties which kept him too busy to do so. And I was happy to press the lift button for myself.

I was also able to tackle the catering arrangements for staff, which were both too hierarchical and too inconsiderate of the need to offer junior staff food of a decent quality. On the top floor of

Lothbury was an antiquated cafeteria, looking like what I remembered to be the old ABC restaurant which my aunt Maud had taken me to on my regular visits to her in the Potteries. I was told that it had not been refurbished because there was not much demand for it. With the help of David Edmonds, who had been principal private secretary to Michael Heseltine at the Department of the Environment and latterly chief executive of the Housing Corporation, who we were fortunate to recruit as our head of property, we created a first-class buffet service, bistro style restaurant in its place, and the result was that those of our staff in the City flocked in. We also got rid too of the concept of separate messes for senior people. There was a gloomy room where senior people who were nonetheless not deemed to be senior enough to go to the board dining room, could take their lunch together, separate from more junior staff. This denied them lunch-time exchanges with their own more senior managers without giving them the opportunity to meet junior staff informally. Twenty of them lunched in stranded and torpid isolation. We also changed the most senior dining room. We brought in round tables, and opened it to everyone in the bank who wanted to have a more special lunch. These changes were in part about giving messages that the organisation should not be obsessed by status. They were in part about simply giving people a more decent and relaxed atmosphere in which to meet. Sadly few of the very senior management ever went to lunch in the upstairs bistro. Indeed they increasingly took a light meal at their desks. This partly reflected increased pressure of work, but I suspect that they found it difficult to adjust to the habit of lunching only with those of their own standing in the bank.

In one sense it could be suggested that the atmosphere I have tried to recreate is about trivialities and does not touch on the real work of the bank. But to me it represented some of the outward and visible signs of an organisation which quite simply was behind the times and in some respects frankly arterio-sclerotic. This was not going to be an atmosphere to attract the more talented, dynamic people who would increasingly be needed to shape the bank's activities in future. The bank had traditionally been light on graduates at the top. A traditional clearing banker had left school at sixteen or eighteen at a time when higher education was much less universally available. They worked their way up through every job in the bank, including the machine room, or logging the deposit of securities in longhand, or coping with other routine administrative tasks in what was a paper-dominated system.

Yet banking was fast becoming more competitive and requiring a greater understanding of marketing, risk, and the combination of using a mix of personal and technological skills. All this called for a decent graduate intake. It was telling that in 1992 Derek Wanless became the first ever chief executive of NatWest to have been to university. Derek had decided from his early years to devote his considerable talent to the bank on a long-term basis. Most of the good people from the graduate intake who had joined with him had left early - in many cases frustrated by the extent to which they were asked to carry out routine activities, to subscribe to a hierarchical and deferential system, and by the general lack of buzz or enjoyment, which permeated the entire institution. For institution it was, rather than a modern business. But it is business activities to which it is now time to turn.

15. BLUE ARROW: IN AT THE DEEP END

The 1980s were a remarkable and exciting decade. The government which Mrs Thatcher so courageously led was pledged to reverse the assumption which had become pervasive within the civil service that the primary aim of government should be the successful management of inevitable decline. The power of the trade unions to prevent change had become increasingly unacceptable in a rapidly-moving world and was challenged head-on. The tax system was restructured to foster enterprise and encourage entrepreneurs. State-owned industries were privatised with the aim that they should become more efficient. Competition and the rights of consumers were increasingly elevated into pole positions. Inevitably, and rightly, the banking industry was not immune from the drive for change. During these years there was increasing deregulation of City activity. "Big Bang" as it was called, enabled institutions to move into areas of financial activity from which they had previously been excluded. This obviously intensified competition but it increased the risks of institutions entering areas they did not properly understand and also called for more sophisticated skills. And the demand by institutional shareholders, more interested in short-term results than long-term success, and for ever greater returns on capital became increasingly strident.

For many years, indeed centuries previously, banking had been a solid, staid, mostly admirable and worthwhile occupation. In "A Tale of Two Cities" Dickens gives us a glimpse into the fusty rooms of a bank in the City of London at the end of the eighteen century:

"Tellson's Bank by Temple Bar was an old-fashioned place, even in the year one thousand seven hundred and eighty. It was very small, very dark, very ugly, very incommodious. It was an

old-fashioned place, moreover, in the moral attribute that the partners in the House were proud of its smallness, proud of its darkness, proud of its ugliness, proud of its incommodiousness. They
were even boastful of its eminence in those particulars, and were
fired by an express conviction that, if it were less objectionable, it
would be less respectable."

A little later Dickens describes the staff of the venerable institution: "Cramped in all kinds of dim cupboards and hutches at
Tellson's the oldest of men carried on the business gravely. When
they took a young man into Tellson's London house, they hid him
somewhere till he was old. They kept him in a dark place, like a
cheese, until he had the full Tellson flavour and blue-mould upon
him. Then only was he permitted to be seen, spectacularly poring
over large books, and casting his breeches and gaiters into the general weight of the establishment."

For a long time after this glimpse of life at Tellson's Bank,
the needs of the customer and the aims of banks had roughly run
in harness together. Customers had wanted an institution where
their funds could safely be lodged, could be available on demand,
or if they had significant surpluses to current requirements, placed
on deposit accounts. Access to those funds for many years was only
gained by personal visits to the bank during limited opening hours.
But most of these customers had welcomed the introduction of the
hole in the wall service till which meant that money was available
at any time of day or night and that they did not have to stand in a
queue at the counters. Some customers had also wanted overdraft
or other loan facilities for personal or business needs.

From the point of view of the bank these needs meant that
much of banking work was humdrum administration and processing. For those who made progress in the bank and were given
lending and management responsibilities, the aim was to be sensibly prudent, responsible in behaviour towards the customer, and
increasingly to play a part in the local community. The strength of
banks was measured by the size of their assets, or loan base which
in turn reflected the volume of funds which customers had placed
on deposit, which the bank was able to deploy as part of its business.

The major hazard, common in the 19th century, but virtually unheard of in the 20th century was a loss of confidence in the bank. This would lead to customers all withdrawing their funds - "a run on the bank" - which the bank could not instantly recall from the borrowers to whom they had lent the deposited funds. So, almost everything was aimed at maintaining confidence in the bank. This is why banking halls used to be so grand. This was the explanation of John Maynard Keynes, who had little regard for bankers. At the time of the First World War he was scathing. He criticised the bankers for their failure to respond appropriately to the financial crisis at the start of the war, blaming the low calibre of directors and managers. He called one bank chief cowardly, another selfish, and the rest were "timid, voiceless and leaderless". A little earlier he had written that "the bankers completely lost their heads and have been simply dazed and unable to think two consecutive thoughts". Before the war he had lectured students that "leading financiers, being unable to follow an argument, will never admit the feasibility of anything until it has been demonstrated to them by practical experience".

But the success of a bank such as NatWest over many years reflected the way in which decent, often shrewd school-leavers, who in those days lacked the opportunity of a university education, had worked their way through to become managers with a limited range of important tasks which called for continuity and prudence. The bank manager, like the general practitioner, was a figure in the local community. He - and it was invariably he in those days - would always be part of local Rotary, often a pillar of the golf club, respected and liked.

Before Big Bang and the liberalisation that went with it, a well-run bank did not suffer over-greatly from the stresses of competition. The attitude of government and the Bank of England was that it was broadly helpful for the banks to make a reasonably good profit when the economy was making progress, provided that they were willing to come to the help of the system and give support in times of crisis.

I do not wish to suggest that banking was an easy occupation, nor do I want to belittle what NatWest had achieved. The bank's history, size, profitability and large customer base did not happen by accident. The bank had been, by and large, built up by the kind of manager who is good at running a ship which is sailing in steady seas. But the climate was changing, and squalls and storms were buffeting the ship. In such conditions a different type of manager was called for.

NatWest had also, to its considerable credit, been a meritocratic bank, and this contrasted with Barclays where there had been a tradition of blue blood. The prototype was that of a school leaver who, at 16 or so joined the bank and started in the machine room of a branch, working his way up had worked pretty well. What was to prove difficult was the need for wider skills, greater experience and training for a rapidly changing world. This, through no fault of their own, exposed limitations in many of the more senior traditional bankers.

Banks have always had to be careful how they balanced their lending portfolio and there were times when banks got into trouble for too hotly chasing particular areas of activity. Lending to property companies in the early 1970s was a classic example. But for all that most of the activities called only for relatively limited skills although for a very large number of people. When I joined NatWest there were 110,000 employees - only a handful were graduates. Many had joined the bank at age 16 with a view to working their way up. We were the largest employers of school-leavers in the country. Computers had made an impact, but there were still mountains of paper and ledger-work which were labour intensive.

We had some 3,250 branches when I arrived in 1989. They varied from large city or town branches to small ones rather akin to corner shops. The branches varied in quality enormously. In some the standards of customer service were high and imaginative. In others they were dismayingly like an old-fashioned post office. In my first wide-ranging series of visits across the country, I was astonished to find the difference between branches of the same organisation. There was no feeling of common or consistent standards of service, or of attitudes or of a universal commitment to best practice. Physically the branches varied enormously. Some had been decently refurbished. Others were simply shameful in a modern world. The windows were all too rarely used for a decent display. Tom Frost told me ruefully early in my time: "Of course, we at NatWest have overall the worst branches". It was almost as if it was a fact of nature rather than reflecting as it did a failure to make the necessary investment or adapt to the modern world. In the same way, most of our technology was old-fashioned. The director then responsible explained this by telling me that we had "legacy systems". The main reporting system in branches when I started, and for a considerable time after, was the "WEO" system, which stood for Westminster Electronic Output" - a new computer system proudly introduced by the Westminster Bank prior to the merger which formed NatWest in 1971.

The acceptance of a processing mentality, of a primarily administrative function, coupled with a lack of appreciation of what was needed to draw customers into their branches when they could increasingly withdraw their money from the service tills - or holes in the wall - was indicative that the bank was failing to grasp quickly enough the challenges which competition and consumer expectations were bringing.

In the wake of Big Bang, these challenges were growing apace. Banks were more competitive with each other in marketing to business and corporate customers. They were now able to sell their customers the full range of household insurance, general insurance, mortgages, pensions and the widest range of personal, financial services. This called for greater awareness by staff, who had to make the most of customer contact however slight, and who needed to understand the range of products available. Branches needed to become much more like shops which customers could either want to enter - a tough task - or at least feel comfortable in. Small business clients, a large and very important group, were served from the branches. By contrast, medium sized and larger corporate clients were no longer dealt with from individual branches, but generally from specialised commercial centres.

In this commercial area NatWest had adapted much more quickly. We had given specialist training to many of the brighter bankers who were eager, professional, visited their customers and were generally much respected. One of the most heartening aspects of my time at NatWest was the strength of our corporate bank and the way it continued to adapt its services to meet a wider variety of needs for specialist loans. The part of the bank which served what were known as mid-corporate clients remained consistently as good as any in the market. This was very satisfying since by serving them well we were making a really worthwhile contribution to the growing resurgence of the national economy and its commercial underpinnings. With this corporate banking strength also went the high quality and innovative venture capital arm.

We also owned Ulster Bank, which, despite its name, was very active and widely regarded in the Republic as well as Northern Ireland. This bank remained dedicated to customers in a period of change, maintained the soundest of lending policies, and was steadily to improve its performance across what was to become a very volatile economic decade. It was always a real pleasure to visit both parts of Ireland to find such a high regard for Ulster Bank amongst politicians, businessmen and personal customers, and to witness the standards and quality of so many of its staff.

But these strengths and weaknesses inevitably took some time for me to appreciate. Indeed on arrival I found the sheer size of the bank daunting. At the Bar I had always worked as part of a small team handling a case. It would be possible for me to know every detail of what was happening, and the individual strengths of the members of the team. The only two organisations for which I had been responsible had been small ones, the Bar Council and the Takeover Panel. In each case it had been possible for me to be fully involved in all important areas of activity. But it was part of my personal culture shock of going to NatWest to appreciate how different my role had to be in the future. In the past, the chairman had rightly or wrongly been seen by most as an elegant figurehead. When I asked Tom Frost what he saw as my job, he responded rather nebulously that it was to "add value" to the bank and added that there were plenty of people capable of doing the banking. I was to find all too soon that all was not well with the banking and that I needed to get to grips with the issues involved. For, as I will tell in a moment, our loan book had gone badly wrong. In the meantime I had to get used to the fact that I would inevitably carry responsibility for a whole range of activities in which I simply could not have detailed knowledge and had to trust to senior management who would in turn have to trust more junior management. Throughout my time at NatWest I did not find this temperamentally easy since my whole training had been to master every detail of my cases.

But one clear and immediate area for action was the corporate governance of the bank. It was urgent to reduce the size of the board, to make sure it had the opportunity to consider the real issues for which it was responsible, and to include some who were at the leading edge of modern business practice. I saw all directors individually. It is never easy for people to stand down and this was perhaps particularly true in the case of NatWest where the billet was a comfortable one and membership of the board gave standing in the community. But those asked to retire at the next annual general meeting agreed to do so with good grace. In April 1990 our numbers came down from thirty to nineteen, including six executive directors.

Also included were three new and very valuable non-executive members. George Quigley, chairman of Ulster bank, Ian MacLaurin, chairman of Tesco and Martin Taylor, a chartered accountant and deputy chairman of Hanson Trust. The two latter appointments in particular demonstrated that I was trying to bring a different type of experience to NatWest, and prompted The Times to comment that I clearly meant business in the restructuring of the board. We were later to add other business leaders such as Sir Michael Angus, who was chairman first of Unilever and then of Whitbread and Sir John Banham who was director general of the CBI and later chairman of a number of substantial public companies.

Ian MacLaurin was to be a valuable director until he left the board in 1996 when Tesco decided to enter banking and so became a competitor. His contributions were down to earth, clear and in-cisive and both strong and helpful as to how our retail business needed to change. He found, as I did, the atmosphere of the bank complacent and difficult to change. In his autobiography 'Tiger by the Tail' he said this: "The trouble with the establishment at Nat-West was that they thought they were fantastic, and they treated their own people and their customers accordingly. The contrast with Tesco was extraordinary. Where we maintained a dialogue with our people and our customers as a matter of company policy, it seemed to me that the hierarchy at NatWest had little time for either. The world was out there, somewhere, peopled by sundry debtors and creditors, but all safely distanced from the cloistered retreat of Lothbury."

He was also acute enough to sense that I was grappling with the same difficulties and summed it up this way: "Since my first days at Lothbury it was clear that Bob Alexander was determined to drag the NatWest into the twentieth, if not the twenty-first cen-tury, and I still wonder whether there were elements within the hierarchy who did not take kindly to this radical agenda. Maybe I was imagining things, but it seemed to me that during my first cou-ple of years in Lothbury, I was caught up in a culture-clash between the old and the new."

For me this was a pretty good summary. I often felt at Nat-West that I was having to fight too hard to modernise the system. Ian also implies, and again I feel this, that I was only partially suc-cessful even though I was there for the best part of ten years. The Bar Council and Takeover Panel, as small organisations, rather like a sailing dinghy had responded promptly to a new hand at the tiller. The bank was much more like a stately ocean liner - powerful but slow to turn, and unable to manoeuvre flexibly in the choppy and changing seas.

I also feel that the bank lacked a passion to attract and serve customers. Too many staff tended to look on the bank as an in-stitution providing a public service, rather than a business seeking customers for profit. In part this was admirable, but this approach was unsustainable in an increasingly competitive market-place.

Nor could some challenges be promptly resolved. The bad debt crisis which was to hit us from the end of 1990 affected the bank's performance and results for the next six or seven years. It was to be no less than four years from my arrival before the stain of Blue Arrow on the bank's reputation, was to be finally removed. A report of the DTI inspectors, as I have previously indicated, had been critical. It had also reinforced the belief that the bank tried to contain the problem by an insufficiently probing and stringent internal report. It was clear that prosecutions were likely to follow. In the event, those put on trial were a number of senior executives of the two NatWest investment bank companies involved. The case did not come for trial at the Central Criminal Court or Old Bailey as it is more commonly known, until February 1991. It lasted for a year and 4 days - at the time the second longest criminal trial on record. During the trial the judge dismissed the charges against two of the individual defendants and against both County Nat-West and NatWest Investment Bank. At the end, four of the five remaining individuals were convicted and the fifth was acquitted. These convictions were to be overturned on appeal in July 1992.

During the trial there was day after day of evidence high-lighting the criticisms of the bank which had a corrosive effect on the confidence of management and our staff. What I had speedily learned was that press criticism is almost more damaging internal-ly in its effect on employees than the reactions of customers who tended to stay pretty loyal. But for members of staff to be regularly questioned by customers, or joshed in the pub in the evenings, in-evitably took its toll on them and on morale. All this made it a very difficult time for the organisation.

I had initiated a series of reports to every board meeting on the Blue Arrow case. Initially I had hoped it would be over by the end of 1991 but this was to prove far too optimistic. After the trial, I felt at last that we were going to be able to put Blue Arrow behind us. In this I reckoned without The Economist. In March 1992 it published another long article repeating most of the initial charges it had made. Its contents disregarded much of the evidence given at trial and the outcome of the proceedings. It suggested that something was still rotten in the state of NatWest, not least that Tom Frost, the chief executive, had been party to the initial decision to camouflage the fact that the issue of Blue Arrow shares had not been successful, and also to the cover-up. It included claims that NatWest had failed to supply crucial documents to the inspectors, and had supplied "clean documents" without handwritten notes made by Tom Frost, and that he had given incorrect evidence to the trial.

The Economist is rightly a very highly regarded magazine, or as it describes itself, a newspaper. It is normally seen as thoroughly responsible, factually accurate, and healthily controversial in its comment. It is highly influential in national and international business and banking circles. So this renewed attack on the bank's integrity was potentially devastating and put the clock back to where it had been before the prosecutions started. I believed that we had to tackle this article head on or there would be a permanent cloud over the bank. All my instincts suggested that we had no alternative but to ask the DTI to reopen its enquiry to bottom-out the claims which The Economist had made. Since it was just before the 1992 general election, I felt there was no time to lose before government went into limbo for the election campaign. There was no time to consult our board fully. I wrote immediately to Peter Lilley, then Secretary of State for Trade and Industry, explaining why it was critical that allegations should be looked into thoroughly. He responded immediately by agreeing to reopen the enquiry, a notable example of prompt and decisive government action.

Our board understood the reasons why I had chosen this course, although they were all disheartened that it had become necessary. Tom Frost, in particular, had spent some gruelling days in the witness box during the criminal trial and would be needed to devote a good deal of time to presenting his case to the enquiry. He agreed, although initially he was understandably reluctant, that he should cease to carry the full-time responsibility of chief executive - and chief executive of a major bank is a sometimes daunting full-time task - and become a deputy-chairman for the next eighteen months until he was due to retire. This was clearly a disappointing end to a forty year career which had taken him from entry as a school-leaver to the very top of the bank.

There were some, too, though only one dared to tell me so, who were concerned that the DTI enquiry might uncover damaging new facts. The new enquiry, chaired, as the first one had been, by Michael Crystal QC, an able and powerful commercial lawyer with special knowledge of insolvency, looked again rigorously into all that had taken place. This, too, took time. It was not until 1993 that it published its report. To my relief and gladness, it firmly nailed the most serious criticisms which The Economist had made. In particular it vindicated Tom Frost, which was most welcome to all of us.

The Blue Arrow incident, and the damage it did to NatWest could at last be put behind us. It was merely for the final rites to be performed or so it seemed. But The Economist disappointingly did not publish a full account of our exoneration at first and merely inserted one tendentious and wholly inadequate paragraph. My relationship with the newspaper during this second enquiry had been a slightly uneasy one. In 1991 I had become a trustee of The Economist and prized greatly the opportunity to be one of those who could support the independence of the editor. I had offered to resign when we took up the cudgels against The Economist after the early 1992 article. I did not want the editor, Rupert Pennant-Rea, to feel that I might in any way be influenced in my general views by the fact that we were locked in conflict. But with his full consent it was agreed that I would simply stand aside from any involvement as a trustee until the Blue Arrow incident was finally closed.

When The Economist responded inadequately to the second Crystal report, we had to write threatening legal action. Rupert Pennant-Rea, a highly able economist and journalist with whom I have always enjoyed warm personal relations, came at once to see me and accepted that a full and proper apology should be made. He wrote it himself, and after a four year battle to establish the correct facts and clear the bank from unfair imputation, it was good to read this article in the next issue: "An article that we wrote last

March ... contained assertions and suggestions which led to an official investigation into one of Britain's biggest banks ...The investigation concluded that the nub of our article was wrong. This page sets the record straight."

The essence of that article was that the role played by Nat-West in the Blue Arrow affair was greater than the inspectors had been told. The Economist said that 'the trial raised new questions. How much had the chief executive of NatWest, Tom Frost, known about the affair? Had the Bank of England performed its supervisory role properly?' It was this article which prompted ... Lord Alexander to ask the DTI to reopen its investigation ... In this second investigation, the inspectors received 304 written submissions and took oral evidence from 109 witnesses. The inspectors reached a number of unequivocal conclusions, which can be summarised in the following terms: we have received the fullest co-operation and disclosure of information from the National Westminster Bank Group, its officers and employees. We are satisfied that senior officers of National Westminster Bank PLC did not deliberately withhold from the (County) inspectors relevant information and documentation bearing on their role and knowledge of events. We have investigated a number of other allegations of dishonesty and impropriety which have been levelled at senior officers of National Westminster Bank PLC. We are satisfied that there is no substance in any of these allegations ... We therefore apologise to NatWest, the Bank of England, and the individuals to whom we referred, and retract these claims absolutely."

It had been a long haul. Those who chose me to lead the bank had been right in thinking that legal skills and judgement would be important in this affair which was so vital to the reputation of the bank. There were long-term lessons which we had learned. One early one for me was the importance of ensuring that the bank had in future a legal adviser to fulfil the role akin to that of general counsel in companies in the United States, a lawyer, almost certainly a solicitor, at the top of the company who could bring real, wide-ranging judgement to bear on whether transactions should be entered into. There is too much of a tendency these days for law firms to be asked to advise whether conduct is legally permissible, without being asked for a broader view as to whether a client is walking too close to the tightrope or failing to fulfil the spirit of the law. Another lesson, now I think universally accepted, is that serious claims of misconduct against an organisation should be investigated by outside professional advisers. If NatWest had done this in the first place, there would almost certainly have been no DTI report and possibly no prosecutions. But what mattered more than anything is that the cloud over the bank had finally been lifted. But the price in terms of customer perceptions and staff morale over six long years, had been a high one.

16. A DELUGE OF BAD DEBTS

In my first years Blue Arrow had proved far from the only problem and not the greatest one in its lasting effect. Economic bust, and bad debts were to play havoc with the bank.

Before I entered banking I saw bankers as being extremely cautious and unimaginative about making loans. What I did not appreciate but was to come to learn very quickly is that the basic economics make it is sensible for a bank to be fairly risk-averse. Winning a majority of cases, say 70% at the Bar, is the mark of a highly-successful practitioner. But in banking the odds are very different. Some risks must obviously be taken. Some loans will prove irrecoverable, because of mistaken judgement or sheer bad luck on the part of the customer. Equally the bank has to judge what is the right interest rate for the particular risk accepted. But for the bank to be profitable, and speaking in broad terms, it needs to recover about 98% of its loans. Any less and the sensitivities mean that its profits will speedily vanish. There are few areas of life which call for what must sometimes seem an impossibly high success rate. Good banking intrinsically involves a high degree of caution. This was to become all too plain in 1990 about a year after I had joined the bank. From the United States, from Australia, from our domestic lending market, there were to be acute financial problems which took several years to address. Those from the United States and Australia came first.

NatWest had grown over three centuries by its business development and acquisitions of other banks in the United Kingdom, often small regional banks, into one of the most powerful banks in the country. The largest merger was when the Westminster joined with the National Provincial bank in 1970.

It took a long time to assimilate the two cultures. When I joined some 19 years after the merger, people still spoke to themselves as being an "old" Westminster or an "old" National Provincial man. One of the reasons why the bank payroll was so large was that very few steps had been taken to achieve the productivity gains which the merger should in theory have brought.

But at the end of the 1970s the bank decided that the time had come to expand overseas into the United States. It was to step outside the markets it knew and understood, and in which it had a strong position. An attractive case could be made for doing so. The United States as the strongest economy in the world, had the potential for further growth at a rate higher than could be achieved in the United Kingdom. There were also times when the United States' economy was buoyant at the same time when the UK economy was sluggish. And in any event competition policy before that time would almost certainly have prevented further expansion here at home.

The broad plan was ambitious. No less than to start on the east coast of the United States and gradually expand retail and commercial banking right across the country. A start was made with the acquisition of a New York bank, which was to become NatWest Bancorp in what was unquestionably one of the most dynamic financial markets in the United States. All went well for some years. By the late 1980s profits which had grown regularly were coming in at the rate of about $200 million a year.

Some small banks had been added to the initial investment and the prospect seemed promising. The footprint of the bank was mainly in New York and later in New Jersey. There was a high degree of confidence at NatWest about future performance. John Tugwell, the then senior executive responsible in London said to me that Bill Knowles, the chairman of the US business, "always delivers his targets".

So there was some concern, when in the autumn of 1989 those responsible in London began to discover cracks in the standards of the lending book in United States. This rapidly turned to alarm when the extent of the problems were bottomed out. The US economy was going through a phase of only moderate confidence - the rough and ready measure being that people were replacing their cars every four years instead of every three - but the dramatic bad debts which we sustained represented a deeper failure. We had committed too much money in doubtful property loans. We had plunged into doubtful or even improbable sectors of the economy, most notably projects for developing electricity plants from urea. We had over lent to Donald Trump. He was to plunge into Chapter 11 administration and incredibly we had no real security for our loans. The only so-called security turned out to be a pledge on gaming machines in a casino in Atlantic City. Most noticeably, bad debts plunged to create a loss for 1991 of over £170 million. It took some years of stringent management gradually to free ourselves from the problem debts.

Not surprisingly directors and indeed shareholders asked whether we were right to be there. With hindsight it is easy to be scathing about the poor management of our US banks. There were two essential problems. Banks which are well-established in their own home countries, are the first choice of customers who are putting forward good loan propositions. What newcomers in the market tend to get offered is the proposals that the larger banks will not take on, which are intrinsically higher risk. Yet the new entrant may feel it needs to grasp them in order to build its share of the market. This is, as we were shortly to discover in regard to Australia as well, one of the elementary dangers of assuming that because a bank has skills in one market, those skills can be transferred to other countries. A second problem had been the failure of NatWest management in London to oversee properly the lending book. Here their basic banking skills should have come into play. But it became clear that there had been too little close control and those responsible for managing risk at headquarters in London were all too unaware of the state into which the lending book had fallen. There had been far too much lending on doubtful property proposals. So often the trap into which banks have traditionally fallen.

Recovery from this major setback was obviously to be a long haul. When Derek Wanless succeeded Tom Frost as chief executive, early in 1992, there was a clear opportunity to dispose of this loss-making banking, albeit at a much higher cost to NatWest.

The opportunity of axing loss-making businesses, and promptly writing off the loss, is one which is often tempting for a new chief executive as then only the sound businesses are retained and he takes much of the credit for recovery. It is a well-known "macho" approach from a new incumbent. Both Derek and I resisted this temptation and he steadfastly oversaw the management of the US bank back into profit. John Tugwell moved to the US and proved outstanding at hands-on management of the bank. By 1995 this had been achieved, the prices for banks in the United States were fairly good, and it was clear that NatWest could not invest the sums needed to build the bank to the ever-increasing scale which financial institutions were aiming for without a wholly unacceptable diversion of capital from our basic businesses. So Derek then recommended a sale.

Some members of the board were reluctant, because in principle they preferred growing businesses to selling them, but the more rigorous and logical argument succeeded. We sold out to Fleet Financial Group Inc for $3.6 billion. Even so we had to write off £690 million in our 1996 accounts which reduced our headline profits and highlighted to the world that NatWest's attempts to bank in the United States had not been a success.

Problems in the United States were disappointment enough. But their discovery in 1991 was almost immediately followed by almost a carbon-copy resulting from NatWest's attempt to enter retail banking in Australia. The Australian government had decided to open up the markets to competition by issuing a dozen or so new banking licences. NatWest applied for and gained one of these licences. This lead again to an entry into a foreign market where local banks such as National Australia Bank and Commonwealth Bank dominated the market. The Australian economy moved into recession by 1990. This revealed the cracks in NatWest's Australian lending policies. The same pattern of conduct we found in the United States had cloned itself across the Pacific. There had been unwise loans on the security of property, no doubt to borrowers whose propositions had been declined by other banks. NatWest management in London did not have enough knowledge of the Australian market to oversee the quality of our lending. In 1990 the Australian bank made a loss of £37 million, which increased to £47 million in 1991. But for the strength of the parent bank, the Australian subsidiary was in such a precarious state that it would have lost its banking licence. We had to shore up the operations during the recovery process by a large injection of capital. This Australian failure, like that in the United States, took a good number of years to resolve until we were able to sell the rump of that business. In retrospect the bank had lacked the skills, or the international knowledge, to venture outside its home shores.

NatWest had become one of the strongest UK banks because over the years it had mostly conducted a shrewd and sound banking policy. I had been told early on in my time there were plenty of people with the skills to carry out our banking well. But the optimism expressed proved all too soon ill-founded. Such highly-concerning problems, as well as the UK recession, quickly made me realise that I must learn a good deal more about the principles of lending. We clearly needed sharper and more skilful controls to ensure that we knew what the risks were that we were taking on and were able to manage those risks properly. On my suggestion the board appointed one of our executive directors, John Melbourn, a highly experienced and intelligent banker, to a post with the somewhat cumbersome title of Director of Group Risk. Looking back, it seemed to have been a weakness that there had been no member of the board who had a specific portfolio highlighting their accountability to ensure that there was really close control over lending and other risks. For lending is, as I have already mentioned, fundamental to the sound conduct of banking and allows for very little margin of error.

For two major overseas subsidiaries to be holed below the waterline was gloomy stuff. But this setback was soon to be overshadowed by the dramatic turnaround in the British economy which went almost overnight from "boom" to "bust". The economy had been in a poor state when Mrs Thatcher came to power. In

1976 it had become so weak that Denis Healey, then Chancellor of the Exchequer, had been forced to call in the International Monetary Fund to support the UK economy. This Fund principally exists to help lesser developed or emerging nations. It was a considerable shock that one of the more mature economies of the world should have to seek its help. The problems overshadowed the fairly short premiership of James Callaghan and, together with a winter of industrial strife, led to the loss of the 1979 election. Mrs Thatcher and Geoffrey Howe, a conspicuously successful Chancellor of the Exchequer, nursed the economy back to sound health.

Through the mid 1980s, encouraged by deregulation, opportunities for competition and breaking the stranglehold of the trade unions, our economy started to make better progress than at any time since the Second World War. Under the six year chancellorship of Nigel Lawson this rate of progress became ever stronger and by the end of 1988 it was clear that there was a boom to which a brake should be applied. Inflation rose to 11% and the interest rates were raised for a time in autumn 1988 to 12%. But the boom went obstinately on and confidence still remained high. All the major banks, spurred on by this confidence but also by competition with each other, continued to lend strongly to businesses and not least to small businesses. Banks made their customers offers of unsecured loans to take second holidays. It was a time when junk mail was at its height, and Mrs Thatcher for one was certainly strongly privately critical to me of the banks. There was something of the feeling abroad that we had cracked the economic cycle and the economy could continue to grow indefinitely without, as normally happens, an easing off or even a time of recession. But in early 1991, about the same time as our problems in the United States and Australia were growing, the bubble burst and one of the sharpest deluges which businesses and banks had ever seen poured down, not least on NatWest.

Throughout 1990 people had been expecting the unprecedented period of boom to come to an end. But, fuelled by the confidence of the previous years, it was slow to do so. So when the economic cycle turned, it did so dramatically. In the five years to

1990 growth had averaged 3.9%. By contrast in 1991, the economy plunged into recession of -1.4% and for the five years from 1990, growth was to average no more than 1.4%. It became an extremely difficult time, both for individuals and for businesses. During this time Lord Forte, the immensely experienced hotelier, who had seen all economic conditions since the Second World War, told me when I confided to him that it was like running round putting buckets under a leaky roof, that it was the most difficult period in his lifetime in which to manage a business. Economic instability plays havoc with business and personal lifestyle planning. Take interest rates. Over the seven years from 1987, when the Conservatives won their third general election victory, to 1994 they oscillated between 5 and 15%. The combination of rapidly changing interest rates and the inevitable change in personal spending patterns, brought about by the recession, meant that the legitimate hopes of decently run businesses and reasonably prudent individuals, were thrown helplessly off course. Such a change in an economic style is bound to be bad for banks. It also throws the spotlight upon them because they are simply unable to support all the businesses which have been thrown into difficulty by the stresses of the times.

But these difficulties were heavily compounded by the over-optimistic lending policies which the banks had followed in the years of the boom. Personal customers got into difficulties, not least with their unsecured loans and their credit card borrowing. Interestingly one of the highest levels of bad debts on credit cards came from the professional classes. But the main problem was that of small businesses. In the enterprise economy fostered by the Conservative government, there had been a dramatic growth in small and medium sized businesses during the 1980s decade of growth. By 1994 businesses employing less than 250 people were contributing 56% of corporate output product and 61% of private sector employment. The small business sector covered a variety of businesses. Some were "lifestyle" businesses such as part-time design work or selling done from home. Others ranged from the corner shop, to the development of small property and construction companies. Most were hard, risky work for their owners. Our survey showed that most of these small businessmen who were our customers, worked a 70 hour week, including time snatched on Sunday afternoon to fill in forms for the government. Few of these businesses went on to become significantly larger and break through into mainstream corporate activity. A combination of pressure of hard work, risk of failure, and other lifestyle demands, meant that many small businesses had only a limited life span, the average at this time being about six years.

NatWest had developed a leading position in the small business sector which it saw as both potentially profitable and also supportive of worthwhile economic development. UK banks as a whole had supported small businesses far better than their continental counterparts and were to continue to do so. Part of this support had been by lending to small businesses. This was a relatively risky operation and meant that even in good economic times the margins on the loans had to be greater than say, mortgage lending or lending to large companies. The recession started to bring bad debts, increase the risk, and the bank looked to compensate by raising the margins to match the higher degree of risk. Perfectly understandable and necessary in business terms, but inevitably the customer saw this as the opposite of helping them through in a time of difficulty when orders fell away.

This tension between the needs of the bank and those of the customer, erupted from time to time in the recession, and there was a good deal of criticism in newspapers of banks for being insufficiently supportive of businesses in difficulty. It was an old cry which is always heard in a recession. This time it was harder because banks had been too optimistic in their initial assessment of risk. Many of their small business customers had been dependent on loans and the bank was effectively carrying the equity risk of the business without the potential of the reward on equity which successful businesses achieve. In the jargon it was said that we were taking equity risk for debt reward. In any event there was a clear mismatch and for NatWest, as the leading lender to small businesses, the problems were bound to be dramatic. We had to make a large provision against bad debts in 1991 and for some years to come. The overall dramatic fall in profits of the banks in these years, illustrate vividly the effect of the recession, together with losses flowing in from the United States and Australia.

In 1989 the profits of the bank had been a healthy £1.4 billion. In 1989 the operating profits before bad debts had been some 13% higher, but they had been reduced because we had written off the overhang of the bad debts arising from lending to the third world as part of the recycling of oil monies a decade earlier. So our declared profits, after providing for bad debts fell to £400 million in 1989. In 1990 there was a modest recovery to just over £500 million. But in 1991, with our personal lending book looking ragged, we were only in profit to the tune of £110 million. The pattern for the next few years was of slow growth from this very low base.

The overall effect of these difficulties was corrosive. There were many bankers who worked tirelessly to try to help their customers through this acutely difficult part of the economic cycle. Yet there were a large number of customers who could not be helped further and whose situation became impossible. Nor was there scope for the bank which was under stress itself, to take risks. So from having been over-confident in risk assessment in the days of the boom, the bank became very risk-averse. Not surprisingly, people were to remind us of the old adage that a bank offers you an umbrella when the sun is shining but takes it away when the rain comes. The dramatic reduction in profit over the years also meant that the bank could not invest as highly as it wished to in some areas of developing business and even in basics such as property refurbishment and technology.

For me there were a number of simple lessons. In a sense these were simpler because they came from this early practical, and difficult, insight into the fortunes of banks and their customers, rather than flowing from any formal economic training. The first was that economic stability is the vital foundation for any sound economy. In the three decades between 1960 and 1990, for example, the French and the German economies had managed to maintain broad stability as the foundation of their strong growth. By contrast our own UK economy had been much more volatile, and the boom and bust which spanned the beginning of the 1990s, brought home the toughest lesson of all. I think it was then finally realised that there was no worthwhile trade off between inflation and high employment. The government of John Major, and indeed the Prime Minister personally, became passionate in the view that low inflation was an absolute key to a sound economy. This culminated with the setting of an inflation target which was arguably the major achievement of Norman Lamont as Chancellor of the Exchequer. The pain of the recession brought about a consensus that it was better to be prudent about inflation and pursue long-term steady growth than take risks with the economy.

So the recession finally brought home, at notable cost, a commitment to low inflation which all major political parties now embrace. It also brought at long last a valuable discipline to the way in which interest rates are fixed. In the past the final responsibility lay with the Chancellor of the Exchequer. He was able to, and did, make changes in interest rates to meet the perceived needs of the moment and sometimes at short notice. This is illustrated vividly in Nigel Lawson's autobiography, "View from Number 11" - the most informative political biography of the last decade. It showed how there were many meetings, sometimes called at short notice, between teams from the Bank of England and the Treasury. There was no indication of the advice given by the Bank of England, which was never made public. All we knew was that at the end, the Chancellor might or might not raise interest rates. Sometimes there were political pressures. Mrs Thatcher was often reluctant to see interest rates raised because of the impact upon home-owners. The Lawson account gives the impression of regular meetings of large teams from the Bank and Treasury, without any indication of who played what parts. By contrast we now have a much more disciplined approach.

The Labour government, on coming into office in 1997, took the giant step forward of giving the Bank of England operational independence. So the government sets the inflation target, but the monetary policy committee of the Bank of England takes the decision on interest rates which are appropriate to meet these targets.

There is now clear accountability placed on the Bank of England, a much more ordered and professional approach to decision-making than in the past, and the duty publicly to explain the reasons for their decisions. The governor appointed by the last Conservative government, whose term was renewed by the present government, was Sir Edward George. This meant that the Bank had a highly experienced and able central banker as its head. All these factors made for a sea change in expertise and professionalism.

We in NatWest, and I personally, could only be one relatively small voice in urging commitment to low inflation, and an independent Bank of England. What we could influence much more directly was our own lending standards. In 1992 I called for an in-depth review of what had gone wrong in our lending policies and what the lessons were for the future. Some of our professional bankers were a bit dubious about this exercise, taking what seemed to me a somewhat fatalist, or laissez-faire view that banks simply make money in good times and do much less well in bad times. The outcome of the review was highly pertinent. What it showed was that there had been a great variance in lending standards between different areas within the bank. This had reflected the pressures on individual managers from their competitors, the differing skills of individual managers and the degree of optimism about the economy felt in different areas of the country. But it also reflected a lack of central guidance and support. It quickly became clear that it was possible to have databases covering, for example, small businesses, dividing them into sectors and sizes and so appreciating the degree of risk involved in each type of business, on a much more sophisticated basis than ever before. This was to prove helpful in future lending but also valuable in advising customers of their business prospects at the outset.

We became able to give a much more informed service to small businesses, and for the most part to avoid giving them encouragement by making a loan which it was not prudently sensible for them to take out. We were able to create a group of much more knowledgeable small business advisers. To me this was deeply interesting and satisfying. My own father had been a one-man business as a garage owner, and as a barrister I had also been engaged in practice on my own account without others where you are only as good as your last case and where many of us have needed to depend on the bank. In these years at NatWest we set up a branch in Fleet Street which at times was a model of its kind for small businesses, devoted to the work of lawyers and most notably barristers, and therefore understanding the difficulties of getting going early in a career at the Bar, and the uncertainties that might occur through the flow of work or even misfortunes such as illness, as well as the funding difficulties for new entrants.

One of the primary roles that I believe financial institutions can continue to play is through greater and more concentrated expertise in the business sector and so encourage the development of new businesses with potential, and to show prudence where the opportunity is less promising. The small business sector will remain a very important part of our economic activity. There are less and less large businesses offering lifetime employment, greater need for greater flexibility of skills, and more people preferring the opportunity of individual expression that comes from running their own business. But the clarion call from a bank should always be caution about taking out loans, even though this may lead the customer at the time to grumble that the bank is being less than fully supportive.

Our lending review also threw up one more general lesson. Our lending generally had been rapid. In the two years to 1990, our total lending had increased by about 30%, well above the level of economic growth. By contrast the sensible level of lending growth for a mature bank should be broadly in harmony, although possibly slightly ahead, of the general level of economic progress. Ideally this should be broken down so that the rates of lending growth match the differing growth rates in the various sectors of the economy. This was the central lesson of our review and I saw it as a critical base for sound banking.

In the light of this review, we were to put into place guidelines for future lending. A sensible degree of caution and regard to the economic growth trends; risk assessment which would increasingly be helped by technical information to include what was often called "credit-scoring"; a consistent check as to whether our lending was growing faster than the economy generally, together with a keen watch on particularly volatile areas such as the property sector. I had learned early and painfully in my time in banking that there were no prizes for customers or banks in aggressive lending policies. To be responsible lenders to responsible borrowers was fundamental. We might lose an element of profit. But we had far more chance of dealing fairly on a continuing basis with customers and of steadily increasing our own business. Not an overdramatic approach and one which would never be perfect. Judgements for and against individual lending requests remained to be taken many times a day by our lending managers. We had to stand firm to resist the pressures of institutional shareholders driving for an ever-higher short-term return on capital. But one of the lasting satisfactions for me of my time at NatWest was that we returned the lending book to sound order, and maintained it. When I left in April 1999, our debt levels for the year in which our profits were over £2 billion was down to just under £500 million - the lowest since 1988. We had obviously been considerably helped by the development of a stable economy, but we had also increased our own skills and sophistications. NatWest by then may not have been as dynamic as everyone might have wished, but it was rock-solid with responsible policies and sound risk management. It was also dealing much more consistently, responsibly and therefore supportively with our customers.

17. REBUILDING THE BUSINESS

During the Blue Arrow saga, Derek Wanless, as I have already mentioned, became chief executive of NatWest. He represented the ablest of the new generation of younger managers, coming up through the ranks. Born in Newcastle-upon-Tyne he had a grammar-school education. He then won a scholarship funded by Nat-West to my own Cambridge College, King's and joined the bank in the early 1970s. He was a very able mathematician and gained a first class degree. He was keen on football, retained fierce Geordie loyalties, and was also a fine chess player. On joining the bank, his legitimate but unwavering and clearly expressed ambition had been to become chief executive. Where other able graduates got frustrated and left, Derek simply did every job extremely well. He won respect and liking, and came through the system with uncharacteristic speed compared with normal progress in a clearing bank. The bank played to his strengths, giving him early regional management experience in the north of England. But sadly, and almost incredibly, what it did not do was widen and deepen the breadth of his experience by sending him for a time either to its operations in the United States or to work in the wholesale financial market division. So his strength was inevitably as a retail banker. He had the ability speedily to grasp the issue involved in both the United States and our commercial activities, but he was not as sure-footed in those areas solely because he had not been given any experience of them. He became chief executive earlier than expected and at a time of acute difficulties. The resilience and determination he brought to coping with an immense number of problems at once has been given less credit than it deserves.

When Derek Wanless became chief executive, the Blue Arrow issue was still very much alive, the cracks in the US and Australian banks were all too visible, and the recession at home was biting and bad debts were pouring in. Managing out these problems was to take five years or so and called for a firm steady hand and considerable patience. Derek showed these in abundance. He brought to his task a highly logical mind, the power of analysis, and a methodical and consensual approach to management. He helped me in the task of sharpening up the issues which should be reported to and debated by the board. He set in train, and here his own experience was invaluable, the reshaping of the retail bank so as to improve our technology, control of risk and the way in which services were offered from our branches. He was not afraid to take up the challenges of rationalisation. These were not easy.

During the time I was at the bank, the number of retail branches was reduced from 3,250 to less than 2,000 - which was still probably too many. The number of employees was reduced dramatically from 110,000 to less than 70,000. The profile of those employed changed sharply. When I joined, the great majority were school-leavers. As Derek reshaped the bank, the administrative tasks were increasingly dealt with by technology and so our recruitment consisted increasingly of those who had acquired higher skills and we employed very few school leavers. The profile of the needs of employees was changing fast, emphasising that successive governments have been so right to prioritise a widening availability of university education and skills training. There was suddenly no room for the school-leavers who for so long had been the mainstay of the bank. All this meant that Derek had for the first time in the bank's history to set in train a redundancy programme which we sought to handle as sensitively as possible with our trade unions. This "downsizing" as it was called in the jargon was necessary but it was an un-enjoyable part of the job. Derek had a well-developed sense of fairness and overall we probably handled it as well as we could. But it was bound to promote personal anguish for those affected who assumed they would have a job for life.

There were other traditions within the bank that had to be changed. The bank had historically been very reluctant to employ anyone who had not grown up in its service from their youth. Spe-

cialist functions such as those of finance director, property director, technology manager, company secretary, community relations
officer, and so on had all been assigned to long-serving employees
who had reached their career limits in banking and were simply
redeployed. Inevitably this meant that they did not have the professionalism in the individual areas which was increasingly necessary in highly specialist and competitive activities. It was surprising that this trend continued through the 1980s, and it was
necessary to make changes fairly speedily. Derek and I established
the modern approach of hiring people for these appointments who
had had the relevant training, had earned good reputations in their
field, and who were capable of bringing some innovative thinking
to areas which at times seemed pretty moribund. Perhaps most
surprisingly of all, the leaders of the vital task of risk-management
reporting to John Melbourn had a lot of banking experience but
none of highly specialised risk-management training needed in the
increasingly sophisticated financial services world.

Another area where the bank lagged behind was in its equal
opportunities policy. One had existed formally for a number of
years but in practice the management of the bank was unable to
shake off the chauvinist habits of generations. When I arrived,
a substantial majority of the banking employees were female, but
they were almost exclusively employed in the lower clerical jobs
or as secretaries. Only a tiny percentage of management, including the junior management levels, were female. Early in my time,
I asked unusually for a chairman, for an opportunity to attend a
regular meeting of the regional executive directors to get to know
them. I enquired what steps were taken to promote and encourage the development of women. The only response I got was from
one director who said "I challenge them on mobility". What he
meant was that he put them through the hoop in seeing whether they were as prepared as the male bankers to move house if a
change in job should require them to do so. There was no hint that
there ought to be flexibility, adaptability or consideration of any
separate needs which women might have. When Derek became
chief executive, I had an ally in seeking to change attitudes.

I decided that we should join Opportunity 2000, an organisation for the promotion of women's interests which was being launched by Elspeth Howe. We publicly committed to an aim that one third of managerial positions should be held by women by 2000. I am often sceptical about the value of targets, but in this case nailing our colours to the mast was the only way of driving home the message internally and ensuring we made the right progress. We met our aim. Disappointingly we did so mostly by bringing women through only as far as junior management posts. When I left, none of the most senior management positions were yet held by women. Even now, Royal Bank of Scotland, which acquired NatWest after I had left, has no female executive director.

One of the advantages of a modern, technocratic chief executive was that he was not bred in the stuffy traditions which had been previously deeply ingrained within the bank. I have mentioned how as chairman I found it hard to get used to the fact that I could only know a small amount of the detail of what was going on, meeting only a small proportion of our staff. When I went out on visits, which I did as often as possible, I particularly wanted to meet the younger staff who seemed to me to be often more eager, focused on customers and open to innovation, than their more senior colleagues. This is not to decry senior management. Undoubtedly a forty year career in the service of the bank would blunt the edge and appetite of many of them and breed a hierarchical and bureaucratic approach. I always encouraged staff to ask me questions about any aspect of what we did. They responded well and did not hesitate to grill me about the value of the role of the board and indeed of the chairman. From time to time this approach was contrasted with that of some of the older senior executives (but not Derek or Martin Gray, who ran the retail bank for most of my time there), who felt that the old-fashioned command culture should continue to prevail.

One of my concerns was how, when the skills level of the bank in all areas needed to be increased, we were going to attract and keep good young people if we did not have a thoroughly positive, open culture. In part I think I helped to lessen the stuffiness of the bank. But it was hard work.

One of the other problems which Derek had to tackle was the ossification which existed in the retail bank. I have touched on the lamentable state of our branches and technology, but the problems went deeper. Staff had for generations been trained for two skills only. To render an administrative service and to operate as lenders to their customers.

Big Bang gave banks greater opportunities of marketing a wider range of products. This was hard for many established bankers to come to terms with. Nor was it easy to achieve in practice. The bank had, at the end of the 1980s, sought to encourage staff to market these services, and brought in for the first time a system of targets and bonuses. These inevitably brought difficulties in their wake. Some staff felt that this drove them to seek to push their customers towards products which they might not need. Others found difficulty in establishing what the actual needs of the customers were, and so found it hard to offer a comprehensive service. The bank had begun by over-estimating the potential advantage which it would have as it widened the scope of its services. There was talk of a "captive" customer base. There was little understanding that most of us as retail customers had over the years only given two cheers for our bank. One of the advantages of being an outsider was being able to see the bank through the eyes of the customer. I also had a complaint postbag which made interesting if sometimes depressing reading. However, I was later to learn that a large number of letters addressed to me were intercepted by well meaning staff and marked with a stamp which said words to the effect: "Not seen and not replied to by the chairman". These words must have conveyed the false message that customers and their complaints did not matter to me.

In the past, the bank had tended to answer many of these complaints with a degree of disdain and on the assumption that the bank was always likely to be right. We began gradually to change this and to treat complaints as giving us a customer opportunity if we were able to respond constructively and flexibly. But the recession also brought its stresses. When customers went into unauthorised overdraft, charges automatically arose. At the time retail banks saw these charges as an important part of the bank's income. By contrast, the customer saw them as being arbitrary and hitting even good customers who might inadvertently have gone temporarily into the red. I call these charges "tripwire" charges because there was no real sense attached to them. They were gradually dismantled.

We carried out some of the non-banking services well. Nat-West had an admirable insurance broking arm, run by a relatively young team, keen to help, which always impressed me and which I personally still use. Our attempts to sell life assurance and pensions were less successful. To a great extent this was true of the industry as a whole.

"Cross-selling" as it is called, has yet to be proved to be successfully achievable. Sometimes what the banks did was actively harmful. When the opportunity arose at the end of the 1980s for financial institutions to offer the opportunity for customers to leave established occupational pensions schemes and take out individual pension policies the industry plunged eagerly in. Too many were encouraged to change from company schemes to personal ones which simply were not as good. The result was very damaging to many customers and to the confidence and integrity of financial institutions. The financial institutions went in, and NatWest sadly was one of them, with inadequate training, often poor checking on the circumstances of the customer and the value of existing policies, and the result was the pensions mis-selling scandal. I experienced the consequences of this from both sides of the industry.

When the problems arose there was rightly a call for investigation by the Securities and Investments Board - the SIB - and for redress to customers who had been harmed. This task was a large one, and took a long time. I experienced the problem from differing angles. It turned out that NatWest had been involved in pensions mis-selling, though no more but no less than most others in the industry. In 1994 I was asked to become deputy chairman of the SIB, which was then the chief city regulatory authority and performed many of the functions now vested in the mammoth Financial Services Authority.

The SIB, under the leadership of Andrew Large, carried out full enquiries into the mis-selling of pensions and recommended a series of stringent measures of redress. This involved all banks setting up highly labour-intensive and costly systems to check with all customers, whether those customers possibly had a claim and to ensure that they were met. At one stage NatWest had a department in a special building, engaged on this full-time task. The cost of this exercise was high, and substantial financial costs had to be incurred to make the reimbursement that was due to compensate customers. What also was deeply concerning was that senior management in none of the banks appeared to have picked up at an early stage what was going wrong, or to have monitored well enough the activities of their pensions' arm. It was a sobering example of how chairmen and boards of directors who tried hard to invest on sound ethical principles could not ensure that systems were being operated to high standards, or that we were being fair to customers. It is also an illustration of why it can never be assumed that even the most reputable of financial institutions is always operating in the interests of customers.

Coming from a family background where my parents had little pension provision, and from a professional background in which I had been tucking away my self-employed pension contributions, I felt that this episode was a real rebuke to the standards of financial institutions. I was to have one other, and very different contact with pensioners. Early in my time at NatWest I was shown a list of the largest loan exposures we had to customers. To my surprise and concern we had out on loan to Robert Maxwell's companies, no less than a sum of £1.2 billion, for which we had no security. At the Bar I had been engaged in one case against Robert Maxwell, where he had treated a leading Swiss banking family very badly. He had been severely criticised in a DTI report with regard to his stewardship of Pergamon Press, although for some reason the predecessor department of the DTI had never used its power to apply to the courts to have him disqualified as a company director.

His general reputation in the City was to put it mildly not a good one, and there was at least one merchant bank which had declined to act for him because of its assessment of his character.

When I asked why we were so exposed to him, I was told that he had a long-standing banking relationship, and that Robert Maxwell had never let us down. My reaction was the terse one that he almost certainly would at some time in the future. This advice was heeded. Banking relationships of this size cannot speedily be reduced first because of the need to be fair to the customer but also because of the risk that dramatic action would bring down the company concerned. But by the time Robert Maxwell went over the side of his yacht in 1991 we had reduced our outstanding loan to £350 million and there was security for all of it. We had to handle the issue sensitively because there were initially risks that long-standing Maxwell employees would lose their pensions. We took this into account in deciding how we would set about recovering the outstanding balance and were commended for the way in which we did so in a report of the Parliamentary Committee on Social Security, chaired by Frank Field. This was a vivid example of the need to make an assessment of character before making large loans which are essentially dependent on the trustworthiness of individuals. It also highlighted that not even company pension schemes provide total security, particularly if companies self-fund them or rely on stock market gains to take "pension holidays" running the risk of underfunding the pension schemes against any stock market downturn.

The future of pensions has become a very considerable issue and the potential uncertainty and scale of the problem is not yet as widely appreciated as it ought to be. The number of employees engaged in large companies, with the expectation of life-time employment, has fallen sharply. Most new pension schemes no longer offer the previously generous and secure terms which related to final salary. They have increasingly been switched to defined contribution schemes where the risk of a market uncertainty falls on the employee. All this means that increasingly people will be dependent on making their own personal pension provision. In the first place there is a need for people to understand that it is important to start making contributions as early as possible to secure the potential of a good pension. Many young people very understandably take the view that with their early years of getting established in their career, taking out a mortgage and starting a family, pension provision comes well below the immediate pressures which are on them. Added to this is that the standard of pension offered, and the advice available, comes not uniformly high. This makes it difficult for people to choose, and as the pensions mis-selling scandal showed, it is not simply enough to rely on an apparently reputable provider. The suggestion has been made that there ought to be limitation on the number of pension packages available on the market and that approved packages should be the only ones allowed on sale. The task of guiding and regulating the industry, and of encouraging more sophisticated financial understanding will become an increasingly hard challenge to government and the FSA, and grows in significance every year as the average age of the population increases.

18. THE PERILS
OF INVESTMENT
BANKING

By the end of 1996, the long haul to restore sound underpinnings to NatWest was showing marked progress. Blue Arrow was well behind us. There was much greater strength to our domestic lending and the bad debts which appeared in the recession had been largely written off. So had the poor lending from the United States. Overall, between 1991-96 NatWest wrote off bad debts to the tune of £7 billion. The US and Australian retail subsidiaries had been disposed of. Investment was being made, although progress was slow, as was modernising the lumbering giant of the domestic retail bank. The UK economy had slowly turned and was making a cautious recovery. We were at last moving forward again. Or so it seemed until with no real warning, our investment bank ran into difficulties.

Big Bang had for the first time given clearing banks the opportunity of owning and developing investment banks. There were two views as to whether it was wise to do so. Some believed that the capital strength and the understanding of the risks of lending which the clearing banks would bring would enable them to do well. Others thought that stolid clearing bankers would not be able to understand or control the bright stars of investment banking or the whiz kids of the complex wholesale financial trading markets. Barclays and NatWest, then the two biggest clearing banks, had decided that it was right to diversify by adding investment banking arms. NatWest already had a good treasury business, led by Martin Owen, together with a more modest but still appreciable business in the capital markets. They had for some years owned a small investment bank, County Bank. They also added a sound stockbroking firm which had long been based in Edinburgh, Wood Mackenzie.

Initial progress was patchy. The treasury and capital markets business continued to do fairly well. The investment banking business of County NatWest, after a modest but decent start, was to a large extent derailed by Blue Arrow which meant that clients for years steered clear of dealing with them. This created an overhang for the equities business and in two successive years this relatively small area of activity ran into a loss of £50 million each year. By 1990 this understandably caused anxiety within NatWest and there was anxious consideration as to whether the equities business should be closed. The business itself produced a careful paper showing that we could get back into profit within two years. The main board debated at length the wisdom of keeping this business. It was the only time I can remember when the board was so split that I took a vote. The decision was strongly in favour of giving the business the opportunity to survive and grow.

I had my doubts about this, but the majority was a clear one and my own City experience too limited to gainsay what were perfectly decent arguments in favour of the course we took. At times progress was a bit bumpy. At our annual general meeting in 1991, I was asked what were our plans for the business. I responded that we had accepted the confidence and plans of management that they could get back into profit within two years. A follow-up should have been predictable, but no-one had anticipated or debated how it should be dealt with. "What will you do if it continues to make losses after that time?" I was asked. I responded openly, "We will have obviously to consider whether it has a future". Those in the equities business itself were openly critical of me for doing so, suggesting that I had damaged the prospects of the very recovery we were seeking. They had some support for this in the financial press. By contrast one or two industrialists, such as Sir Derek Birkin, the tough and experienced chairman of RTZ, commented that I could hardly have said anything different without suggesting that we were too soft on non-performing businesses, or indeed without potentially misleading the markets. At all events the issue of closure did not arise because the business did get back to profit within the two year period for which the board had allowed.

As our main business gradually developed, Derek recommended, and the board fully supported, that we should expand the investment banking business. We made a number of acquisitions. A US business called Greenwich in the capital markets business. A small US investment bank called Gleacher & Co. After some attempts unsuccessfully to woo UK investments banks such as Warburgs, when it ran into difficulties and eventually sold out to UBS and Rothschilds, we found that the only apparently good UK investment bank available to us was the comparatively small Hambro Magan. Rupert Hambro, one of the founders of this bank, had by then gone his separate way. There was not total enthusiasm for the acquisition. The bank was very dependent on the personal skills of one of its founders, George Magan, who had earlier worked at Morgan Grenfell, closely together with Roger Seelig. But Martin Owen, who was by then the chief executive of NatWest Markets, strongly urged that we needed an investment banking arm to support and develop our equities business and we agreed to make the purchase. This acquisition proved disappointing, and the business seemed to loose its sparkle. George Magan, who subsequently became treasurer of the Conservative Party was widely thought to have lost the hunger for business which he had when working for himself.

A more worthwhile acquisition was that of Gartmore. This fund management business was headed by the able Paul Myners, who also brought some rigorous new thinking to the senior executive team. This business was acquired for £472 million, and after a difficult patch, grew in strength and shortly after I had left was sold for a value of £1,030 million in 2000.

Our attempts to build an investment bank at the time seemed sensible and logical. But they did not appeal to institutional investors. They preferred profits today rather than investment which might improve returns tomorrow and they regarded the returns from investment banking as inherently risky. They also compared Barclays and NatWest, which were pursuing similar strategies, with Lloyds, which under Sir Brian Pitman was doing strikingly well in the retail markets, and obtaining a huge annual rate of return on capital, which at one time rose to very nearly 35% (34.9% in 1997).

The typical clearing banker and investment banker were like chalk and cheese. I heard that, shortly after Big Bang, the blue merchant bankers referred to their new clearing bank colleagues as "grammar school boys in Marks & Spencer suits". The clearing bankers were suspicious of both the old merchant banking types and the newer market dealing colleagues. They saw them as flash, and out for a quick profit, and far more interested in their individual bonus than in the well-being of the company. For all the limitations of the traditional clearing banker I found them easier to like and respect. Some investment bankers, like Alton Irby and Chip Kruger and most of the thoroughly decent stockbroking team, were good to work with. But I did not easily empathise with traders. Ultimately the view that the clearing bank and the investment bank were like oil and water was to prove correct.

Within the investment bank there were strong characters who did not take kindly to the supervision, which they saw as bureaucratic, imposed by retail banks and expected by the Bank of England as our chief regulator. For Derek and his colleagues, it was a constant struggle to see that they were kept sufficiently informed. For all this, it appeared that there were good control procedures in place and certainly we had satisfied our auditors when in February 1997 we announced our annual results. Two days later, Derek came to me visibly shaken by the discovery that one of the bond-trading books contained losses which had been made over several months and concealed by those responsible. In theory this should be prevented by the checks and balances and controls within what is called the back office. But as other financial institutions found, and the collapse of Barings was the extreme example, losses can be concealed with the connivance or simply lack of vigilance of only a small number of people in an individual area of business. Whatever increased technological controls are put in, this is still an inherent risk within a trading business. We found that losses of over £90 million had been concealed and that the results we had so recently announced had to be publicly restated. This was later to happen in a dramatic way to the Bank of Ireland with their US subsidiary.

There were the inevitable long running, time-consuming and dispiriting regulatory enquiries. We made certain that, contrary to the Blue Arrow case, there was an outside investigation and we kept the markets and the Bank of England fully informed. This took some months, it was bad for the way in which our competence was seen in the outside world, and internal confidence was dented. At the same time our equities business started to go into loss again and we had to review its future. By September we decided firmly that we should sell it, and over the next few months went through a very difficult process of selling a loss-making business to a combination of Deutsche Bank and Bankers Trust. We owed a good deal in this rescue act to Chip Kruger, who headed the Greenwich business and Alton Irby, who was the second in command at Hambro Magan. Their negotiating skills in this sort of situation were greater than those of our own senior executive team and we relied on them to extricate us as well as they could from a difficult situation.

By the end of 1997 we were finally out of the equities business and our investment bank had been very substantially pruned. Barclays had much the same experience with an uncanny coincidence of timing and they, too, bowed to the pressures. But fifteen years of attempts on the part of both banks to build their investment banking had ended in failure. I believe that we had to try to create a successful investment bank. Not to do so would have been seen as defeatist, and leaving the field open for competitors to usurp our position. But with the benefit of hindsight we were bound to fail. The business was and is very risky, and the shareholders receive inadequate reward for this risk. Most of the reward goes to the employees concerned, leaving the shareholders to foot the bill for losses. The economics have much in common with professional football - where the footballers command high incomes, and the shareholders are left with little.

All this meant that 1997 was a disappointing and unhappy year for us and indeed for me personally. I had taken a good deal of quiet satisfaction from the recovery we had slowly made from many difficulties, which were threatening the foundations of the bank at the time when I joined. But I, along with the whole board, fully supported our management team in the development of our investment bank. Stockholders were obviously concerned by this setback. Whilst we had recovered from our earlier difficulties, they were wondering when we would make greater progress and the area of investment banking suggested to them that we were accident-prone. Not unnaturally press criticism, fed by investors, focused on Derek Wanless and myself and there were newspaper reports that investors were suggesting that each of us should go. These statements were very hard to pin down. Even the reputable financial press was prepared to publish anonymous statements, which led sometime later in another context to a complaint from Martin Taylor, then chief executive of Barclays, that investors who were prepared to criticise in this way should be prepared to put their names to the criticism.

I felt that investors who might feel like this were entitled to talk to me about it so I wrote to some twenty of the senior figures in the institutional funds. Perhaps naively I was surprised when only one of them took up the offer. Increasingly through my time at NatWest I felt that institutional investors were not over-impressive. They virtually never attended company AGMs and only sent junior representatives to the conferences at which results were presented and where there was an opportunity to question the chairman together with chief executive and finance director. When they did meet privately with senior management, we had to be cautious in case they were hoping to gain the advantage of some private information. Added to this their concept of the function of the ownership of the business was a narrow one. They were interested, and only interested, in profitability. They were wholly indifferent to the standards of service that were given to customers, unless it led to a reduction in profitability. They were indifferent to fair treatment of employees. They appeared to accept that banks had to make a moderate contribution towards community activities, but they took absolutely no interest in them. Unlike some of the financial analysts who work for stockbrokers and advise clients on the buying and selling of stock, known in the trade as the "sell side" analysts, they had no sophisticated understanding of the business. They appeared to have little interest in the long-term future and progress of any individual business or indeed sector of industry. I came to think, as others have done before and since that this blinkered concept of the responsibility of ownership of a business was increasingly a weakness of modern capitalism.

I suppose in partial defence of their approach, it can be said that many of the investments which were institutions managed were held by pension funds of businesses which took all too short a term view of the performance of those whom as business managers they invested for short-termism. But it hardly makes for easy motivation of those who work in a business. Trying to serve customers, to enhance the opportunities for employees, to develop new skills and markets, and to add something back into the community, was the satisfying part of my time at NatWest. As a shareholder, and understanding the philosophy of capitalism, I naturally wanted us to work in a way which enhanced the share price and the dividend to which many of our individual investors attached importance. But the sheer distance at which the owners of the business kept themselves, and their apparent lack of wider values, made this aspect of the job less satisfying than it might have been.

19. FAREWELL TO BANKING

These difficulties, and the sniping in the press, made 1997 a not particularly happy year. It brought one other real disappointment. I had always thought it to be odd that NatWest as one of the leading banks in the country, had such a small share of the market in mortgages. We had about 20% of the country's personal customers, almost one third of the small business market, yet our share of lending for house purchases hovered at about 3%. Yet to me it seemed that the first and most worthwhile reason why personal customers might want to borrow, might be to help finance the acquisition of their home. In a society where house prices had consistently risen and where 70% of homes were owner-occupied, the need to get a foot on the housing ladder was and is one of the early ambitions of many young people, once they start to earn moderately well at work. Lending for mortgages was, too, inherently less risky than other personal lending. It seemed to me that it ought to be a central activity of a major bank. By 1997 there was an increasing realisation that some of the leading financial institutions might merge together and it seemed sensible for NatWest to look for partners. Our clear first choice was Abbey National. Over the previous decade, under the able leadership Peter Birch, as chief executive, Abbey National had converted from a building society, entered the traditional banking market, and was seeking to widen its activities into the wholesale market. The fit was a good one. Derek and I approached Sir Christopher Tugendhat, the chairman of Abbey National, and Peter Birch. We were turned down, although it was rumoured at the time that Peter Birch was himself in favour of the merger but that his chairman's view prevailed. Peter has since confirmed this to me and expressed the view, which I share, that the futures of both banks would have been stronger if the merger had been realised.

After this disappointment, we also explored the possibility of a merger with the Prudential, at their suggestion. Their insurance business in this country would have been a valuable enhancement of our own relatively small presence in those markets. But they were also very active, through a subsidiary, in the retail markets in the United States. We had just withdrawn from those markets, one of the reasons being because we felt it was difficult to control from a distance the activities of subsidiaries in that country and that the financial risks of imperfect control were unacceptable. Whilst Prudential tried to reassure us on this, we agreed to go our separate ways.

These discussions, and the fact that I was no longer particularly enjoying banking, prompted me to consider that summer when would be the right time for me to leave NatWest. When I had joined, I had stipulated, and the bank had also thought it right, that I should not serve for more than a maximum of ten years. In 1993 I had briefly toyed with the thought that, as Blue Arrow had been resolved, and as Derek had made a good start as chief executive, I might leave to pursue other opportunities. Overall at that time, I felt that I was making a worthwhile contribution, was deeply interested in many of the challenges of the bank, and wanted to see through the process of recovery. But by 1997, when I had just turned 60, I was clear that I wanted to leave the bank in time to have the opportunity to pursue other activities nearer to my heart. In the discussions with Abbey National, I had let Christopher Tugendhat know that if the merger went through, I would be very content to stand down shortly afterwards, which would raise the prospect that he would be the obvious person to succeed me as chairman of the merged group. In France on my summer holiday, I decided that I should stay another year or so, or find a successor if I was wanted to do so, and leave not later than the annual general meeting in April 1999.

This timing also gave me the opportunity to support Derek in recovering from the blows which had been sustained by the investment bank saga and in encouraging him to speed up the process of change in our retail bank and to increase profitability and to put down what were increasingly sound foundations. He, sometimes more even than myself, was being publicly criticised without any acknowledgement of his achievements in working through the burdens of his difficult inheritance at NatWest. Some felt, and there was something in this, that he was too much of a consensus leader and did not have the flair or drive to take a bank forward to the next stage. I believe he had earned the opportunity to counter these criticisms and thought one of the advantages of my going soon would be that another chairman could form his own judgement as to how long Derek should lead the management of the bank.

When I got back from France, I at once told my board colleagues of my decision. They encouraged me to search over the next year, under the guidance of our nominations committee, for my successor. I was glad to do so as I had come to care a good deal about the health of the bank to which I had given eight tough but interesting and often enjoyable years of my working life. It had many strengths. In some areas, such as our insurance services and corporate lending, its standards had always been high. In other areas there was a growing professionalism. What particularly excited me was the quality and enthusiasm of our younger staff.

The field for my potential successor was not a wide one, still we felt that it should be someone either with wide City experience or with a track record of running a successful business. We looked at potential candidates both from inside and outside our existing board. There were not many outsiders who seemed a potential prospect and who might be available, and on enquiry they fairly quickly fell out of consideration. Within our board, there were two possibilities, Lord Blyth, experienced and successful chief executive of Boots and Sir David Rowland, who had followed a long career in insurance broking by achieving the almost impossible task of effecting a settlement between the Lloyds insurance markets and the names with whom they were in litigation with about large losses. James Blyth ruled himself out of consideration by telling me he could not be available until 2000. The choice of David Rowland was widely supported by my fellow directors, by Eddie George and

Howard Davies at the FSA, who were our principal regulators, and by Derek and his management team. David had intellect, courage and the enthusiasm for the task and he emerged as the clear and obvious choice. My last year at the bank went well. The benefits of radical change in our retail bank were beginning to come through. There were no unpleasant surprises of the kind which I had almost come to think were an integral part of banking. In 1999 we were able to declare profits of over £2 billion, easily a record for the bank, as was our return on capital of 20%. The share price was at an all time high of over £15.00 in April 1999. This was some five times as high as it had been when I joined the bank, which meant that we had not served shareholders, including myself, too badly.

When I left NatWest I had thought that the aim was to consolidate on the progress that had been made in the last few years and to look in the course of time for a merger with another large financial services company which would be a good fit. David Rowland, who was able to take a new look at the strengths and weaknesses of the bank, was concerned to accelerate this process. He arranged, and I gather this was his personal decision, although supported by Derek, the acquisition of Legal & General - one of the two largest UK life assurance companies, and very highly regarded as an efficient and profitable business. I suspect that one of his motives for speed was his belief that the management team at NatWest needed strengthening and that the chief executive of Legal & General, David Prosser, would give valuable leadership. He had experienced financial advisers in J.P. Morgan and David Mayhew of Cazenoves. What they do not seem to have considered is that this acquisition might make the bank vulnerable to a take-over bid. But the financial markets were lukewarm. They doubted that the merger would give the synergies which were predicted, and they thought the price which NatWest was paying was too high. There was also an underlying feeling of discontent with the quality of NatWest management.

So the Bank of Scotland saw their opportunity to make a bid for NatWest, which was initially received well. The assumption made by the markets was that this would open a wide-ranging bidding process amongst banks generally and that other large institutions would come in and top the Bank of Scotland bid handsomely, and so drive the share price of NatWest and the whole banking sector upwards. This did not happen. The only other bidder to appear was Royal Bank of Scotland, which made an offer only slightly ahead of that from its rival Scottish Bank. The Bank of Scotland had apparently, but surprisingly, not anticipated the need to increase their initial bid, were unable to do so and Royal Bank of Scotland succeeded without there being any real premium for NatWest shareholders arising from the loss of control of their company. This mattered less to institutional shareholders than to personal shareholders, since almost all the institutions would have held shares in Royal Bank of Scotland. But it was hardly an impressive price.

After my departure from NatWest in April 1999 I obviously lost touch with the details of what was taking place inside. But certainly with hindsight it seems to me that the bid for Legal & General was a mistake. The insurance company had not even been on the possible agenda of bid targets in my time and the market doubts that the benefits of cross-selling would be achieved were understandable. The public knowledge that one of David Rowland's motives was his doubts about Derek's leadership abilities soon made Derek's position impossible. He was asked to resign on immediate notice, which was a sad and unjust end to what over more than thirty years had been dedicated and able service to NatWest. The same financial advisers who had supported David Rowland in the potential acquisition of Legal & General at once changed their tune. This bid was dropped, and they advised David to shore up his defences by agreeing to sell off businesses, including even Ulster Bank which had been so very successful over the long term. In effect the defence tactic was to clone the plans which Bank of Scotland had indicated they would put in place if they succeeded in gaining control of NatWest. Such a defence seemed pretty barren when it was put forward and, in spite of David's tireless vigorous and almost single-handed attempts to resist the offer, the bid succeeded. This was a sad and probably unnecessary end to the independent existence of NatWest, although Royal Bank of Scotland wisely recognised the value of the name by continuing to use it for its retail branches. But I was a spectator of all this.

I believe that the progress that we had made was regarded by shareholders as promising, but the bank was still on probation. Royal Bank of Scotland exploited NatWest's vulnerability and, I suspect, they felt that they had snapped up the bank just in time. Much hard work had been done, and this was not yet reflected in the share price.

I had no regrets at leaving NatWest in April 1999. The excellent secretarial support, and the invaluable chauffeur service, obviously disappeared. But I had regained my freedom. The Bar is an individual, sometimes maverick, profession, where each of us takes individual responsibility for what we do. There is competition but companionship, and the deep warmth of friendships. There is a generosity of spirit between members of a profession which can be rich in opportunity, and bring exciting victories and disappointing defeats, and where laughter is rarely absent from evening conviviality. This was the atmosphere in which I had worked for a long time and the change to the bank had come as a culture shock. I think the atmosphere in the bank grew much better, much less stuffy and even quite a lot less bureaucratic, during my time. But even so, I never felt that I quite fitted in to what was a staid, orthodox, administratively driven huge institution where laughter was not often heard.

How might my end of a ten year term report have read? Perhaps something like this: I helped to move the bank from a weak and dispirited state to a confident outlook with the right foundations for a profitable future. But I had not managed to make a sufficient change in the culture of the bank - we were aware of the need to compete for the customer, but we lacked the single-minded determination required to succeed.

The Royal Bank of Scotland brought this single-minded determination, and I believe that the NatWest staff have risen to the challenge. I would dearly like to have realised this transformation myself. Perhaps this transformation could only be brought about by the shock of a take-over, and by transferring control to executives who are consumed by the will to succeed. I suspect that the NatWest staff who remain are the better for this change, and that their customers are better served. Whilst inevitably the experience is brutal and distressing for many, this infusion of new blood and new vision is one of strengths of the free market system.

I became on good terms with a large number of able and fine people in the City. But the competitive atmosphere meant that with a few exceptions we always had to preserve a distance from each other. Notable amongst the exceptions were Wyn Bischoff of Schroders, Willy Purvis of HSBC and the generous-spirited Brian Pitman of Lloyds. There were others whose advice was always promptly available - fine people such as Eddie George, Howard Davies and David Walker. But it was a much more lonely, regimented existence than my own profession of the law. Internally there were a few particularly valuable colleagues. Apart from a good working relationship with Derek, I especially valued the warmth and friendship of the wise and supportive Sir Sydney Lipworth, who, when he ceased to be chairman of the Monopolies and Mergers Commission, had responded positively to my request that he should join us as a deputy chairman, and Sir George Quigley, the extremely thoughtful and dedicated chairman of Ulster Bank.

On the other side of the balance sheet, there were opportunities I could not have dreamed of if I had stayed solely in the narrow discipline of the law. To understand more about and engage in economic decisions, to have an insight into the demands of managing a large business, to engage widely and actively in issues affecting a community, such as promoting equal opportunities for our young staff, and encouraging the work we did to help teach financial literacy in schools were all rewarding. So too was the challenge of dealing with the key issues affecting the business. At the Bar we are very much engaged in one-off advice or conduct of a case and after it is all over, simply tie up the tape and lose our association with those particular clients. There was the satisfaction of having effectively one client, to whose affairs I had to commit myself deeply, for some nine years.

There were opportunities too, to take part in the wider work of the City. The governor of the Bank of England regularly took advice and views from the chairman of the major banks. I was to serve successively as director of the Stock Exchange, which was only partially satisfying as the organisation searched not always convincingly for its own role. I moved on to become deputy chairman of the SIB, where my legal knowledge as well as City experience was able to contribute a little to what was a wholly professional and worthwhile regulatory body. I enjoyed greatly the way in which we were able to widen our international experience - in Hong Kong, Singapore, Australia, Thailand, Indonesia, China, Japan and even taking an opportunity to visit our small office in Russia. We had regular involvement with the United States, not least during the years when we had visibly to be seen to support the effort of our US colleagues to work through their difficulties.

Best of all was the chance to take part in the International Monetary Conference. This conference, not to be confused with the unwieldy junket of the International Monetary Fund, consisted of about one hundred bankers who were elected almost invariably because of their position in their own banks. So at these conferences we were able to meet the chairmen of the hundred leading banks in the world. This attracted good speakers, very interesting and revealing discussions, and informal opportunities of getting to know our peer group of bankers from across the world. The presidency of the group was considered by many bankers to be the highest position which a commercial or clearing banker could attain and it was certainly an honour. So I was surprised by, but eagerly accepted, the invitation to be president in 1997. We had a memorable meeting in Interlaken, the elegant Swiss town in a valley in the Bernese Oberland. Jim Wolfensohn and Helmut Kohl, then still at the height of his remarkable career as one of Germany's strongest Chancellor's, led those who made the journey to talk to us. It was a splendidly heartening interlude in an otherwise sobering year, and it was one of the happy memories I shall carry from the kaleidoscope of experiences at NatWest. I tried hard, learned much, achieved some change, been partially successful in driving the bank forward, and had gladly participated in wider aspects of life than would ever have been available to me at the Bar. But it was time to move on, and not to hurry my next choices. My only firm plan had been to get tickets to a lot of matches in the Cricket World Cup, to take a short and much needed course in drawing at the Slade School of Art, and to have a generous tranche of time of idleness at our home in France.

20. FREEDOM

My first taste of freedom was to enjoy as much as I could of the Cricket World Cup. This was to prove something of a let down. I saw several fine preliminary matches at Hove, Trent Bridge, Bristol and Taunton. But England were a real disappointment and were knocked out in the early rounds. There was a thrilling semi-final between South Africa and Australia at Edgbaston and the result went in Australia's favour by a freak run-out in the last over. But I could not go because the memorial service for Lord Denning was held on the same day. The final at Lord's was an anti-climax. The always unpredictable Pakistan were dismissed cheaply by Australia who won by the margin of 9 wickets early in the afternoon.

But for all its disappointments the World Cup provided light relief from a task I had taken on for the Chancellor of the Exchequer, Gordon Brown, shortly before I left the bank. This was to try and work out a tax strategy which would help to revive the shipping industry and the numbers of skilled merchant shipping officers. The issues sounded as dry as dust. But an unlikely alliance of John Prescott, the Deputy Prime Minister and a former seaman, and Lord Sterling, a long standing Chairman of P&O, was rightly concerned to see if the decline in the industry which had been taking place for 20 years or more could be halted. They drew attention to the traditional reliance of the United Kingdom on this industry. I was to put it in my report in these words.

"Our shipping industry and the skills of our seafarers have been a crucial part of our success as a trading nation ... they have in turn bred internationally regarded shore-based industries including the supply of marine equipment, ship building, ship repairing, ship broking, freight futures, maritime finance, maritime law and arbitration, marine insurance and ship classification. This success has never been achieved without cost: Cabot's great voyage, Drake's opportunism and Admiral Rodney's fight with the Dutch for control of the American trade routes demanded courage, verve and investment. Yet they paid off handsomely and are a part of our history of which we are justifiably proud."

But concern for a strong shipping industry was not just based on nostalgia. With the growth of world trade the shipping industry was continuing to expand globally. Competition was intense. We still had a significant share of the industry with many world class operations. But for all that it was in steady, continuing, decline. Vast training grants and tax breaks had helped to slow the pace but something more radical was needed.

In July 1998 the Government had set out clear aims for an integrated shipping policy based on promoting the growth of an efficient UK-owned merchant fleet, the greater employment and training of British seafarers especially officers, and encouraging UK ship registration. John Prescott had committed himself strongly to reviving the industry and believed that relying on foreign supply too heavily was too risky. For its part the industry had indicated that it would be willing to commit to a firm training programme for cadets if the tax regime was changed in its favour. They said that they would do their best to increase the numbers in training by 25% over several years. This was seen to be "make or break" time. It was this that had brought the Government, the industry and the trade unions together in a partnership to try to secure its future.

With this impetus my task was not too difficult. We simply had to put British shipping in the same position as that of other European countries. This led to the concept of what was elegantly termed as "tonnage tax". This species of tax had been adopted in Greece, Norway and the Netherlands and was in the process of being put into place in Germany. It was central to a package of measures to make the industry financially competitive. It operated by ignoring actual profits and computing a notional profit on the basis of the number and size of ships operated. It taxed this profit, rather than the commercial profit, at the normal corporation tax rate. The art was to set the tonnage rate so that the notional profits, and hence actual corporation tax paid, were minimal. I described this as "an ingenious device for obtaining virtual tax exemption compatible with international tax treaty obligations". But no one had put forward any alternative scheme for stimulating the shipping industry. What was also heartening was that the concept of a low tax environment in this form to help the shipping industry be more competitive had been clearly endorsed by the European Union in its guidelines on maritime state aid. Europe on this occasion had certainly been ahead in ensuring that this industry could have a chance of being competitive. All arguments pointed towards introducing the tax. Our merchant shipping officers are highly regarded throughout the world. A strong merchant shipping industry was valuable as a support to the Royal Navy. The on-shore industries such as ship broking, finance and law would all benefit from a reverse in the decline of the industry. The activities of the Baltic Exchange are but one example.

Lord Sterling, whose forceful persuasiveness I had first experienced when I had acted for him in a legal dispute, pressed for me to resolve the issues speedily. This was not difficult. I had prompt and able help from the industry and notably the Inland Revenue, especially the able and highly objective Jenny Williams, who was then the director of the Business Tax Division. She helped me work out the complexities with the figures and on one occasion very fairly pointed out that part of the formula I had suggested would work against the industry and not achieve my aim. This was a classic example of a talented civil servant at work. I had started work just before leaving the bank in April and was able to deliver my report in July. What was especially rewarding was that within a fortnight Gordon Brown adopted its recommendations and set in train the complex formula for legislation needed to achieve them. What is even more rewarding is that the measures seem to have had a positive effect.

What also opened up for me shortly after leaving NatWest was the opportunity to arbitrate and mediate in some international commercial disputes. The Saturday before I left NatWest my friend, Michael Payton, the senior partner of the outstanding shipping law firm, Clyde & Co, had telephoned me and asked whether I would accept nomination as an arbitrator. Why me? I pointed out that I had no direct experience of taking part in legal proceedings for 10 years and might well be out of date. He countered that the agreement required one of the arbitrators to have 10 years experience in business. This meant there was a limited choice available amongst lawyers. So we agreed I should dip my toe in these waters.

This, together with mediation, have turned out to be a very worthwhile part of my life in the last few years. It meant going back to familiar territory. Arbitrations are effectively the same as court cases only they are heard in private with a rather higher degree of informality. Mediation is a way of trying to resolve disputes by bringing the parties to realise early on the strengths and weaknesses of the positions they have taken up, and encourage them to reach a settlement avoiding the financial and emotional cost as well as the uncertainty of adversarial litigation. All this brought me back to my old discipline and life of the law which for all my excursions into the financial world remained my lasting love. It also gave me the opportunity to be joint head of a fine set of chambers, whose members apart from myself largely practice in insolvency, at 3/4 South Square, Gray's Inn. A large added bonus is that my eldest son David, a member of those chambers, persuaded both them and me that this was the right place for me to go and then organised that I should have the room next door to him. To give legal advice, to arbitrate and mediate, and very occasionally to be prepared to argue a constitutional case is my great good fortune and since there is no retirement age I can go on some time yet. It will be clients who decide when the time has come that my services are not worthwhile and I should stop.

What I did not want to do on leaving NatWest was to follow the well-trodden route of becoming a non-executive director of several companies. I had been fortunate enough to serve for six years on the board of Rio Tinto, the international mining conglomerate and Total Elf Fina the large French oil company. Both were extremely well-run, managed and focused businesses. There were occasions when the non-executives could make a real contribution as when Rio Tinto decided not to bid for British Coal and when it acquired control of the Australian mining company, CRA. Likewise there was a fascinating year in which Total acquired in quick succession both Petrofina, the Belgian oil company, and Elf, its leading French rival. But for the most part the task of the non-executive was monitoring decisions, asking probing questions, and testing financial controls through the work of the Audit Committee. In a really well-run company there was not that much for non-executives to do. I was fortunate in that these were the only two directorships I took on.

For by contrast in a badly run company or one which, like Marconi, lurched into a wrong strategic direction, there would be relatively little the non-executives could do except possibly change senior management. They might voice their misgivings but the management team were closer to the action and had great knowledge of the facts and would almost invariably carry the day. By the same token it was almost impossible for the non-executives to detect financial malpractice or corruption within the company. They were inevitably highly dependent on customer controls which they could police but only to an extent, and on the outside auditors. This was a rather unsatisfying role at the best of times and carried responsibility without really effective power if things went wrong without their knowledge. In recent years the position has become even more dramatic. There have been some spectacular management failures with the understandable reaction that even more responsibility has been placed on non-executives. I think many of the expectations of what non-executive directors can achieve are simply unrealistic. Yet in an ever more litigious world they are, as the directors of Equitable found, extremely vulnerable to the misery and cost of protracted law suits. I have become ever more glad that I stood right aside from this only partly satisfying and potentially perilous role.

Yet in 2001 I had one very different role which deepened my renewed relationship with the world of the law and brought me much satisfaction and happiness. This was as Treasurer of Middle Temple. The title "Treasurer" fortunately did not mean that I had to keep the books. It meant that I was effectively head for a year of the Inn of Court which had contributed to much of my life. I had lunched there in the splendid 16th century hall, where the first public performance of Twelfth Night had been given, most days of the week during my time in practice at the Bar. Lunch was not lavish, was speedy, but gave me the opportunity to see many lifelong friends regularly. In court barristers are inevitably adversaries. But out of court it is the most friendly, helpful and loyal of professions. I had become what is called a "bencher" of Middle Temple in 1979 which gave me the opportunity of getting to know on friendly terms many senior judges whom I admired. This gave me an insight into their characters and work. It also meant that I could enjoy rather more in the evening what Stanley Baldwin called "the pleasures of the Temple". This dining, with fine wines and stimulating if sometimes parochial conversation is very well caught in a scene in David Hare's play "Murmuring Judges".

The four Inns of Court have a more serious function. Every student of the Bar has to join one of them. This brings them into contact with other students and barristers and gives them an opportunity to get a feel for the values of the profession. Middle Temple has a fine library, light refreshment facilities for students, and an education programme which sits alongside that of the more formal training in law and practice given by the Bar Vocational Course. When I was a student there was no formal or informal training in advocacy except the opportunity to conduct the occasional mock trial after dinner. This had changed dramatically in recent years. The development of advocacy courses at the start had been spearheaded by two senior QCs, Michael Hill and Michael Sherrard. This meant that the Bar had become possibly the only profession outside medicine in which senior practitioners gave a lot of their time to train young advocates in the techniques and skills of this trade. It means that unlike when I started young barristers have some practical experience of how to conduct a case before going into court for real. They are not just exposed to wind and weather on the Spartan hillside.

The Inns of Court are cautious, even conservative, institutions but are still capable of evolving. I mentioned earlier my frustration that I when I was a student it was necessary to eat 12 dinners in each of 3 years. By the time I had become Treasurer this had shortened to 12 qualifying occasions during a single year. I was able to change the extent to which these occasions were dinners by introducing a course of lectures and receptions which meant both that the students could hear fine speakers and wider aspects of life than technicalities of the law and also mix more freely with barristers. They have proved very popular and tend to attract audiences of about 250, six times a year. We were fortunate to start with speakers as interesting as Chris Patten and Nicholas Phillips who spoke of the BSE Inquiry. A wide range of talents amongst lawyers has made sure that the interest value of the series is strong.

There were other changes which I was able to make. It was important to try and bring the bench or governing body of the Inn closer to our other members, especially students. New benchers had traditionally given an "account" of themselves in private to the other benchers after dinner. We changed this so that they gave their speeches to all barristers and students in the large hall. This modest reform drew an enthusiastic reaction from the students because speeches were informal, and showed those who were at the beginnings of their career that people from all sorts of backgrounds and ranges of practice had come through to do well. On a slightly larger scale we were able to start some major building works. We bought a large dilapidated office building in Fleet Street and converted it into decent accommodation for barristers. This explains why the profession was concentrated in the Inns of Court and it has helped over centuries to build a collegiate spirit. We also started at last on the modernisation of the kitchens of the Inn. This had last been carried out in 1912 and must have failed every health and hygiene regulation. After a full tour of the old kitchens I found it difficult to eat in the Inn for at least a week. Now there is a state of the art, modern kitchen, decent facilities for staff who had been remarkably stoical in dreadful conditions and we are an immensely popular choice for weddings and other celebrations.

It was a fine feeling to spend a year as head of the Inn which had given me so much since I started as a student for the Bar. But in one sense it was quite long enough. The number of formal dinners eaten by the legal profession must exceed those in any other walk of life. But there is one splendid occasion I shall always remember. I was allowed to ask friends from all the areas of my life, the law, politics, the City, the theatre and cricket. From our temporary kitchen in a portakabin the chef somehow did this sparkling occasion proud. By coincidence, a deeply satisfying one, this dinner on 21 November 2001 was exactly the 40th anniversary of my own call to the Bar. The only nervous moment was when Baroness Thatcher, sitting opposite Lord Woolf, the Lord Chief Justice, started to expound her views on the European Union. Harry Woolf started to make his diametrically opposed view fairly clear and I had to weigh in quickly to change the subject. After dinner there was the amusing vignette of students gathering around Baroness Thatcher in one room and others gathering around John Major in the room next door. Each responded warmly to the students and was wholly unaware of the competition from the other. This happy evening would have confirmed the views of those who firmly believed lawyers carouse together until the early hours.

Another warm evening was the last visit of the Queen Mother on what sadly proved to be her final public engagement. She came to dinner in December 2001, as she had done each year. She was our senior bencher and remembered the wartime blitz which shattered much of the Temple and the Elizabethan hall. I recalled this in my short speech of welcome and she intervened to say "I still remember those fragments". Only the previous week she had entertained a party of students on an advocacy weekend at her home at Windsor Great Park, mixed with the crowds outside church on a cold morning and then stood talking to all of us at her party for an hour. She and the Inn had a deep mutual affection and she was a remarkable supporter who cared passionately for our legal system.

One of the pleasures of being Treasurer was the contact it gave me with students. I have always enjoyed the company of the young which was one reason I unhesitatingly accepted an invitation in 1998 to become Chancellor of Exeter University. The tasks of a chancellor are very part-time consisting mainly of presiding at degree days, giving general advice, and helping with fund-raising. At Exeter there is also the most important task of chairing the group which selects a new vice-chancellor. The key figure in any university is the vice-chancellor. This is an immensely wide ranging role from ensuring that academic standards in all the schools are maintained to representing the university widely on the national educational scene. Sir Geoffrey Holland, a former very senior civil servant, was my first vice-chancellor who did much to raise the standards of the university which had temporarily dipped in the mid-1990s. He also steered through the creation of a medical school for the university, then construction of a fine building for our Centre of Islamic and Arabic Studies, and the partnership which with the aid of European Union money established a Combined Universities in Cornwall. The creation of the first new medical school in the country to be set up for 40 years and of new university facilities in a county previously without them was a notable double.

Exeter's involvement in Cornwall stem from its history as an integral part of the region. It had been established early in the 19th century as the University College of the South West. Full university status had been achieved in 1955 when it became the only university to receive its charter from the Queen directly on a visit to the campus. Exeter is a particularly fine campus university set in rolling Devon countryside but close to the centre of the city. It contributes much to the economy of the regions and its innovation centre reaches out to local businesses. It has remained true to its roots. But as it prospered it increasingly developed international and national strengths especially in the arts, law and economics. In part it is the beautiful campus which helps students thoroughly to enjoy the Exeter experience. I have never met one of our graduates who has spoken other than warmly about their time at university. We also have a good record in the value employers place on the general skills and employability of Exeter graduates. At one time it had a reputation as a "green welly" university. This was not easy to change and we still have to work very hard to make certain that we can contribute to giving proper access to university to those who come from less advantaged backgrounds. Our geographical location does not make it that easy. We have to concentrate many of our efforts in this direction in the South West peninsular. But it is crucial.

No one is more passionate about the importance of fair access to universities than our new vice-chancellor, Professor Steve Smith, who took up his post in 2002. He is a brilliant international political scientist with the gift for leadership which took his department at Aberystwyth University from a rating of 3* to 5* in a short time. He has a gift for management, a tough but inclusive leadership style and immense commitment. He quickly made his mark in the broader educational world when he supported tirelessly the case for "top up" fees. He made the imaginative flagship commitment to using a substantial tranche of the additional income to providing 1400 bursaries of £3,000 a student.

Universities have been starved of resources for 20 years or so. It is remarkable that the standards remained as high as they have. This is a great tribute to the dedication of academics and the important administrative team. Our administrative team at Exeter was led for almost 15 years by Ian Powell, who steered imaginative development without putting the university into deficit. His successor David Allen, previously registrar at Birmingham, is playing a key role in making certain that the university buildings and other facilities are constantly improving. The reality is that universities can never be adequately financed by the state. Each of us has to hunt for money for research and develop a programme of giving from former students to be increasingly self-financed. One of the great strengths of US universities is the extent of their endowments built up over many years and the ingrained habit of graduates of giving generously to their former university. This habit is so far hopelessly underdeveloped in this country. Many graduates who were fully financed to go to university by the government have not yet realised that those days are over and that their successors need tangible help. The annual income which Harvard receives from its endowments equals the total capital sum of the endowment of Oxford University. This disparity is great in every area. Salaries of academics are much higher in the United States. They also have more time for research because they have about half the number of pupils to teach as do academics in this country.

Another feature of Exeter is the way in which our guild of students manage the student and community affairs of the university. A team of them is elected each year. Each has a different portfolio, is granted a sabbatical year, and the team has responsibility for managing their own budget. Their enthusiasm, dedication, and the imagination of youth enables them to generate an outstanding range of student activities. Particularly impressive are those dedicated to helping others, either by raising funds or holding camps for children to go to on holiday. The best of modern youth is marvellous and I always look forward to the Friday at the end of degree week when after I have shaken 3,000 or so hands we go to the students graduation ball at Powderham Castle. The new graduates, flushed by success but with mixed feelings about leaving the university, dance the night away until dawn comes through the mist across the fields by the River Exe. We have a great affection for the university and feel really fortunate that it is part of our lives and that they make us so very welcome.

One of the bonuses, too, of my frequent visits to Exeter is the opportunity it gave to discover more of Devon and Cornwall. Devon attracts more tourists than any other single county in the country but it is large and spread out enough not to seem over-crowded. Exmoor is a landscape jewel not known at all. Cornwall was traditionally a place packed for six weeks in the short summer holidays. With the dwindling of the tin and china clay industries it became the poorest county in England. But recently it has received a real shot in the arm from being granted Objective 1 status by the European Union with funds for development, and support from the Regional Development Agency and the government office in the South West. The Tate Gallery in St Ives, the Maritime Museum at Falmouth, the University and the Eden Project are all fine attractions. They add to the excitement of sparkling gardens such as Trebah, Durgan, Trellissick, Trewithen, outstanding at rhododendron and azalea time the rediscovered Heligon, the fairy tale castle of St Michael's Mount, the house and gardens at Lanhydrock, and so I could go on. There are long beaches, coves, Fowey Harbour, Padstow, now famed for its restaurants spearheaded by Rick Stein, all in all there is a buzz which the county has not felt for generations.

Exploring Cornwall has proved a lasting if sporadic joy. So did rediscovering Warwickshire and cycling along the old converted railway track at Stratford during my time with the Royal Shakespeare Company. As did travel ranging from Old Trafford in Manchester to Peshawar in Pakistan for the MCC tour. All of these have been important parts of my post NatWest years which I shall say a little more of. They have so far been rich, fascinating, busy years. They are so worthwhile. Well worth it for the kaleidoscope of different experiences in areas of life about which I am passionate. The freedom to follow my enthusiasms for 40 years of focused career commitment has been even more rewarding than I ever dreamed.

21. CRICKET

When I went to NatWest I was fortunate that there was a long standing tradition of sponsoring cricket. In my early years in the tough times of the recession of the early 1990s the opportunity to combine my cricketing sponsorship with meeting clients at various country grounds was an oasis of relaxation. The final of the Nat-West Trophy was always played at the beginning of September and often produced a very exciting finish. Perhaps the more remarkable was in 1993, in Sussex, when my own county made the immense score of 321, which made them apparently certain winners. But Warwickshire broadly kept pace throughout their innings and with the help of the magnificent century by Asif Din overtook the Sussex score as dusk deepened in the last over. In the tea interval the then Sussex secretary had come to me and ask whether the cup was insured. This seemed to me dangerously close to taking victory for granted and from that moment on I had superstitiously become anxious that Warwickshire might overhaul our score. So it proved, but it was an unforgettable one day match.

For much of its long history the MCC was responsible for running English cricket. Our national sides toured under the MCC colours. But in the 1960s structural changes were agreed to the game, which meant that the Test and County Cricket Board took over selecting the sides and managing English cricket. This was the governing body for the sport at the time of the Kerry Packer challenge to the cricketing establishment but in time, it evolved into the English Cricket Board. MCC has membership of this board, along with representatives of the counties. But it no longer runs English cricket. For a time the club did not find it easy to come to terms with this change in its role. Yet MCC still has considerable influence, responsibility and opportunity. Lord's is admired by cricketers and cricket lovers everywhere as the home of cricket and over the years one of the key functions of the club has been to make sure that its ground development is of a commensurate standard. MCC retains overall responsibility for the laws of cricket, and has always played a leading role in discussions with all the wide ranging cricketing interests as to what changes should be made. The club also has a wide range of cricketing fixtures. It sends high quality teams, often including some former test cricketers, to countries which are currently not of test match status but are strengthening their skills. Bangladesh before it became a test match country was very much nurtured by MCC teams. So currently are Kenya and Bermuda. This cricket is played by a comparatively small number of playing members out of a total membership approaching 20,000. For many years the President of MCC was also Chairman of the International Cricket Council. This, too, changed with the increasing professionalism within the game and the growing role of the ICC as the ultimate governing and coordinating body for the international game.

The MCC committee had often included senior lawyers. In the 1990s both Lord Griffiths, who had been a fine fast bowler for Glamorgan, and Mr Justice Popplewell, who had been wicket keeper in the great Cambridge side in 1950, had served as president. I suspect it was their idea that I should be asked to stand for election to the committee. The committee consisted, as it generally does, of some fascinating people from different walks of life united by a passion for game. In my time the membership has included Colin Cowdrey, Ted Dexter, Tony Lewis, David Gower and Mike Gatting to mention only some of those of the fine cricketers amongst its members who have captained England. Our members at any time include those skilled in estate management and finance and marketing which give the club access to an immense range of skills to support the senior management team. During my time, this team was lead by Roger Knight, as secretary and chief executive, who had played cricket for no less than three counties, Gloucestershire, Surrey and Sussex, had come close to playing international cricket, but who was also a fine school master and briefly head of Worksop College before taking up his role at MCC. Roger's considerable strengths lay primarily in the cricketing and the administrative areas and over the years he attracted an increasingly strong staff to support him at the club. Notable among these were David Batts, who joined us as his deputy to bring great commercial experience from a prior career in hotel management. In Tony Dodemaide, a former Australian test cricketer who later played for Sussex, we had a fine leader of cricket and Colin Maynard, was a most knowledgeable, committed membership secretary.

There are normally between six and eight meetings of the full committee every year. At my first one we were immediately asked to take a momentous decision as to the design of the new media centre which the club planned to build at the opposite end of the ground from the pavilion. The choice was between a relatively conventional design and a somewhat futuristic overall lozenge. I liked the lozenge, and slightly to my surprise so did all but one of the other members of the committee. So what was to be described in the press as "Al Jolson's lips" when we unveiled the scheme was swiftly chosen. The novelty was even greater because the construction was of two hulls of vessels, one upturned on the top of the other, built by Pendennis, a ship builder from Falmouth in Cornwall, who had never before put together a building. The project was overseen for MCC successively by Brian Thornton and Maurice de Rohan, who did us a great service by bringing a most unusual construction to completion. It has become a building instantly recognisable throughout the world, a great success with the media and an additional visitor attraction at the ground.

I was still at NatWest when construction was taking place. I was due to be in Cornwall one weekend and had arranged to visit the Pendennis shipyard. The week before a senior corporate bank manager came to see me and advised me not to go to the yard because of the risk that the Pendennis account was in such a state that facilities might have to be withdrawn. I reluctantly accepted the view that I should not visit the yard at that time, but also made the point forcibly that it would be extremely embarrassing if the company which was constructing the media centre at Lord's were to be brought down by NatWest with its reputation for sponsoring and supporting cricket. In the event Pendennis was nursed through, completed the media centre excellently and is, I believe, an increasingly thriving business.

The other major construction project which the club had to undertake was the demolition of the old grandstand built during the 1920s and its replacement by a modern, more handsome stand with greater entertainment facilities and, most importantly, much better views. This was achieved within budget and within the two year time frame which we set ourselves.

But if the development of the property went really well there were some other issues which proved harder, and temporarily drove a wedge between the committee and some of our members. The first was the potential admission of women. This could not be achieved without a change in the rules which in turn required a two-thirds majority of those who voted. Such a majority is never easy to achieve, although two resolutions had in the past gone through with a bare majority in favour but not with the large majority needed. When Colin Ingleby-Mackenzie, the splendid, larger than life personality who had been one of Hampshire's finest cricketers and had led them to the County Championship in 1961, and who was president between 1996 and 1998, came back from a visit to Australia, he pointed out that even in that country which is traditionally regarded as a haven of male chauvinism women, had now been admitted to the cricket clubs in Melbourne and Sydney. He believed our position to be really out of step and vulnerable in a world in which women increasingly watched cricket, wanted to play cricket, and where the MCC was not merely a members' club but had a public role to fulfil in support of the game. He asked a small group of us, led by Anthony Wreford, a committee member with great professional skill in marketing, if he would manage a campaign to try to persuade members to vote in favour. Since this involved a change to the rules we needed a two-thirds majority. Some members felt, and this was understandable, that our efforts were a re-run of a recent attempt to admit women members which had been unsuccessful. They saw it as a refusal to accept the verdict of the jury. We by contrast saw it as critical to the way in which the club would be held to move forward and meet the expectations of the modern world.

We mounted our campaign with the help of a number of meetings, some of which I chaired, at which we listened to the concerns of members but also of those who have supported the change. I remember at one of these meetings being told by a member that he liked women very much but did not like them in his club. Another member expressed concern that he might have to give the seat in the Long Room which he had taken early in the morning of a day's cricket and offer it to a woman who came into the pavilion. We made it clear in the course of these meetings that we were not going to allow women to jump the queue on the list of candidates and that they would be treated equally with men. In the end we scraped the necessary majority but only just. It is in fact very difficult to secure a two-thirds majority. I was to find this again when at the end of the my presidency we only just carried a resolution to increase subscriptions above what had been a very modest level for the facilities offered to members.

But there was no doubt that after the vote there was a lurking discontent among those members who felt that the committee had somewhat railroaded through the issue of the admission of women. They all too soon had another complaint which they could take up against the committee. Back in 1987 the then president had indicated that members would not be charged for admission to any game at their ground. This gave rise to a real complication at the time of the 1999 World Cup, of which several of the rounds and the final were due to be played at Lord's. The English Cricket Board insisted that members should pay for their seats as part of the income to English cricket.

The committee could theoretically have taken the view that in the light of what had been said some years ago, the price of these tickets should be paid for out of the general funds of the club. But we felt it would be more equitable for individual members to pay for their own tickets rather than to charge indirectly those members who would not be going to any matches. What we got wrong, as we later admitted, was that we failed to consult members as to whether we should charge them for tickets and they felt that the committee had behaved high-handedly. We on the committee undoubtedly had to learn a lesson from this mistake. We needed to realise that our members fell into three categories. There were the vast majority of them who simply wanted the opportunity to buy their tickets for big matches and be proud of their membership of MCC. There was another group which was interested in the material which we put out in the regular MCC newsletters. But there was a third and relatively small number of those who wanted to know more about the way the club was run and to be consulted informally about how decisions were taken. We put in place a regular series of members' forums at which they could learn what was coming forward by way of proposals from the committee and be given an opportunity to comment on them ahead of meetings. These were led by Charles Fry, a fine cricketer who tirelessly chaired our membership sub-committee and later became president of the club. It has done much to defuse any grounds of complaint and make members who wanted to be involved feel that they are closer to knowing what is actually going on. It also helps the committee to keep in touch with their views.

But unfortunately the height of the discontent took place during the presidency of Tony Lewis. This gave him an undeserved hard time during his presidency. He had to take responsibility for a situation which he had done nothing to create. Fortunately he has stayed involved with the club and now has succeeded Ted Dexter as a rigorous and imaginative chairman of the cricket committee. This manages all our cricketing policy and contributions to the game. It speaks much for the support which MCC has from former players that in succession its last chairmen have been Cowdrey, Dexter and Lewis. Not many clubs can boast of support at that level. Their standing and knowledge give our decisions immense influence. Perhaps the most notable of these decisions was the inspiration of Colin Cowdrey, taken forward by Ted Dexter, to try to bring back into the game, what has been called the ethos of the Spirit of Cricket. This contains simple principles designed to encourage fair play, to avoid intimidation and cheating, such as appealing when you know someone is not out, and was sadly much needed. Some of us were concerned that in putting this idea forward, MCC could appear to be going against the tide of the times and trying to promote old fashioned values. But the idea caught on and it was supported by an annual Spirit of Cricket lecture given by towering figures in the game such as Richie Benaud, Barry Richards, and Sunil Gavaskar. The concept and the way in which it was framed was adopted by cricket associations as far away as New South Wales and Victoria.

This was particularly important because Gavaskar said in his lecture the falling off, and the sledging and aggravation, were unfortunately led by a small number of cricketers who were members of the finest cricket side in the world. It has always seemed a great pity that one of the most wonderful of teams has regularly let itself down in this way. This is not least so because in many aspects of the game the leadership of Steve Waugh, an inspired cricketer with a great sense of cricketing history, has been such a thrilling example. No one who saw that team on its visit to England in 2001, and I was fortunate enough to be president of the MCC, will ever forget its skill and indeed genius. But I believe that in the end it is vital for any sport to be conducted with the sense of fair play and decent behaviour, which for the most part exists in games as different as golf, snooker and tennis. The ECB have been very supportive of the Spirit of Cricket initiative which is an illustration of the way in which MCC with its standing in cricket can help influence the game for the good.

During Tony's presidency I had been chairman of the Arts and Library Committee. This was a group responsible, together with Stephen Green our long-standing curator, for maintaining the MCC cricket museum and our book collection but also engaging in new artistic initiatives. They started a scheme where young artists went for a time on English overseas tours and created a series of paintings, some of which were retained by MCC and many were bought by members. This proved a great success and also meant that MCC was able to have, at last, a portrait of Ian Botham, painted on a balcony in Pakistan by Nick Botting and portraits of Michael Atherton and Alec Stewart by Andy Pankhurst. Andy was the young artist on the 2002-3 tour to Australia and famously captured the moment when Steve Waugh completed his 100th century off the last ball of the day at the Sydney Cricket Ground. We have now built on this initiative by introducing a scheme which encourages young cricketing photographers. We also acquired a sculpture of WG Grace, and commissioned sculptures of "a batsman" and "a bowler" which are now positioned prominently around the ground. Again this committee was able to draw on talented writers, art dealers, and curators amongst our membership. The museum is sadly not visited enough. It is included in the regular tours of Lord's but on big match days inevitably it is mostly visited when rain stops play. The Ashes are probably the best known item in the collection and they consistently surprise visitors by how modest the urn is in size. But overall the collection, including the pictures on display in the Long Room, is a treasure trove of cricketing memorabilia.

Under the MCC rules the incumbent president nominates his successor. This may seem undemocratic to the modern age but overall as a system it seems to have worked remarkably well. But when Tony Lewis asked me to lunch one day I had not expected that he would offer me the opportunity to succeed him. I was thrilled and did not hesitate. I am probably the worst cricketer ever to have been president of the MCC in a long time, although Tim Rice thinks, I suspect wrongly, that he is a close competitor for this doubtful accolade.

Whatever the reason of his choice, it was to bring me one of the best experiences I could possibly have. One of the really fine aspects of the MCC is that the committee and most of the members are so supportive of the president. If he, and I am sure that one day this will include she, makes a half-good speech he gets immense support and enthusiasm. There is a generosity of spirit, and a back-up from management, which could not fail to make it a memorable year.

In the winter the duty and pleasure of the president is to represent MCC at some of England's overseas tours. I went first with Roger Knight to Dacca in Bangladesh for that country's inaugural test match against India. Since it became a test playing nation, Bangladesh has not achieved much success. The standard of cricket was probably not high enough for it to be granted test match status so early. Yet there is no doubt that in a desperately poor country where there is a passion for cricket, and where those who run the game are determined to reach out into the outlying parts of the nation to find talent, the opportunity to play test cricket was a great fillip. The first match was preceded by an evening where all the local crafts, dances and music of Bangladesh were on display. The President of Bangladesh attended the first day where we all sat in the pavilion in splendid rattan chairs. Bangladesh had a good day to start with although by the end of the match India supremacy asserted itself strongly.

We flew from Dacca to Lahore, a graceful, spacious city of the former Indian Raj where England were to open their test series against Pakistan. We saw three days of rather slow cricket in which England cautiously built up their position. The series was to end with a thrilling climax in Karachi which we did not see, where in gathering gloom England succeeded in snatching the series victory at the end of a thrilling run-chase. This achievement was a real tribute to the determination of Hussain as captain and his major players, and not least the batting of Graham Thorpe. Roger was a good friend from university cricketing days with the former Pakistani captain, Majid Khan. We stayed with Majid and travelled with him and his wife, Ceema, right up to the Afghan border. From the military outpost on the North West frontier we were able to see Torkham, the other side of the border. We reached the frontier by train travelling through the mountainous country, with many refugee camps, with much of the population apparently on the move and many of them including youngsters carrying guns, which even then suggested how difficult the area was to govern. We were told that we were in a land of drug barons. All this was in autumn 2000, almost a year before the assault on the United States of 9 September 2001 heightened the awareness and importance of this desolate, wild, rugged and hard to police area of the world.

We then came back to Islamabad, stopping at a wonderful virtually deserted city of Taxila which lay on the great silk route to the south of India. Pakistan has a fascinating cultural and scenic heritage if the country ever becomes settled enough to allow the development of structured tourism. To see it with Majid was an especial privilege. He was known throughout Pakistan, knew exactly where we could go safely, and his presence ensured a warm and friendly reception wherever we went.

Cricket is a passion in Pakistan. In Lahore I gave a talk for the British Council on "The Law, Shakespeare and Cricket," drawing on three topics which are of keen interest in both our countries. The questions which followed were almost exclusively on cricket. Test matches are not well attended because people find it difficult to get the time free from work. There are great crowds for all the one-day internationals. The development of cricket has been difficult over recent years, from time to time for security reasons. Mainly because of a political stand-off with India the Pakistani team has not always been able to play a full list of fixtures. They have some immensely talented players although their team performance is often unpredictable, as was notably seen in the final of the World Cup at Lord's in 1999 when they lost abjectly to Australia.

The autumn visits to countries I had never been to before were a highlight. So, too, was the trip in March 2001 to Sri Lanka to watch the final test at Colombo. The series between the two sides was level and the first two days of the match were hard fought. At the end of the first day each team had scored rather over 300 and there was nothing to indicate the drama that would follow that Saturday afternoon. Sri Lanka then collapsed badly on their second innings and none of their very talented batting line up scored many runs. They were all out by teatime. In pursing the score England had their own fair share of adventures and it was left to Thorpe, who earlier in the day had completed a fine 100, to bat for the second time and steer his side home. When I met him the night afterwards he said that the team led by Hussein had learnt to "dig deep into itself". Certainly the wins in the two series that winter had taken a great deal of determination as well as skill.

No one had contributed more than Thorpe himself, who became ranked as one of the top batsmen in the world. It is very sad that family misfortunes have made his later performances more mixed although his return to form with a century against South Africa at The Oval in the summer of 2003 was a fine come back and a great contribution to our victory over South Africa.

After the memorable winter tours the next onerous duties of the president involved hosting home matches at Lord's. The wonderful Australian team of 2001, rivalling Bradman's great side of 1948, was too good for England in the test match. The only sad moment of my presidency was standing in the middle at Lord's as the presentations were made in front of a capacity crowd hoping for more cricket at shortly after midday on a Sunday of bright sunshine. Many former Australian cricketers had come over for the tour and it was good to meet characters as varied and interesting as Sam Loxton and Neil Harvey. I was also able to have Arthur Morris confirm a story which he told about Bradman's epic duck when bowled by Eric Hollies in his last test match at The Oval. Morris has often been accosted by cricket followers who have asked him whether he witnessed the occasion. His response invariably is "yes, I was batting at the other end, and I managed to score 196". Yet it is Bradman's failure to score and so bring his test match batting average over 100 which has passed into legend.

My year as president passed all too quickly. As a very average cricketer I had no hesitation in the choice of my successor. Ted Dexter was one of the greatest and most exciting English cricketers since the 2nd World War. He had acted as chairman of selectors, which is never an easy task in English cricket, and then had increasingly devoted himself to helping the MCC. He was a name to conjure with throughout the cricketing world and he proved a stylish and committed president. The role of the president, as will be obvious from what I have written, is largely ambassadorial and is spent watching cricket, entertaining guests, and making short speeches at lunches and dinners. The more mundane work of the club is guided by the chairman of the committee and I was asked if I would take on that task for three years. This was very welcome since I loved my involvement with the MCC and it meant that I did not have to step aside immediately after my time as president. The work load of the chairman is more nitty-gritty and concentrated, but the time commitment is a good deal less.

My predecessor as chairman, Sir Michael Jenkins, had reshaped the constitution of the MCC so as to focus on work of different committees with the help of an executive board. When we put these changes to the members we suggested that they would be reviewed after three years. They asked a group headed by Sir Scott Baker, now a senior judge, to look at the way in which the club was working and as to whether we were meeting the needs and wishes of members. Broadly speaking this group endorsed our new approach although it rightly suggested that the rules of the club should be totally rewritten to make certain that they were up to date. Writing rules is a long and arduous task and we were fortunate that Nigel Peters QC, another barrister member of the committee, was prepared to work on the task so tirelessly with some other lawyer members. In one sense this could be seen as a tedious nuts-and-bolts exercise but in the modern world a club of the size of MCC, with so many members, with such a large budget, and with the responsibility of playing a public role in cricket we needed to be satisfied that it was effectively run.

When I had joined the committee there was no executive board. This meant that the only forum for discussion of the way in which the recommendations of one sub-committee, say cricket, interacted with the work of another sub-committee, say marketing, was the main committee. But a committee of 20 could only give broad guidance and could not work through issues in detail. This now became the task of the executive board, consisting of Roger Knight, David Banson and their senior colleagues together with myself, the president for the time being, Oliver Stockton as chairman of finance, and the chairmen of the other sub-committees. This meant that tighter and clearer recommendations should be put to the main committee. It still left that committee with the important role of deciding the broad policy issues, evaluating priorities and also pointing out where the executive board might want to reconsider detailed proposals. This, together with the ever strengthening quality of the staff who were recruited, meant that the management was able to act with more authority and confidence. Decisions were better informed and more effectively communicated.

One of the principal tasks of each generation of temporary custodians of the MCC has been to ensure that our building programme is consistently maintained and upgraded for our great ground. Once we had completed the grandstand we needed to turn to the playing area itself. The drainage of the outfield was inadequate and sometimes this had meant that we had not been able to start play quickly enough after heavy rain. We decided to replace the entire outfield during the closed season between September and April 2002-2003. This was a very tight assignment in terms of time and any delay would obviously have been little short of disaster. The project was masterminded by Tony Dodemaide, our head of cricket, who organised the replacement of turf grown in the Midlands and supervised the entire construction process. It was only when this started and the giant excavators were in, digging several feet down below the square to allow insertion of new pipes and a porous sand base beneath the turf that we were able to see what a large work of civil engineering was involved.

We offered the old turf, which had been there since the pitch was first laid in 1814, for sale in small pieces or if members wished, in slightly larger tranches for them to put in their gardens. The take up was good and relatively little of the turf was wasted. The appeal of having turf from Lord's on which all the great cricketers of the past had walked and played was irresistible to many of our members. The idea of selling it reflected credit on our increasingly enterprising marketing department. The work went so smoothly, we were lucky with the weather that winter and Tony appeared so relaxed and quietly confident about progress at all stages that it would have been easy for us to underestimate this very considerable achievement. He deservedly became Chief Executive of Western Australia's cricket in 2004 which gave him the chance to go back to live in Australia.

The new outfield was finished on time and within budget. Tony also led the way in preparing on a pilot basis drop in pitches which should if they work successfully enable us to play more cricket on the square every summer. So we were alert to trying to keep our cricketing facilities state of the art. At one time we thought this would necessarily lead us to having floodlighting on the ground. But we have increasingly gone slowly on this idea because it is far from obvious how often we would be able to use it effectively in an English summer. Some county clubs, including Sussex have experimented bravely but the jury must be very much still out as to whether floodlighting is to become part of the mix of English cricket. In Australia with a more consistent climate, and long warm evenings the day/night match can be fulfilling entertainment. But I suspect this will never be so in any large scale way in this country.

The most memorable part of the built heritage of Lord's is the pavilion, designed by Thomas Verity in 1889-90. At the heart of the pavilion is the Long Room, with its traditional high chairs, where members congregate and through which the players have to come on their way out to the wicket. The players come down the wide stairs from their respective dressing rooms and pass through the ranks of spectators and out through the centre door. A good performance is rapturously received by the members, by contrast a stark failure can be greeted by a dismal silence. After we had completed the grandstand and the outfield the pavilion became the next part of the building programme. It needed not only extensive general maintenance but an enhancing of the facilities on the top floor to make them a source of pride and pleasure. These works were expensive, costing about £8 million but the members rightly had no hesitation in authorising this expense.

One of the vexed issues which arose during my chairmanship was the need for the ECB to decide whether the English team would play in Zimbabwe. By the end of 2002 the regime of President Mugabe increasingly had a wretched record of tyranny, slaughter, repression and breach of human rights. It had been suspended from membership of the Commonwealth. But some of the games in the World Cup taking place in South Africa in early 2003 were scheduled to be played in Zimbabwe. One of these was a game between England and Zimbabwe. By the time the English team arrived from the tour of Australia it was clear that it was going to be an extremely difficult conundrum for the ECB. The players were doubtful as to whether they should go to Zimbabwe on moral grounds. They later became concerned for their safety and security. The Foreign Office intervened by saying publicly that the English team should not make the visit. This was at a time when there were no sanctions against doing business with Zimbabwe or against airline travel to that country. This intervention made the task harder for the ECB who, unlike the Foreign Office in making its gesture, carried the financial responsibility under its contract with the ICC if it did not play the match. England would also lose points in the tournament. The Australian Prime Minister, John Howard, a keen cricket lover, had taken a more pragmatic view that a ban on playing in Zimbabwe might be desirable but that it should be a general ban and not imposed by individual countries. The ICC, and the South African host government which felt its great debt to Zimbabwe for the way in which the African National Congress Party had been sustained during the years of apartheid, were adamant that the only reason for not going to play in that country would be on grounds of safety and security. They were clear that there was no risk to the players. Australia dealt with the problem by flying in one evening, playing one match and flying out.

The issue was most sensitive of all to England because of our long past colonial responsibility for Zimbabwe. There were some MCC members who felt that we should protest against the ECB going to Zimbabwe at all. This in part reflected a belief that MCC's influence was probably greater than it was, and also the view of some of our members that although we did not run cricket any longer we were a spirit of the game. We felt we should not express our view publicly, because it was very easy to strike attitudes from the sidelines when we did not carry the responsibility for the decision and the potential financial loss it could cause to English cricket. So we expressed our view privately to the ECB and ICC that it would be inappropriate, given the regime in Zimbabwe, for an English team to play the match there. But the real influence on the decision was to be the views of the players which they discussed and expressed to David Morgan, the new chairman of the ECB, and Tim Lamb, the chief executive, over long and anguished meetings in South Africa. The dilemma for the ECB was extremely difficult, given the insistence of the ICC as organisers of the tournament that they ought to go to Zimbabwe. But in the end the overall view of the players was that they should not go and the ECB supported them. It was not difficult for those of us without the responsibility to take the view that England should not play cricket in Zimbabwe. But for the ECB it was an immensely difficult decision and whatever they did was inevitably going to be criticised.

The MCC members who felt we should have spoken up publicly about Zimbabwe came back to the issue at the end of 2003 since England were due to tour Zimbabwe for a test series in November 2004. The ECB started to consider the issue at least a year in advance and once again the Foreign Office expressed a view that it might be unwise for the tour to take place. This fell short of being a government instruction, and again it would not involve the government in any responsibility to compensate English cricket in the event that there was financial loss from the cancellation. Some of the members of our committee wanted to go public with an MCC view against the tour, but they were persuaded that it would be right to allow the ECB to take its decision responsibly and in its own time although we made our views known. But again the decision was not an easy one for the ECB as it was highly unpopular with other members of the ICC. The view of the ICC is that the only factor which ought to interfere with matches should be a direct government instruction or the inability to play them safely on security grounds. This is understandable given the variety of different countries and governing regimes which play test cricket. The ICC point to the need of the country hosting a test series for the income to support the promotion and development of the game. They also argue that calling off a test series is not going to bring down a regime when all other forms of trade with that country are permitted. But in practice in the current state of public and government opinion shared by many of the players who would have to make the tour, the ECB had no choice but once again to call off the test series.

I was fortunate enough to have 10 years closely involved with MCC. They were years of mixed fortune for English cricket when we were able to win test series against every country except Australia. The then Australian team raised the standards of the entire sport. English cricket struggles to compete with Australia. The doyen of cricket writers, John Woodcock, once suggested to me that this in part stemmed from the automatic covering of wickets. History showed that English victories had often been achieved on pitches affected by rain which suited our medium pace and spin bowlers. But Australia's attitudes to sport and their climate probably make it likely that they will normally have the edge over us.

The task of the ECB is not an easy one. The majority of their funds come from television income gained from the broadcasting of test matches. With this income the ECB has to support an infrastructure where there are 18 first class countries all of whom rely on subscriptions from the ECB for more than half their income. The ECB also has to support the very fine new cricket academy created at Lilleshall together with their work helping to develop grass roots cricket. Cricket is played in far too few schools, and the summer term ahead of exams is now much briefer than when I was young. The clubs have to play a large part in encouraging youth cricket and discovering talent.

MCC may not now run English cricket but it has a clear and important future. We must strive continuously to give the best possible facilities to our members and to meet their needs as the premier cricket ground of the world, where all cricketers wished to play and dream of scoring a century or taking five wickets in an innings. Both achievements are recorded on a board in the dressing rooms. The MCC also has to work tirelessly to continue its touring programme overseas helping those countries which are still below test status. We will continue to play a large range of matches across this country and to promote the Spirit of Cricket. We can also help the ECB achieve some of the projects which they consider important to cricket which can be supported and financed under the name of MCC. It is an exciting, fulfilling task, uniting cricket lovers, bringing together fascinating people from different walks of life, together with fine friendships and laughter. To be part of it more than compensated slightly later in life for my having been such a very average player.

22. THE ROYAL SHAKESPEARE COMPANY

For me, as for so many, William Shakespeare was the deepest influence in my study of literature. His mix of language, insight, philosophy and paradox had fascinated me as a student when I read English literature at Cambridge. His immense range reached, as Michael Boyd, the Artistic Director of the RSC, was to put it to me years later, "From court playwright to courtyard playwright". He captured people and human dilemmas. Tragedy, comedy and romance are the essence of his work, in all their moods, passions, vulnerabilities and positions in life.

During my busy years at the Bar the theatre was part of my relaxation and hinterland. But as so often happens in life my connection with the RSC began by accident. I was telephoned by Lord Ackner, a senior law Lord, and told that a trial was being arranged for charity in Middle Temple to decide whether the works of Shakespeare might after all have been written by an Elizabethan courtier, Edward de Vere, the 17th Earl of Oxford. Over the years there have been regular expressions of disbelief as to whether a man who received a relatively brief grammar school education, was unfamiliar with foreign parts or royal pursuits, left virtually no traces of his own handwriting, whose daughter was illiterate, and who apparently possessed no library, could possibly have produced the works of William Shakespeare.

This had led to the idea that they were written by Sir Francis Bacon, a great scholar of the time, or that Christopher Marlowe somehow escaped assassination in the tavern at Deptford in 1593 and lived in hiding fulfilling his genius. The 17th Earl of Oxford was entered somewhat later in the stakes, the case based on circumstantial evidence that he had some ability as a poet but for various reasons had to disguise his identity as a playwright. He did, however, have access to all aspects of life such as foreign travel and the royal pursuit of falconry which gave him the knowledge that Shakespeare was supposed to have lacked. A circumstantial argument was mounted that he was most probably the author.

The trial was to take place before three judges. I was asked to organise a team of barristers and went straight to the top to secure my friend and chambers' colleague Sydney Kentridge QC, together with two rising juniors, David Anderson and Richard Slade. We agreed that I should take the case for the Earl of Oxford, and that Sydney should argue on behalf of the "man from Stratford" as the sceptics tended to deride him. For me this meant reading a huge tome by an American lawyer called Charlton Osborn who was totally committed to the cause of the Earl of Oxford. I did so during the summer as we stayed by a lake in Maine with friends. The argument was long, painstakingly and passionately put together but in the end I believed unconvincing. So did the judges after a marvellous day in the autumn in the Elizabethan Hall of Middle Temple where it is believed that the first public performance of "Twelfth Night" was given. We had a packed house, not a footfall could be heard during the seven hours of hearing, with a cast of witnesses including the leading Shakespearean scholar Professor Stanley Wells. Sydney rightly drew attention to the fact that our argument was based on speculation as he could point to certain pieces of evidence such as records of payments to Shakespeare in account to books of the time, a diary entry by John Massingham, a student of Middle Temple, and the dedication to the First Folio by Shakespeare's colleagues after his death. The judges understandably decided that a modest amount of fact is preferable to a great deal of conjecture and we duly lost.

What I did not realise was that this exciting diversion would mark me out to Sir Geoffrey Cass the chairman of the RSC, as promising material to become involved with the company. Shortly afterwards he approached me to chair the newly-founded development board, aimed at raising private funds for the RSC. It was the time when all arts organisations were realising that they could no longer depend simply on public subsidy and takings at the box

office and were having to become more active to promote sponsorship and private patronage. This needed a marked change of
culture within the RSC because there were those who felt that the
involvement of private funders could become a corrupting influence on artistic decisions. The danger was and always will be there,
but we gradually persuaded people that we had no choice but to try
and that we should try to manage any potential conflicts. Over the
next years our development board achieved some success, notably
with the gift of £3 million as part of an endowment for actors from
the Weston Foundation under the impetus of the remarkably phil-
anthropic Garry Weston, who so successfully guided the fortunes
of his company, Fortnum & Mason.

The RSC has its home in Stratford-upon-Avon, where for
many years there was a summer festival season. The genius and
energy of Sir Peter Hall created the modern Royal Shakespeare
Company with certain key underlying aims and values. The RSC
sought from the outset to deliver outstanding performances of
Shakespeare, but also of other classical theatre works and new
plays. It aimed to do so through building an ensemble company
where actors worked together, often for several years and developed
their skills through playing a variety of roles. The effect was electric
from the start. Peter was supported by the finest actors. The RSC
nurtured most of the talent later to reach the top of theatre and
film in this country, such as Peggy Ashcroft, Judi Dench, Kenneth
Branagh, Antony Sher, Simon Russell Beale, and Sinéad Cusack
to name but a few. In 1960 he brought the RSC to London to the
Aldwych Theatre, from where it was later to move to a longer-term
home at the Barbican. Peter's skills as a theatre director, intensity allied to sensitivity, and sheer charisma, all made him the most
influential theatrical visionary of our generation. He went on to
nurse the National Theatre through the stop-go of its gestation and
long delayed birth. Stephen Fay, his biographer, says that without
Peter Hall we would have had one National Theatre in this country
but not two. His remarkable achievement was to be part of the
creation of both across a mere time span of less than 20 years when
the national budget was short and the country was widely seen to

be in economic decline. Both theatres contribute immensely to the vitality of theatre in this country, and both are rightly subsidised, although each wishes at all times that its subsidy should be greater. Almost all RSC performances are loss-making, which is hardly surprising since a full Shakespeare cast can involve 24 actors and some of the classical and new plays may not have the wide, popular appeal to which the commercial theatre has to give the highest priority.

The RSC has always aroused controversy. There are some who love it with a passion, and there are some who see it as a bloated institution ever demanding more from public funds when smaller theatres have to scrimp and scrape for crumbs. Its finances have see-sawed. When Adrian Noble became the Artistic Director in 1990 he inherited a deficit of £4 million. Over several years he gradually brought this down, but it spiralled again during 2002 after the RSC left the Barbican and experimented with a London season at the Roundhouse. Theatrical companies have always lived dangerously as the histories of Garrick and Sheridan in the great age of the theatre in the late 18th century vividly demonstrate. Theatre demands innovation and experiment, and will always have its share of failure. It cannot be managed like supermarket stores and its sales and margins cannot be predicted with anything like the same confidence as groceries and bank loans. Much can be achieved by flair, and dominant single talent as was shown by David Brierley over so many years at the RSC. But without some conscious approach to management discipline, waste and inefficiency can develop to an unacceptable extent especially in a large organisation operating on more than one site. This increasingly became the case for the RSC in the 1990s operating a full, virtually year-round programme at Stratford and a complete schedule at the Barbican as well as its touring activities right across the country with residences at Newcastle and for a time Plymouth.

The organisation simply became over-stretched, which Adrian recognised was a danger to its work and overstrained its finances. In 1995 he decided to axe half of the annual programme at the Barbican which immediately brought him under fire from the metro-centric critics. But it soon became apparent that there was need for the RSC to rethink its strategy more imaginatively, more widely and come forward to the Arts Council with a plan that would underpin its finances. The Arts Council encouraged the RSC to enter what is called its stabilisation programme which acknowledges that an arts company may need to refocus some of its work but also pledges financial help to make the change.

In 2000 Sir Geoffrey Cass indicated that he would bring his long, dedicated and skilful term as chairman of the RSC to an end. He suggested to myself and the board that I should succeed him. Over the previous year he had made substantial changes to the board. There were some long-standing stalwarts such as Sir Eddie Kulukundis and Professor Stanley Wells, but most of us came comparatively fresh to the task. We were eager to play our part, but not yet fully bedded-in when Adrian came to our first away-day meeting in January 2001 with an outline proposal for change. This was the start of three years which were going to be challenging, anxious, difficult and often disappointing. But they were to end with Michael Boyd in place as the new Artistic Director who will lead the RSC to ever-finer heights and with our finances recovering to the extent that we were able to slash our deficit by £1.5 million.

I was honoured and excited to be asked to be chair of the RSC. After leaving NatWest I had rather hoped that this might happen and this had encouraged me not to respond to suggestions for what I saw as less appealing public jobs. Marie and I bought a small flat in Stratford, a delightful bolt-hole in a modest block called Avonside, with a marvellous location looking out onto Holy Trinity Church where Shakespeare was baptised and buried, with a fine view of the Avon, and in short walking distance from the theatre. For all the importance of the RSC being seen nationally and internationally, and not least in London, Stratford is its home and power-house. Without a successful and holistic artistic and management company based there its work could never be successful for long.

It is vital that actors who come to Stratford and are away from home can be made to feel welcome, cared for and wanted. This was brought home to me by Sir Nigel Hawthorne, who returned at the age of 70 to play King Lear in 2000 and told me how saddened he had been by the lack of interest and support when needed. Those who run the RSC must care passionately about Stratford, about the Midlands and about creating a warm, family atmosphere for the company. Marie and I realised this and we gave parties for artists in the flat after performances. They were immense fun, and went on until the early hours. The zest for conversation and company felt by members of a profession which is immensely demanding, often ill-rewarded and uncertain was very obvious and their appreciation immensely touching. We were to make some good friends amongst them.

The Stratford experience, and the contacts with artists and some of the management company, were to be a real pleasure over the coming years.

But our enjoyment of the pleasure was to be darkened by the difficulties and by the problems which led to the RSC becoming labelled, and we all know that newspaper labels stick, as a "troubled" company. At the January meeting Adrian explained to us that he would like to leave the Barbican almost completely, to perform in a wider range of theatres in London and to originate some of our work there. He believed that this would give us a greater chance of attracting back some of the RSC actors who were reluctant to come to Stratford. He also felt that we would be widely welcomed in the London theatre scene and have a good chance of available theatres. He felt we needed to look at the issues swiftly because if we did not give notice that we were discontinuing our management agreement with the Barbican Centre, which was part of our package with them, we would have to continue for another five years. The board readily agreed that he, and Chris Foy, the new managing director, assisted generously without fee by McKinseys, the management consultants, should look to see whether a viable and detailed artistic and business plan could be prepared.

Over the next few months we considered in some depth the way in which the ideas were developed. There were several dominant strands to the argument. We considered that, with the opportunities available to actors in television and their wish to be in London, the RSC was struggling to attract the finest artists and creative teams to Stratford. The RSC's standards of performance were generally high, but not as often as outstanding as they ought to be. The average age of the audience was rising as we were not appealing to the younger age groups. Many who did not come to the RSC were said to consider us "exclusive and expensive". Part of the answer was to offer shorter contracts of six months or less. This meant change to the mix of the traditional ensemble companies and to the scheduling pattern.

There was a feeling that the location of the Barbican was unattractive to many, and that while the theatre itself had much to offer the overall surroundings were flat and unattractive to artists and many audiences. So the idea was to continue to perform some work in the Barbican but embark on a "caravan" model using different theatres to give the flexibility to stage productions in the most appropriate theatres at the most suitable times. It was recognised that the subsidy from the Corporation of London, which the Barbican were already indicating they wished substantially to reduce, would be lost. To meet the extra costs our commercial or enterprise activities and private fundraising could be stepped up. We also needed to proceed swiftly with the creation of new theatre spaces at Stratford.

We were under pressure to take a decision because of the Barbican deadline. A great deal of work went into the plan and the budgetary forecast for the next five years. These took account of the likely operational deficit over the transition period but also of the expected grant from the Arts Council towards the cost of change. Our board endorsed the proposal in May. We were encouraged by the support of the Arts Council representative, Kim Evans, for the general thrust of the change although she made plain that they would need to look at the financial proposals very carefully.

There is no doubt that looking back at it there was over-optimism in the plan. We too readily assumed the availability of times and on terms attractive to the RSC of London theatre spaces. A timetable for potential redevelopment at Stratford was unrealistically short. The figures predicted from commercial income and private funding were simply too high for an organisation which was still in its comparative infancy in those areas. We were understandably driven by the strong belief of artists and board alike that we could never refocus our strategy and meet the needs of stabilisation without ending the obligation to play throughout half of the year at the Barbican. But looking back on it, it would have been much better if we had tried to negotiate the transition more gradually, which perhaps we might have done if the relationship between the artistic management of the RSC and the Barbican had been more sympathetic and friendly. What, too, we were told was that the senior figures in the artistic community, notably Peter Hall and Trevor Nunn, were strongly supportive. Each of them was later to tell me that this was simply not so.

The proposal was initially received reasonably favourably in the press. In the late summer we presented a feasibility study for the redevelopment of the theatres in Stratford. This ambitiously involved the knocking down of the existing Royal Shakespeare Theatre, designed by Elizabeth Scott in 1930 and since heavily modified, and the building of a single-space theatre designed specifically for playing Shakespeare, to operate in tandem with the marvellous, smaller Swan theatre. This was the preferred choice of our redevelopment committee at the time, although they made plain that they would listen carefully to argument and test the proposal against other ideas.

What really torpedoed Adrian's plan at the outset was the way in which he and Chris Foy decided to put it into practice. At our board meeting in January 2002, we were presented with the proposal for "making a splash" in London with three plays at the Roundhouse running from April to July with the same production then moving on to Stratford for the summer festival. But these proposals showed a potential operating deficit of almost £2 million more than that which board had already sanctioned. Chris Foy, who presented in Adrian's absence, sought to justify this by pointing out that we could economise on the one-off costs of change. But this sleight of hand missed the point. What it meant was that we could anticipate higher operating costs for several years to come. The firm commitment to put this programme in place had apparently already been made. This gave me a thankless dilemma. My instinct was to ask for plans to be halted and for the budget to revert to what the board had already sanctioned. But with the company in a controversial period of change this would have created massive uncertainty and undermined confidence, possibly to the extent of destroying the whole institution.

I spent a sleepless night before writing to Adrian who was unavailable on the telephone, protesting strongly at what he had done and asking him to seek to reduce the operating costs. He did not reply and when I chased him, he simply wrote that Chris Foy was handling the issue.

By then Adrian was on sabbatical leave. He had a clear entitlement to this leave under his contract and had not taken it for many years. The opportunity arose for him to direct "Chitty Chitty Bang Bang" and, as so many theatre directors have done over the years, to make some money privately. It was very unfortunate that this chance came for Adrian at the time when he was really needed to devote his maximum energies to change at the RSC. I warned him that he would be heavily criticised, and so it proved. What I had no inkling at all of was that as soon as "Chitty" was launched, he would come to me, as he did in April 2002, and say that he had decided to give notice to terminate his contract with the RSC. He wanted to announce this immediately. My first reaction was anger, because Adrian had always said that he was committed to seeing through the change which he had initiated. It was a time when the company was having a good deal of difficulty with the press and he wanted to make the announcement during the week in which we actually had four press nights coming up for which it was important to secure good reviews without distracting events. But he was adamant.

As my feelings of being thoroughly let down subsided I began to realise that his resignation was in the long-term fortunate for the RSC. To be artistic director of the RSC is to perform an immense, demanding, emotionally-draining task. Adrian had done the job for more than a decade, was clearly fatigued by it and hurt by the criticism. He had a young family to consider and, in the short period of a year or so of overlap I had with him, his commitment had been variable and his judgement increasingly erratic. He is a brilliant artistic director, as his own production of Pericles during the Roundhouse season and his direction of Ralph Fiennes in "Brand" a year later were to remind us. He is obviously very good with his own team. But, even if he had once been good at the wider human challenges falling on the artistic director, he appeared to have lost the talent or energy to reach out in human and sympathetic terms to the company as a whole or to the outside world.

This became clear during the search for his successor. I had to drop all my professional commitments for several months to lead this vital, all-absorbing task. In this I was greatly helped by Lady Sainsbury of Turville, my deputy chairman. Susie Sainsbury was passionate about the RSC, devoted most of her time to the work of the company and in particular to the redevelopment project, and was most generous in encouraging funding from Sainsbury trusts to give the RSC essential and timely help. We held meetings with staff right across the board, and the extent of discontent at the lack of interest by Adrian in the management company as opposed to artists, came across loud and clear. So did it when we met many leading figures in the theatre and arts world who consistently felt that Adrian had adopted an elitist attitude to them and as a result lost the RSC the support and goodwill of many of those who should have been our friends. I began to suspect that one of the reasons why leading actors would not come back to the RSC was the feeling that it was not just a question of length of contracts but because Adrian did not woo them hard enough or make it feel an exciting and attractive place in which to work.

The suddenness of Adrian's departure meant that we had not been able to engage in any succession planning. Some of those who might have been eligible, such as Michael Attenbrough and Nicholas Hytner, had already accepted their posts at the Almeida and the National theatres respectively. But we were fortunate that within the field there were two strong candidates in Michael Boyd and Greg Doran. In the end we felt that Michael had the rigorous mind and deep interest in management which made him the right choice at this particular time to lead the RSC. He had been director of the Belgrade Theatre at Coventry and then made an immense success of a renaissance of the Tron Theatre in Glasgow. We had been fortunate that Greg came to grips so well with what must have been a considerable disappointment. His part over the last few years in our work has been simply marvellous. He was responsible for the unique project of resurrecting five little-known Jacobean plays, and for pairing "The Taming of the Shrew" and "Tamer Tamed." He was able to attract Judi Dench back to Stratford for the first time in twenty years to play the Countess in "All's Well that Ends Well." His energy and engagement are boundless and it is fortunate for the RSC that so much of his finest work came together at this critical time.

In other respects the summer of 2002 was bumpy. The Roundhouse season did attract a younger audience but overall numbers and results and box-office take was disappointing. The way in which Adrian had programmed the season meant that it overlapped with the conclusion of our previous season at the Barbican which caused dismay amongst the artists and did not help the financial outcome. Nor did the resulting inability to programme our festival season at Stratford in good time. The deficit escalated and became really worrying by the end of the summer. The Arts Council were understandably reluctant to release stabilisation monies whilst they felt that the RSC was losing so much money and was unable to say when the bottom had been reached. In the end we succeeded with the aid of a substantial anonymous donation in persuading them to release their funds to enable us to overcome what would have been a real crisis, and start to improve the budgets for the future.

But our difficulties were not over and they were compounded by the fact that the relationship between myself and Susie Sainsbury which had worked so well when we were in agreement, started to break down. We disagreed about the way to approach the Arts Council for stabilisation funds. She felt they were holding back on us unreasonably and wanted us to ask David, her husband, the Minister for Science, to go to see Tessa Jowell, the Secretary of State for Culture, and talk "minister to minister" as she put it with a view to pressure being applied to the Arts Council. I felt strongly that this would sour our relationship with the Arts Council for a long time, and that Gerry Robinson, the chairman, would not take kindly to his decision-making power being hi-jacked in this way. We next, and most surprisingly to me, disagreed strongly on whether Michael Boyd should become the leader of the RSC. Artistic directors traditionally lead the company, and the post had been advertised in this way. But she fought a long and bitter battle arguing that Chris Foy should be joint leader of the company "with equal seniority" as she suggested. She lobbied board members to support her cause, and some of them did so. To have adopted this course would have been disastrous. It would have meant reneging on what we had promised Michael, and he indicated to me that he would decline to take up his appointment on that basis. The issue was only resolved in his favour after a prolonged board debate shortly before Christmas.

This second disagreement led to a very uneasy continuing relationship between Susie and myself. I learned from a mix of board members and members of staff that she had started to raise doubts about my continuing as chairman. She increasingly developed a strong working relationship with Chris Foy, and both of them had misgivings about whether Michael Boyd was committed to effective management. The atmosphere became unpleasant and it was harder to deal with because of the potential financial importance of the Sainsbury trusts for the redevelopment of the theatres at Stratford. I was keen not to lose either her energy or commitment towards the redevelopment and, even more, not to precipitate a departure which could be financially very disadvantageous to the RSC. But I could not take my wish to accommodate her as far as allowing decisions which were plainly contrary to the interests of the RSC.

The spring of 2003 brought a further complication. When we were in Washington for our first residency at the Kennedy Centre, Michael Boyd told me that he felt it was going to be extremely difficult in the interests of the company to continue to work with Chris Foy. I asked him to weigh the position carefully but he felt there was no choice but to write to me setting out his concerns. It would not be the first time that the new artistic director of a theatre company felt that they did not temperamentally work well with the managing director. Michael wrote to me in the summer expressing his views very strongly. We had some anxious board debates before deciding that it was inevitable we should part with Chris. I had sympathy with Michael's view and it accorded with others which had been expressed with me and coincided with my own growing concern as to whether a change was needed. Chris had worked courageously and tirelessly for the RSC, and we recognised this with an appropriate settlement package. Errors in commercial judgement, people management and a penchant for secrecy had cost him credibility inside and outside the company. Meanwhile Michael was reviving spirits in Stratford among the other artists who joined us for the summer season. It was vital to give him the management partner who could help him motivate the company as a spur to its renaissance.

The process of deciding to ask Chris to go was not easy. Several members of the Board who unfortunately were not as familiar with what was happening on the ground at Stratford as I necessarily had to be, felt that Michael was forcing their hand, and that I was supporting him too strongly. Susie was very disappointed at the outcome although she accepted its inevitability. From then on she got ever more vocal in her criticisms of me to other people. She also frankly said to me that it was time I ceased to be chairman because I could not give enough time to the affairs of the RSC. Since I had given large tranches of my time over the previous few years, including the months devoted almost exclusively to recruiting Michael Boyd, this was clearly code language for her now obvious wish that I should not continue. I also felt that I had used up a deal of my political capital with many board members by the way I had backed Michael in the contest with Chris Foy that summer. It seemed to me that the time had come to bow out gracefully.

I did so with a mixture of relief and regret. The relief stemmed from the wish to escape from an unpleasant working relationship where the alternative was the departure of the RSC's most valuable donor. It had also been a challenging, difficult time and there was much to be said for moving on and allowing someone else to take up the helm. I was keen to be able to give more time to my practice and to the increasingly anxious constitutional debate about the way in which the independence of judges should be maintained. My interest in this was professional and as chairman of JUSTICE, the all-party law reform group.

My regret was that by autumn 2003 we had in place not only Michael but also Vikki Heywood, who had been so successful at the Royal Court, and who had come in for the time being as managing director. For the first time I had a combination at the RSC in which I had total confidence and who were a joy to work with. Michael was getting out a marvellous artistic programme for the coming years with Judi Dench, Corin Redgrave, Antony Sher, Toby Stephens all coming back to the company and with exciting plans for the next few years. We had gradually strengthened our financial controls and were now able to reduce the deficit by £1.5 million in December 2003. Optimism about the company was growing. Sir Peter Hall wrote to me expressing confidence in the future under Michael's leadership. We had in his words "a bright future in our grasp". Kim Evans, the executive director of the Arts Council said to me shortly before Christmas that she felt we had turned the corner. We were by then negotiating for a new London home. We reached agreement with the Piccadilly Theatre in January 2004 which should enable the RSC to have an even greater and certainly more regular home in London over the next few years. The long delayed saga of planning the redeveloped theatre spaces in Stratford was increasingly being gripped with the help of Vikki and Anthony Blackstock, the former finance director of the National Theatre.

The RSC will have bumpy times again. It is the essence of theatre, of inventiveness and creativity. But overall it has done pretty well in the 40 years of its modern existence. As Greg Doran once said, "It has lasted longer than Shakespeare's players were ever together". Not every performance is outstanding. But under Michael the company has regained its freshness of approach, has enhanced the strength of its ensemble company and its contribution to the education of actors, and is once again an exciting place to be. As the writer Bryan Appleyard recently said: "If you want to see good Shakespeare, then the RSC is the only place in the world where you can be pretty sure of getting it - and that is saying a lot - everything in fact". It was a privilege to be associated so closely with it even during one of the tough periods in its history. For the future Marie and I will remain keen supporters of the Actors' Circle, our group of major patrons led by Laurence Isaacson and will make forays to our flat by the river to share more great theatrical experiences. We will do so in the firm belief that Michael Boyd will be a truly great Artistic Director of the RSC and that we saw the RSC through turbulent waters and on to the high seas of promise.

Bob Alexander died on 6 November 2005 before he was able to complete his memoir.

CROSSING THE BAR

by Alfred, Lord Tennyson

Sunset and evening star,
And one clear call for me!
And may there be no moaning of the bar,
When I put out to sea,

But such a tide as moving seems asleep,
Too full for sound and foam,
When that which drew from out the boundless deep
Turns again home.

Twilight and evening bell,
And after that the dark!
And may there be no sadness of farewell,
When I embark;

For tho' from out our bourne of Time and Place
The flood may bear me far,
I hope to see my Pilot face to face
When I have crost the bar.

BA pursuing his love of cricket later in life.

INDEX